D0983542

Bible Translations

Bible Translations

A HISTORY THROUGH SOURCE DOCUMENTS

by
Roland H. Worth, Jr.

McFarland & Company, Inc., Publishers
Jefferson, North Carolina, and London

Acknowledgments: Strenuous efforts have been made to obtain all necessary and appropriate permissions to reprint those "source documents" found within this volume. If any oversight has inadvertently been made, notification is requested and appropriate correction will be made in any future edition. The following items were used in this text by permission.

Preface to the *New King James Bible*, © 1979, Thomas Nelson, Inc., Publishers. Preface to the *New American Bible*, © 1970 by the Confraternity of Christian Doctrine. "Gender neutral" extract from *An Inclusive Language Lectionary: Readings from Year B*, © 1984 by the Division of Education and Ministry of the National Council of the Churches of Christ in the USA. *The Lollard Bible and Other Medieval Biblical Versions* by Margaret Deanesly, © 1920, Cambridge University Press. *Luther's Works* (Volume 35) edited by E. Theodore Bachmann, © 1960, Fortress Press; used by permission of Augsburg Fortress. *Coverdale and His Bibles* by J. F. Mozley, © 1953, Lutterworth Press. *Correspondence of Erasmus*; Volume 3: *Letters 298 to 445 (1514-1516)* edited by R.A.B. Mynors and D.F.S. Thompson, © 1976, University of Toronto Press; Volume 6: *Letters 842 to 992 (1518-1519)*, © 1981, University of Toronto Press. *An Introduction to the Revised Standard Version of the Old Testament* edited by Luther A. Weigle, © 1952, reprinted by permission of Thomas Nelson, Inc., Publishers. Extracts promoting the *New American Standard Bible* and *New International* versions from *What Bible Can You Trust?* © 1974, Broadman Press. *The King James Version Debate* by D. A. Carson, © 1979, Baker Book House. Excerpts from *Aristeas to Philocrates (Letter of Aristeas)* edited and translated by Moses Hadas; English translation © 1951, Harper & Row, renewed 1979 by Elizabeth C. Hadas. Introduction from *The New English Bible*, © 1961, 1970, the Delegates of the Oxford University Press and the Syndics of the Cambridge University Press. "The Greek Text of the New Testament" by Frederick C. Grant, in *An Introduction to the Revised Standard Version of the New Testament*, © 1946, International Council of Religious Education; reprinted by permission of the National Council of the Churches of Christ. Masseketh Sopherim, reprinted from the English translation of H. St. J. Thackeray, *The Letter of Aristeas*, © 1917 by Society for Promoting Christian Knowledge.

British Library Cataloguing-in-Publication data are available

Library of Congress Cataloguing-in-Publication Data

Worth, Roland H., 1943–
  Bible translations : a history through source documents / by Roland H. Worth.
    p. cm.
  Includes index.
  ISBN 0-89950-537-6 (lib. bdg. : 50# alk. paper) ∞
  1. Bible—Translating—History—Sources.   2. Bible—Versions—History—Sources.   I. Title.
  BS450.W62   1992
  220.5—dc20   91-52513
  #23140650   CIP

Manufactured in the United States of America

McFarland & Company, Inc., Publishers
  Box 611, Jefferson, North Carolina 28640

Dedicated to the memory of
E. V. Srygley
who, three decades ago,
introduced me to the fascinating saga of
how the Bible was
transmitted through the centuries

Contents

Introduction

The history of the translation of the Bible has been covered many times. My intent in this work is not to compete with these scholars but to supplement their endeavors. Useful and informative as introductory surveys are, the very degree to which they have digested their sources and recapitulated their contents usually results in a loss of the feel of the raw data. By this I mean the peculiarities, the eccentricities, and even the prejudices found in the source documents that the scholar utilizes to reach his conclusions.

In the present context, "source documents" essentially refer to three types of documentation:

(1) *Material composed by the Bible translators themselves.* In this category belong documents from the reformer Martin Luther, the Renaissance scholar Erasmus, Matthew B. Riddle (who worked on the American Standard Version), and twentieth century Catholic translator (and prominent cleric) Ronald A. Knox. In such documents the translators personally discuss their problems, their difficulties, and their attitudes.

(2) *Early material about Bible translations.* When first-hand material from the translators themselves has been lost (or, in some cases, perhaps never existed), the scholar is compelled to seek out the earliest surviving data. For example, what is known about the composition of the early Greek translation of the Old Testament known as the Septuagint — beyond what can be deduced from the peculiarities of the translation itself — comes from the much later Letter of Aristeas and the writings of the first century Jewish scholar Josephus. Both are utilized in this compilation to enhance understanding of the then traditional explanation of that ancient translation's origin.

Also under this heading would come those documents providing biographical information about the translators. Everyone knows about the multi-century prestige of the King James Version, yet few know anything about the men who worked on it. In this volume I single out the career of John Bois to illustrate the caliber of men who produced that classic version.

(3) *Material illustrating then contemporary justifications (and criticisms) of various existing and proposed translations.* Here we delve into the controversies surrounding the proper translation of the scriptural text. These documents include analyses of the perceived faults of the original Revised Standard Version, the inadvisability of producing an "immersion" Bible (from a strong believer in the practice), and an explanation (from a staunch feminist viewpoint) of what is required to "degenderize" the scriptures.

A representative cross-section of Bible versions is discussed, and most (but not all) of the most prominent ones are studied — from the standpoint of someone either defending the translation, attacking it, explaining the reasons for it, or illustrating events surrounding the rendition. In light of the wide variety of sources utilized, it should not be surprising that the theological assumptions (explicit or implicit) vary tremendously. The readings are included for the light they shed on the translations, translators, and translation process rather than because of the particular theologies being advocated.

Each extract is preceded by a brief introduction either setting the material in its historical context or providing other information relevant to its interpretation.

Roland H. Worth, Jr.

ONE

Translations from Hebrew into Greek

I. Pre-Septuagint Translations

1. ALLUSIONS IN THE LETTER OF ARISTEAS

Although the Letter of Aristeas is of main concern to us because of its detailed account of the translation of the Septuagint (LXX), some remarks it makes are relevant to pre LXX translations as well. The words rendered "committed to writing" could refer to the Hebrew manuscripts and their inadequate preservation. However, the more customary usage of the word is in the sense of "translated." Indeed, this would be more appropriate in the immediate context: It is unlikely that many Egyptians could read Hebrew, and concern by the king and his chief librarian over the state of manuscripts they could not read makes little sense; concern over the accuracy of translations they *could* read, however, would provide a more reasonable impetus for a fresh translation.

This assumes that there is at least an historical germ beneath the transparent effort to explain the lack of use of the Hebrew scriptures by Egyptian authors. At least in part, the text sounds like a rationalization by a member of an oppressed minority for his holy books being ignored.

(For a more detailed description of the Letter of Aristeas, see Chapter 2, pp. 5–9.)

To the great king, from Demetrius: At Your Majesty's bidding with respect to the completion of the collection of books in the library, that those which are wanting should be added to the collection and that those in disrepair should receive the proper attention, my efforts in the charge have not been cursory, and I now submit the following statement to you. The books of the Law of the Jews together with some few others are wanting. It happens that they are written in Hebrew characters and in the Hebrew tongue, and they have been committed to writing

1

somewhat carelessly and not adequately, according to the testimony of experts, for they have never benefited by a king's forethought. It is necessary that these books too, in an emended form, should be given a place in your library, for their legislation is most philosophical and flawless, inasmuch as it is divine. It is for this reason that authors and poets and the mass of historians have abstained from mentioning these aforesaid books and the men who have lived and are living in accordance with them, because the views set forth in them have a certain holiness and sanctity, as Hecataeus of Abdera says.

(Source: Moses Hadas, translator, *Aristeas to Philocrates [Letter of Aristeas]*, New York: Harper & Brothers, 1951.)

Toward the end of the Letter, Aristeas makes an even more explicit reference to pre–Septuagint translation efforts. His stress on the failure of Egyptian writers to incorporate such material suggests that whatever efforts had been made were thoroughly ignored by those outside the Hebrew community.

When these proceedings were reported to the king he rejoiced greatly, for he thought that the purpose he cherished had been securely carried out. The whole work was read out to him also, and he marvelled exceedingly at the intellect of the lawgiver. To Demetrius he said, "How has it not occurred to any of the historians or poets to make mention of such enormous achievements?" And he said, "Because the Law is holy and has come into being through God; some of those to whom the thought did occur were smitten by God and desisted from the attempt." Indeed, he said, he had heard Theopompus say that when he was on the point of introducing into his history certain matter which had previously been translated from the Law, too rashly, he suffered a derangement of the mind for more than thirty days; upon the abatement of the disorder he implored God that the cause of what had befallen be made plain to him, and when it was signified to him in a dream that it was his meddlesome desire to disclose divine matters to common men, he desisted, and was thereupon restored to health. "And of Theodectes also, the tragic poet, I have heard," he added, "that when he was on the point of introducing into one of his plays something recorded in the Book, his vision was afflicted with a cataract. Conceiving the suspicion that this was the reason for his calamity, he implored God and after many days recovered."

(Source: Moses Hadas, translator, *Aristeas to Philocrates [Letter to Aristeas]*, New York: Harper & Brothers, 1951.)

2. ARISTOBULUS (AS QUOTED BY EUSEBIUS)

A work attributed to the Jewish philosopher Aristobulus and addressed to Ptolemy Philopator (c. 170–150 B.C.) contains a reference to pre–Septuagint translations. A fragment is quoted by Eusebius in his *Preparation for the Gospel* (XIII. 12), and it is exclusively through this source that it is known to us.

Though it is clear that Eusebius himself took the document at face value, many later historians have questioned whether this "Aristobulus" actually dates back as far as Eusebius thought. Moses Hadas concisely sums up the scholarly reservations:

(a) It is striking that Josephus, to whom the statement that Platonism derives from Judaism would be very welcome in *Against Apion*, fails to mention him; (b) his manner of exegesis seems very like Philo's; and (c) his ascription of spurious verses to Orpheus, Linus, Homer, and others seems strange in a Peripatetic scholar supposed to be a contemporary and perhaps colleague of the great critic Aristarchus.

(Source: *Aristeas to Philocrates*, published for the Dropsie College for Hebrew and Cognate Learning by Harper Brothers, New York: 1951, page 27.)

Regardless of the ultimate origin of the "Aristobulus" fragment, it unquestionably bears witness to a tradition accepted as objective fact by the time of Eusebius in the fourth century. One could contend that the original writer knew of alleged Platonic borrowings from Jewish thought and so concluded that Plato must have taken them from a pre–LXX version. In other words, the similarities produced the deduction that an earlier translation had been produced.

However, it seems that Aristobulus knew of such a previous effort on independent grounds as well, for he is careful to limit the amount of the Old Testament that Plato had access to. He specifies that Plato had access to the account of "the exodus of the Hebrews our fellow countrymen from Egypt" and even "the conquest of the land," which would take us from Exodus (if not Genesis) through Joshua. At first he seems to imply that much more was included in the translation, for he calls it "the exposition of the whole Law." Yet just a little later he admits that "the entire translation of all the contents of our Law" was not made until later and by his reference to Demetrius making the arrangements clearly shows that he has the LXX in mind as the later, "complete" translation. This strange and needless inconsistency would be explainable if the earlier translation was more of a midrash than a strict rendition of the text itself. If the writer had merely been interested in a mythological inflating of the impact of the Jewish Torah, one would not expect any hint that Plato had access to less than all of it.

It is evident that Plato closely followed our legislation, and has carefully studied the several precepts contained in it. For others before Demetrius Phalereus, and prior to the supremacy of Alexander and the Persians, have translated both the narrative of the exodus of the Hebrews our fellow countrymen from Egypt, and the fame of all that had happened to them, and the conquest of the land, and the exposition of the whole Law; so that it is manifest that many things have ben borrowed by the aforesaid philosopher, for he is very learned: as also Pythagoras transferred many of our precepts and inserted them in his own system of doctrines.

But the entire translation of all the contents of our law was made in the time of the king surnamed Philadelphus, thy ancestor, who brought greater zeal to the work, which was managed by Demetrius Phalereus.

(Source: *Eusebius*, translated by Edwin M. Gifford, *Preparation for the Gospel*, volume II, Oxford: at the Clarendon Press, 1903.)

3. MASSEKETH SOPHERIM ("TRACTATE OF THE SCRIBES")

This testimony (I. 7–10) is of very late date, perhaps as late as the eighth or ninth century. The Tractate appears to refer to *two* translations having been undertaken in the days of King Ptolemy, the first by five translators and the second by the famous "seventy" (in other sources: 72) who produced the Septuagint.

This would be compatible with Aristeas' reference to inadequate translations existing in Ptolemy's library before the LXX translators began their work, since there is no specific time frame attached to his remarks as to when they had been undertaken.

However, many believe that "five elders" is itself a scribal misreading: that *ha-zekenim* ("the elders") was misread as *he-zekenim* ("five elders"). In favor of this possibility is the fact that the day the translation was completed is compared to the day the golden calf was finished in the wilderness. This comparison—applied to the Septuagint—became common after Philo due to the effective Christian usage of that version. Its use in regard to a different translation would be unexpected.

However, when the Tractate shifts from the translation of the "five" to that of the "seventy" (Section 9), the transition is marked by the word "Again"—as if something different is being referred to, rather than the previous comment being elaborated upon in greater detail. In addition, the assessment of the work of the "five" seems markedly more severe: In connection with that effort the generalization is made that "the Law was not capable of being interpreted according to all its requirements"; but of the LXX it specifies only "thirteen passages" as being in error. Furthermore, the Tractate approaches the idea of divine inspiration for the LXX by repeating the legend that the translators were put "in seventy [separate] cells" and each man was separately instructed to translate the Torah: "He came in to each of them in turn and said to them, 'Write me out the Law of Moses your master.'" Although literal inspiration is incompatible with the Tractate's listing of alleged errors in the version, certainly divine oversight is attributed to the effort: "God put counsel into the heart of every one of them, that they were all of one mind, and they wrote out for him the Law by itself." In contrast, the work of the five is compared to the day Israel erected the golden calf!

Hence it seems most likely that the Tractate does accept as a reality the existence of two distinct translation efforts in the lifetime of the same king.

The Law must not be written in *ordinary* Hebrew nor in Aramaic nor in the Median language nor in Greek. A copy written in any *foreign* tongue or *foreign* characters shall not be used for reading *in the services,* but only one written in the Assyrian characters.

It happened once that five elders wrote the Law in Greek for King Tolmai; and that day was a hard day for Israel, like the day on which Israel made the *golden* calf, because the Law was not capable of being interpreted according to all its requirements.

Again, it happened to King Tolmai that he assembled seventy elders and placed them in seventy cells, and did not make known to them wherefore he had assembled them; *but* he came in to each of them in turn and said to them, "Write me out of the Law of Moses your master." God put counsel into the heart of every one of them, that they were all of one mind, and they wrote out for him the Law by itself. But they altered thirteen passages in it [to avoid alleged misunderstanding of the intent of the Hebrew text (Oddly enough, fourteen texts were actually quoted in an accompanying list.)].

(Source: Masseketh Sopherim, reprinted from the English translation of H. St. J. Thackeray, *The Letter of Aristeas,* copyrighted 1917 by Society for Promoting Christian Knowledge.)

II. *The Septuagint (LXX)*

4. THE CLASSIC AND EARLIEST ACCOUNT: THE LETTER OF ARISTEAS

To call it "the *Letter* of Aristeas" is somewhat of a misnomer, for it is more of a short history of the events surrounding the Septuagint. Aristeas presents himself as a high official during the reign of Ptolemy Philadelphus (285–247 B.C.). His reliability on peripheral matters not related to the translation has been challenged, but the discrepancies may, in part, be explained by differences between what really happened and the "official" truth as propagated in Egyptian royal and popular opinion. On the other hand, the papyri discovered in Egypt during the second half of the nineteenth century verified that "Aristeas" had an excellent knowledge of the actual terminology used to describe official positions and functions in the royal court.

In regard to his comments describing the translation, there is clearly a considerable amount of puffery added to impress the reader. The extended dialogues between the ruler and his translators seem so inherently improbable that Aristeas is compelled to include a rationale: "For it is the custom, as you surely are aware, to record in writing everything said and done from the moment the king begins to give audience until he retires to bed—a good and useful custom. On the day following, before audiences commence, the actions taken and the remarks uttered on the previous day are read through, and if any procedure is found incorrect it receives rectification."

Another major section of his book is devoted to a detailed description of his trip to Jerusalem carrying the king's gifts and request for translators. Here his digression is looked upon with considerably more favor, it commonly being conceded that there are at least touches of a first-hand narrative.

The author presents himself as if he were an idol-worshipping Greek (Section 16). This seems clearly a fiction unless the writer was a Gentile convert and is speaking in the accommodative sense of "we" praying to pagan deities (Section 16), referring to what was normal practice for Greeks rather than to what he himself was any longer doing. The book has every appearance of being designed as a Jewish apologetic to enhance the credibility and prestige of the Mosaical Law. The translation of that Law is the central motif to the entire work. Much space is devoted to the royal verification of the "wisdom" of the Jewish translators. An apologetic motive becomes explicit when Aristeas explains the lack of reference to the Jewish Law among pagan writers (Sections 31, 312–315) and when he has Eleazar the priest spiritualize the Law's ordinances (Sections 144–147 and 170–171).

This document purports to have been composed about 250 B.C., but a date around 100 B.C. is more readily accepted today. This does not exclude the possibility that Aristeas is reworking an earlier source that actually did date back to the time of Ptolemy Philadelphus.

Although the degree of divine superintendence over the Septuagint is magnified by some later writers into overt inspiration, Aristeas clearly presents the translation as a scholarly endeavor. Some later retellers of the story went so far as to have each translator independently render the text—and for all of their efforts to perfectly agree. Whatever the degree of historical mythology in his account, Aristeas in no way is responsible for this fiction. According to him, the text was decided not on the basis of inspiration nor on the basis of unanimity but on the basis of "wherein the majority agree" (Section 39). Nor did they work separately and alone. Instead we read of "making all details harmonize by mutual comparisons. The appropriate result of the harmonization was reduced to writing under the direction of Demetrius" (Section 302).

Sections 34–40:

The purport of the king's letter was as follows:
"King Ptolemy to Eleazar the High Priest, greeting and good health. Whereas it is come about that many Jews have been settled in our country, some forcibly

removed from Jerusalem by the Persians during their period of power and others who came into Egypt as captives in the train of our father—of these he enrolled many in the armed forces at higher than ordinary pay, and likewise when he judged their chief men to be loyal he gave them fortresses which he built, so that the native Egyptians might be in awe of them; and we too, since we have assumed the realm, meet all men in a very humane manner but your countrymen to a special degree—we, then, have given liberty to above a hundred thousand captives, paying their owners proper market prices and making good whatever injury may have been inflicted through the impulses of the mob. Our resolve in this matter was to do a pious deed and to dedicate a thank-offering to God the Most High, who has preserved our kingdom in tranquillity and in the mightiest esteem throughout the inhabited world. Those in the flower of their age, moreover, we have enrolled in our forces, and to those capable of being about our person and worthy of the trust of the royal court we have assigned offices of state. Now since we desire to show favor to these and to all the Jews in the world and to their posterity we have resolved that your Law should be translated into Greek writing from the Hebrew tongue in use among you, so that these writings should find place in our library along with other royal books. It will be a courteous act, therefore, and one worthy of our own zeal if you will choose elders of exemplary life who possess skill in the law and ability to translate, six from each tribe, so that it may be discovered wherein the majority agree, for the investigation concerns a matter of great weight. We think that we shall bear off great renown by the accomplishment of this task. We have sent upon this business Andreas, of the keepers of the bodyguard, and Aristeas, men whom we hold in honor, to converse with you. They bring with them dedicatory offerings for the Temple, and for sacrifices and other purposes a hundred talents of silver. And if you should write us concerning any desires of yours, you would gratify us and act as friendship requires; be assured that your wishes shall be fulfilled most speedily. Farewell."

This request was readily granted but only upon the pledge that they would be allowed to return after their work was completed (Sections 121–126):

Eleazar, then, selected men most excellent and of outstanding scholarship, to be expected in persons of such distinguished parentage. They had not only acquired proficiency in the literature of the Jews, but had bestowed no slight study on that of the Greeks also. They were therefore well qualified to be sent on embassies, and performed this office whenever there was need. They possessed great natural talent for conferences and discussions pertaining to the Law. They zealously cultivated the quality of the mean (and that is the best course), and eschewing a crude and uncouth disposition, they likewise avoided conceit and the assumption of superiority over others. In conversation it was their principle to listen attentively and to reply appropriately to every question. All of them observed this behavior, and it was in such conduct that they most desired to surpass one another; all were worthy of their leader and of his virtue. One could see how they loved Eleazar and he them from the distress of their parting. Besides writing the king on the subject of their safe return, Eleazar besought Andreas and me too to exert our efforts in the matter as far as we were able. And though we promised to take careful heed of the matter he said he was still deeply distressed, for he knew how the king in his love of excellence regarded it a very great gain, wherever he heard of a man surpassing others in culture and intellect, to summon him to himself. Indeed I have heard of a fine saying of his, that by having about himself just and prudent men he would have the greatest protection for his kingdom, for friends frankly advise what is best. This was surely true of the men Eleazar sent.

Upon hearing that the translators had arrived, the king immediately cancelled all other business to greet them and to pay homage to the sacred scrolls they bore (Sections 172–179):

And so Eleazar, after he had offered sacrifice and had chosen the men and prepared many gifts for the king, sent us on our way in great security. When we reached Alexandria word of our arrival was brought to the king. Upon our admission to the court Andreas and I gave friendly greeting to the king and delivered the letters from Eleazar. Being very eager to receive the delegates, the king gave orders that all the other officials be dismissed, and that the men be summoned. This procedure struck everyone as strange, for it was the custom that those who came on official business gained access to the royal presence on the fifth day, while visitors from kings and prominent cities were barely admitted to the court in thirty days. But he thought that these men who had come were worthy of higher honor and rightly judged the eminence of him who had sent them, and so, dismissing all persons he considered superfluous, he waited, walking to and fro, to greet them on their arrival. They entered, then, with the gifts which had been sent and the precious parchments in which the Law was inscribed in Jewish letters with writing of gold, the material being wonderfully worked and the joinings of the leaves being made imperceptible; and when the king saw the men he began to put questions concerning the books. When they had uncovered the rolls and had unrolled the parchments the king paused for a considerable space, and after bowing deeply some seven times said, "I thank you, good sirs, and him that sent you even more, but most of all I thank God whose holy words these are." And when all with one accord, both those newly come and those already present, exclaimed in a single voice, "Excellent, Your Majesty!" he was moved to tears out of the fullness of his joy. For the strain of the spirit and the tension of honor constrain to tears upon attainment of success. He bade them put the rolls back in their places, and only then did he greet the men, saying, "It was right, my God-fearing friends, first to pay homage to those treasures for whose sake I summoned you, and thereafter to extend the right hand to you; therefore have I done this thing first.

After receiving the translators, the king ordered a seven-day feast in their honor. During it he tested each translator with a spontaneous and challenging question. He came away impressed with their answers. Then the story finally gets to what is of greatest interest to us, namely the actual translating and its immediate reception (Sections 301–311):

After three days Demetrius took the men with him and crossed the breakwater, seven stades long, to the island; then he crossed over the bridge and proceeded to the northerly parts. There he called a meeting in a mansion built by the seashore, magnificently appointed and in a secluded situation, and called upon the men to carry out the business of translation, all necessary appliances having been well provided. And so they proceeded to carry it out, making all details harmonize by mutual comparisons. The appropriate result of the harmonization was reduced to writing under the direction of Demetrius. The sessions would last until the ninth hour, and afterwards they would break up to take care of their bodily needs, all their requirements being lavishly supplied. In addition, everything that was prepared for the king Dorotheus arranged for them also, for he had been so instructed by the king. Every day they would come to the court early in the morning, and when they had made their salutation to the king they departed to their own place.

When they had washed their hands in the sea, as is the custom of all Jews, and had offered prayer to God, they addressed themselves to the interpretation and clarification of each passage. I questioned them on this point too, why it was that they washed their hands before praying. And they explained that it was in witness that they had done no wrong, since the hands are the organs of all activity; in such beautiful and holy spirit do they make all things symbols of righteousness and truth. Thus, as we have said before, they forgathered every day to this spot, so delightful for its seclusion and its clear light, and carried out their appointed task. And so it came about that the work of transcription was completed in seventy-two days, as if this coincidence had been the result of some design.

When the work was concluded Demetrius assembled the community of the Jews at the place where the translation was executed, and read it out to the entire gathering, the translators too being present; these received a great ovation from the community also, in recognition of the great service for which they were responsible. And they accorded Demetrius a similar reception, and requested him to have a transcription of the entire Law made and to present it to their rulers. When the rolls had been read the priests and the elders of the translators and some of the corporate body and the leaders of the people rose up and said, "Inasmuch as the translation has been well and piously made and is in every respect accurate, it is right that it should remain in its present form and that no revision of any sort take place." When all had assented to what had been said, they bade that an imprecation be pronounced, according to their custom, upon any who should revise the text by adding or transposing anything whatever in what had been written down, or by making any excision; and in this they did well, so that the work might be preserved imperishable and unchanged always.

(Source: *Aristeas to Philocrates [Letter of Aristeas]* edited and translated by Moses Hadas, English translation copyrighted 1951, Harper & Row, renewed 1979 by Elizabeth C. Hadas, reprinted by permission of Harper-Collins Publishers.)

5. JOSEPHUS' REWORKING OF ARISTEAS' ACCOUNT

Nearly all of the account that Josephus gives in his *Antiquities* (Book 12, Chapter 2, extracts from which are quoted below) amounts to a paraphrase of Aristeas' earlier version. So close are the two that some scholars have found Josephus useful in confirming the text of Aristeas!

Unlike Aristeas' narrative, Josephus omits the names of the "elders" who translated the text and the lengthy narrative of the king's banquet enquiries of the translators, though he shows that he knew of these incidents by making allusion to both (12.2.7; 12.2.12). Aristeas' spiritualizing of the Jewish Law (through Eleazar the high priest) is omitted, as is all reference to apparent native Egyptian anti–Semitic riots (Aristeas, 37).

Josephus changes Aristeas on a number of minor matters, such as raising the price of a slave from 20 drachmas to the more realistic 120 drachmas (12.2.3) and by altering the number of feast days from seven to twelve (12.2.12).

In Aristeas there is a conscious effort to elevate the prestige of the Jewish Law and community, but in ways that most Gentiles would have considered as straining credulity. Moses Hadas points out that Josephus has eliminated several such elements: "Ptolemy does *not* bear down before the Law seven times (Aristeas, 177), his courtiers do *not* wait on table for the translators (186), he does *not* decree that informers take possession of those who fail to release Jewish slaves" (*Aristeas to Philocrates*, page 21).

1. When Alexander had reigned twelve years, and after him Ptolemy Soter forty years, Philadelphus then took the kingdom of Egypt, and held it forty years within one. He procured the law to be interpreted; and set free those that were come from Jerusalem into Egypt, and were in slavery there, who were a hundred and twenty thousand. The occasion was this: Demetrius Phalerius, who was library-keeper to the king, was now endeavoring, if it were possible, to gather together all the books that were in the habitable earth, and buying whatsoever was anywhere valuable, or agreeable to the king's inclination (who was very earnestly set upon collecting of books;) to which inclination of his Demetrius was zealously subservient. And when once Ptolemy asked him, How many thousand of books he had collected; he replied, that he had already about twenty times ten thousand, but that in a little time he should have fifty times ten thousand. But he said he had been informed, that there were many books of law among the Jews, worthy of inquiring after, and worthy of the king's library, but which being written in characters and in a dialect of their own, will cause no small pains in getting them translated into the Greek tongue: that the character in which they are written seems to be like to that which is the proper character of the Syrians, and that its sound, when pronounced, is like theirs also: and that this sound appears to be peculiar to themselves. Wherefore he said that nothing hindered why they might not get those books to be translated also, for while nothing is wanting that is necessary for that purpose, we may have their books also in this library. So the king thought that Demetrius was very zealous to procure him abundance of books, and that he suggested what was exceeding proper for him to do, and therefore he wrote to the Jewish high-priest, that he should act accordingly.

2. Now there was one Aristeus, who was among the king's most intimate friends, and on account of his modesty very acceptable to him. This Aristeus resolved frequently, and that before now, to petition the king that he would set all the captive Jews in his kingdom free; and he thought this a convenient opportunity for making that petition. So he discoursed in the first place with the captains of the king's guards, Sosibius of Tarentum, and Andreas; and persuaded them to assist him in what he was going to intercede with the king for. Accordingly, Aristeus embraced the same opinion with those that have been before mentioned; and went to the king, and made the following speech to him: "It is not fit for us, O king, to overlook things hastily, or to deceive ourselves, but to lay the truth open; for since we have determined not only to get the laws of the Jews transcribed, but interpreted also for thy satisfaction, by what means can we do this, while so many of the Jews are now slaves in thy kingdom? . . ."

4. Now when this had been done after so magnificent a manner, according to the king's inclinations, he gave order to Demetrius to give him in writing his sentiments concerning the transcribing of the Jewish books; for no part of the administration is done rashly by these kings, but all things are managed with great circumspection. On which account I have subjoined a copy of these epistles, and set down the multitude of the vessels sent as gifts [to Jerusalem,] and the construction of every one, that the exactness of the artificer's workmanship, as it appeared to those that saw them, and which workman made every vessel, may be made manifest, and this on account of the excellency of the vessels themselves. Now the copy of the epistle was to this purpose: "Demetrius to the great king. When thou, O king, gavest me a charge concerning the collection of books that were wanting to fill your library, and concerning the care that ought to be taken about such as are imperfect, I have used the utmost diligence about those matters. And I let you know, that we want the books of the Jewish legislation, with some others; for they are written in the Hebrew characters, and being in the language of that nation, are to us unknown. It hath also happened to them, that they have been transcribed more carelessly than they ought to have been, because they have not had hitherto royal care taken about them. Now it is necessary that thou shouldst have accurate copies of them. And indeed this legislation is full of hidden wisdom, and entirely blameless, as being the legislation of God; for which cause it is, as Hecateus of Abdera says, that the poets and historians make no mention of it, nor of those men who lead their lives according to it, since it is a holy law, and ought not to be published by profane mouths. If then it please thee, O king, thou mayest write to the high-priest of the Jews, to send six of the elders out of every tribe, and those such as are most skilful in the laws, that by their means we may learn the clear and agreeing sense of these books; and may obtain an accurate interpretation of their contents, and so may have such a collection of these as may be suitable to thy desire."

5. When this epistle was sent to the king, he commanded that an epistle should be drawn up for Eleazar, the Jewish high-priest, concerning these matters: and that they should inform him of the release of the Jews that had been in slavery among them. He also sent fifty talents of gold for the making of large basins, and vials, and cups, and an immense quantity of precious stones. He also gave order to those who had the custody of the chests that contained these stones, to give the artificers leave to choose out what sorts of them they pleased. He withal appointed, that a hundred talents in money should be sent to the temple for sacrifices, and for other uses . . . . "And as I am desirous to do what will be grateful to these, and to all the other Jews in the habitable earth, I have determined to procure an interpretation of your law, and to have it translated out of the Hebrew into Greek, and to be deposited in my library. Thou wilt therefore do well to choose out and send to me men of a good character, who are now elders in age, and six in number out of every tribe. These, by their age, must be skilful in the laws, and of abilities to make an accurate interpretation of them; and when this shall be finished, I shall think that I have done a work glorious to myself. And I have sent to thee Andreas, the captain of my guard, and Aristeus, men whom I have in very great esteem; by whom I have sent those first fruits which I have dedicated to the temple, and to the sacrifices, and to other uses, to the value of a hundred talents. And if thou wilt send to us to let us know what thou wouldst have farther, thou wilt do a thing acceptable to me.". . .

11. And these were what gifts were sent by Ptolemy to Jerusalem, and dedicated to God there. But when Eleazar the high-priest had devoted them to God, and

had paid due respect to those that brought them, and had given them presents to be carried to the king, he dismissed them. And when they were come to Alexandria, and Ptolemy heard that they were come, and that the seventy elders were come also, he presently sent for Andreas and Aristeus, his ambassadors, who came to him, and delivered him the epistle which they brought him from the high-priest, and made answer to all the questions he put to them by word of mouth. He then made haste to meet the elders that came from Jerusalem for the interpretation of the laws; and he gave command that every body, who came on occasions, should be sent away, which was a thing surprising, and what he did not use to do; for those that were drawn thither upon such occasions used to come to him on the fifth day, but ambassadors at the month's end. But when he had sent those away, he waited for those that were sent by Eleazar: but as the old men came in with the presents which the high-priest had given them to bring to the king, and with the membranes, upon which they had their laws written in golden letters, he put questions to them concerning those books; and when they had taken off the covers wherein they were wrapped up, they showed him the membranes. So the king stood admiring the thinness of those membranes, and the exactness of the junctures, which could not be perceived (so exactly were they connected one with another;) and this he did for a considerable time. He then said, that he returned them thanks for coming to him, and still greater thanks to him that sent them; and, above all, to that God whose laws they appeared to be. Then did the elders, and those that were present with them, cry out with one voice, and wished all happiness to the king. Upon which he fell into tears, by the violence of the pleasure he had, it being natural to men to afford the same indications in great joy that they do under sorrows. And when he had bid them deliver the books to those that were appointed to receive them, he saluted the men, and said, that it was but just to discourse, in the first place, of the errand they were sent about, and then to address himself to themselves. He promised, however, that he would make this day on which they came to him remarkable and eminent every year through the whole course of his life; for their coming to him, and the victory which he gained over Antigonus by sea, proved to be on the very same day. He also gave orders that they should sup with him; and gave it in charge that they should have excellent lodgings provided for them in the upper part of the city.

12. Now he that was appointed to take care of the reception of strangers, Nicanor by name, called for Dorotheus, whose duty it was to make provision for them, and bid him prepare for every one of them what should be requisite for their diet and way of living: which thing was ordered by the king after this manner. — He took care that those that belonged to every city, which did not use the same way of living, that all things should be prepared for them according to the custom of those that came to him, that, being feasted according to the usual method of their own way of living, they might be the better pleased, and might not be uneasy at any thing done to them, from which they were naturally averse. And this was now done in the case of these men by Dorotheus, who was put into this office because of his great skill in such matters belonging to common life: for he took care of all such matters as concerned the reception of strangers, and appointed them double seats for them to sit on, according as the king had commanded him to do: for he had commanded that half of their seats should be set at his hand, and the other half behind his table, and took care that no respect should be omitted that could be shown them. And when they were thus set down, he bid Dorotheus to minister to all those that were come to him from Judea after the manner they used to be ministered to: for which cause he sent away their sacred heralds, and those that

slew the sacrifices, and the rest that used to say grace; but called to one of those that were come to him, whose name was Eleazar, who was a priest, and desired him to say grace, who then stood in the midst of them, and prayed, — "That all prosperity might attend the king, and those that were his subjects." Upon which an acclamation was made by the whole company with joy and a great noise; and when that was over, they fell to eating their supper, and to the enjoyment of what was set before them. And at a little interval afterward, when the king thought a sufficient time had been interposed, he began to talk philosophically to them, and he asked every one of them a philosophical question, and such a one as might give light in those inquiries: and when they had explained all the problems that had been proposed by the king, about every point, he was well pleased with their answers. This took up the twelve days in which they were treated: and he that pleases may learn the particular questions in that book of Aristeus's, which he wrote on this very occasion.

13. And while not the king only, but the philosopher Menedemus also, admired them, and said, that "all things were governed by providence; and that it was probable that thence it was that such force or beauty was discovered in these men's words," they then left off asking any more such questions. But the king said, that he had gained very great advantages by their coming; for that he had received this profit from them, that he had learned how he ought to rule his subjects. And he gave order, that they should have every one three talents given them; and that those who were to conduct them to their lodging should do it. Accordingly, when three days were over, Demetrius took them, and went over the causeway seven furlongs long; it was a bank in the sea to an island. And when they had gone over the bridge, he proceeded to the northern parts, and showed them where they should meet, which was in a house that was built near the shore, and was a quiet place, and fit for their discoursing together about their work. When he had brought them thither, he entreated them (now they had all things about them which they wanted for the interpretation of their law,) that they would suffer nothing to interrupt them in their work. Accordingly, they made an accurate interpretation, with great zeal and great pains; and this they continued to do till the ninth hour of the day; after which time they relaxed and took care of their body, while their food was provided for them in great plenty; besides, Dorotheus, at the king's command, brought them a great deal of what was provided for the king himself. But in the morning, they came to the court and saluted Ptolemy, and then went away to their former place, where, when they had washed their hands, and purified themselves, they betook themselves to the interpretation of the laws. Now when the law was transcribed, and the labor of interpretation was over, which came to its conclusion in seventy-two days, Demetrius gathered all the Jews together to the place where the laws were translated, and where the interpreters were, and read them over. The multitude did also approve of those elders that were the interpreters of the law. They withal commended Demetrius for his proposal, as the inventor of what was greatly for their happiness; and they desired, that he would give leave to their rulers also to read the law. Moreover, they all, both the priest, and the ancientest of the elders, and the principal men of their commonwealth, made it their request, that since the interpretation was happily finished, it might continue in the state it now was, and might not be altered. And when they all commended that determination of theirs, they enjoined, that if any one observed either any thing superfluous, or any thing omitted, that he would take a view of it again, and have it laid before them, and corrected; which was a wise action of theirs, that when the thing was judged to have been well done, it might continue for ever.

14. So the king rejoiced when he saw that his design of this nature was brought to perfection, to so great advantage: and he was chiefly delighted with hearing the laws read to him; and was astonished at the deep meaning and wisdom of the legislator. And he began to discourse with Demetrius, "How it came to pass, that when this legislation was so wonderful, no one, either of the poets or of the historians, had made mention of it." Demetrius made answer, that "no one durst be so bold as to touch upon the description of these laws, because they were divine and venerable; and because some that had attempted it were afflicted by God." He also told him, that "Theopompus was desirous of writing somewhat about them, but was thereupon disturbed in his mind for above thirty days' time; and upon some intermission of his distemper, he appeased God [by prayer] as suspecting that his madness proceeded from that cause." Nay, indeed, he farther saw a dream, that his distemper befell him while he indulged too great a curiosity about divine matters, and was desirous of publishing them among common men; but when he left off that attempt, he recovered his understanding again. Moreover, he informed him of Theodectes, the tragic poet, concerning whom it was reported, that when in a certain dramatic representation he was desirous to make mention of things that were contained in the sacred books, he was afflicted with a darkness in his eyes; and that upon his being conscious of the occasion of his distemper, and appeasing God [by prayer] he was freed from that affliction.

15. And when the king had received these books from Demetrius, as we have said already, he adored them: and gave order that great care should be taken of them, that they might remain uncorrupted. He also desired that the interpreters would come often to him out of Judea, and that both on account of the respects that he would pay them, and on account of the presents he would make them: for he said, — "It was now but just to send them away, although if, of their own accord, they would come to him hereafter, they should obtain all that their own wisdom might justly require, and what his generosity was able to give them." So he then sent them away, and gave to every one of them three garments of the best sort, and two talents of gold, and a cup of the value of one talent, and the furniture of the room wherein they were feasted. And these were the things he presented to them. But by them he sent to Eleazar the high-priest ten beds, with feet of silver, and the furniture to them belonging, and a cup of the value of thirty talents; and besides these, ten garments, and purple, and a very beautiful crown, and a hundred pieces of the finest woven linen; as also vials and dishes, and vessels for pouring, and two golden cisterns, to be dedicated to God. He also desired him, by an epistle, that he would give these interpreters leave, if any of them were desirous of coming to him, because he highly valued a conversation with men of such learning, and should be very willing to lay out his wealth upon such men. And this was what came to the Jews, and was much to their glory and honor, from Ptolemy Philadelphus.

(Source: Josephus, *Antiquities*, in *Works of Josephus*, William Whiston, translator, four volume edition, volume two, Oakley, Mason & Company, New York: 1869, pages 260–277.)

6. PHILO'S ACCOUNT OF THE TRANSLATION

In this first century account, Philo stresses the accuracy of the LXX but accounts for it not on the basis of the skill and dedication of the translators but on the grounds of supernatural inspiration. While Aristeas has the translators deciding upon their text through mutual consultation, Philo has each of them working separately and yet producing a text that invariably was identical with that of the others.

He refers to a long-standing feast day held by the Jews in Alexandria (with major Gentile participation) in honor of the translation. Although nations have known many different types of holidays, this is probably the only one ever undertaken out of respect for a Bible translation!

From Philo's *On the Life of Moses* (2:5–7) comes this extract:

...And that beauty and dignity of the legislation of Moses is honoured not among the Jews only, but also by all other nations, is plain, both from what has been already said and from what I am about to state. In olden time the laws were written in the Chaldaean language, and for a long time they remained in the same condition as at first, not changing their language as long as their beauty had not made them known to other nations; but when, from the daily and uninterrupted respect shown to them by those to whom they had been given, and from their ceaseless observance of their ordinances, other nations also obtained an understanding of them, their reputation spread over all lands; for what was really good, even though it may through envy be overshadowed for a short time, still in time shines again through the intrinsic excellence of its nature.

Some persons, thinking it a scandalous thing that these laws should only be known among one half portion of the human race, namely, among the barbarians, and that the Greek nation should be wholly and entirely ignorant of them, turned their attention to their translation.

And since this undertaking was an important one, tending to the general advantage, not only of private persons, but also of rulers, of whom the number was not great, it was entrusted to kings and to the most illustrious of all kings. Ptolemy, surnamed Philadelphus, was the third in succession after Alexander, the monarch who subdued Egypt; and he was, in all virtues which can be displayed in government, the most excellent sovereign, not only of all those of his time, but of all that ever lived; so that even now, after the lapse of so many generations, his fame is still celebrated, as having left many instances and monuments of his magnanimity in the cities and districts of his kingdom, so that even now it is come to be a sort of proverbial expression to call excessive magnificence, and zeal, for honour and splendour in preparation, Philadelphian, from his name; and, in a word, the whole family of the Ptolemies was exceedingly eminent and conspicuous above all other royal families, and among the Ptolemies, Philadelphus was the most illustrious; for all the rest put together scarcely did as many glorious and praiseworthy actions as this one king did by himself, being, as it were, the leader of the herd, and in a manner the head of all the kings.

He, then, being a sovereign of this character, and having conceived a great admiration for and love of the legislation of Moses, conceived the idea of having our laws translated into the Greek language; and immediately he sent out ambassadors to the high-priest and king of Judea, for they were the same person. And having explained his wishes, and having requested him to pick him out a number of men, of perfect fitness for the task, who should translate the law, the high-priest, as was natural, being greatly pleased, and thinking that the king had only felt the inclination to undertake a work of such a character from having been influenced by the providence of God, considered, and with great care selected the most respectable

of the Hebrews whom he had about him, who in addition to their knowledge of
their national scriptures, had also been well instructed in Grecian literature, and
cheerfully sent them.

And when they arrived at the king's court they were hospitably received by the
king; and while they feasted, they in return feasted their entertainer with witty
and virtuous conversation; for he made experiment of the wisdom of each individual among them, putting to them a succession of new and extraordinary
questions; and they, since the time did not allow of their being prolix in their
answers, replied with great propriety and fidelity as if they were delivering
apophthegms which they had already prepared. So when they had won his approval, they immediately began to fulfil the objects for which that honourable em-
bassy had been sent; and considering among themselves how important the affair
was, to translate laws which had been divinely given by direct inspiration, since
they were not able either to take away anything, or to add anything, or to alter
anything, but were bound to preserve the original form and character of the whole
composition, they looked out for the most completely purified place of all the
spots on the outside of the city.

For the places within the walls, as being filled with all kinds of animals, were
held in suspicion by them by reason of the diseases and deaths of some, and the
accursed actions of those who were in health. The island of Pharos lies in front
of Alexandria, the neck of which runs out like a sort of tongue towards the city,
being surrounded with water of no great depth, but chiefly with shoals and shallow
water, so that the great noise and roaring from the beating of the waves is kept
at a considerable distance, and so mitigated. They judged this place to be the most
suitable of all the spots in the neighbourhood for them to enjoy quiet and tranquillity in, so that they might associate with the laws alone in their minds; and
there they remained, and having taken the sacred scriptures, they lifted up them
and their hands also to heaven, entreating of God that they might not fail in their
object. And he assented to their prayers, that the greater part, or indeed the
universal race of mankind might be benefited, by using these philosophical and
entirely beautiful commandments for the correction of their lives.

Therefore, being settled in a secret place, and nothing ever being present with
them except the elements of nature, the earth, the water, the air, and the heaven,
concerning the creation of which they were going in the first place to explain the
sacred account; for the account of the creation of the world is the beginning of
the law; they, like men inspired, prophesied, not one saying one thing and another
another, but every one of them employed the self-same nouns and verbs, as if
some unseen prompter had suggested all their language to them. And yet who is
there who does not know that every language, and the Greek language above all
others, is rich in a variety of words, and that it is possible to vary a sentence and
to paraphrase the same idea, so as to set it forth in a great variety of manners,
adapting many different forms of expression to it at different times.

But this, they say, did not happen at all in the case of this translation of the law,
but that, in every case, exactly corresponding Greek words were employed to
translate literally the appropriate Chaldaic words, being adapted with exceeding
propriety to the matters which were to be explained; for just as I suppose the
things which are proved in geometry and logic do not admit any variety of explanation, but the proposition which was set forth from the beginning remains unaltered, in like manner I conceive did these men find words precisely and literally
corresponding to the things, which words were alone, or in the greatest possible
degree, destined to explain with clearness and force the matters which it was

desired to reveal. And there is a very evident proof of this; for if Chaldaeans were to learn the Greek language, and if the Greeks were to learn Chaldaean, and if each were to meet with those scriptures in both languages, namely, the Chaldaic and the translated version, they would admire and reverence them both as sisters, or rather as one and the same both in their facts and in their language; considering these translators not mere interpreters but hierophants and prophets to whom it had been granted with their honest and guileless minds to go along with the most pure spirit of Moses.

On which account, even to this very day, there is every year a solemn assembly held and a festival celebrated in the island of Pharos, to which not only the Jews but a great number of persons of other nations sail across, reverencing the place in which the first light of interpretation shone forth, and thanking God for that ancient piece of beneficence which was always young and fresh.

And after the prayers and the giving of thanks some of them pitched their tents on the shore, and some of them lay down without any tents in the open air on the sand of the shore, and feasted with their relations and friends, thinking the shore at that time a more beautiful abode than the furniture of the king's palace.

In this way those admirable, and incomparable, and most desirable laws were made known to all people, whether private individuals or kings, and this too at a period when the nation had not been prosperous for a long time. And it is generally the case that a cloud is thrown over the affairs of those who are not flourishing, so that but little is known of them; and then, if they make any fresh start and begin to improve, how great is the increase of their renown and glory? I think that in that case every nation, abandoning all their own individual customs, and utterly disregarding their national laws, would change and come over to the honour of such a people only; for their laws shining in connection with, and simultaneously with, the prosperity of the nation, will obscure all others, just as the rising sun obscures the stars.

(Source: C. D. Yonge, translator, *Works of Philo Judaeus*, volume III. London: Henry G. Bohn, 1855.)

7. JUSTIN MARTYR ON DEPARTURES FROM THE LXX AS PROOF OF TEXTUAL CORRUPTION

Writing in the first half of the second century A.D., Justin shared with Philo a confident belief in the inspiration of the Septuagint. In his writings and those of later Christians who shared the same assumption, this belief carried a very important negative implication as well: If the Hebrew text differed from the Septuagint, then the Hebrew must have been the victim of textual corruption. And from this deduction it is but a small step to make the accusation that Justin does in the following extract, that the Jewish scribes had intentionally altered the Hebrew to hide the spiritual truths that the Septuagint so clearly revealed. In chapters lxxi–lxxii of the *Dialogue with Trypho* we read:

"But I am far from putting reliance in your teachers, who refuse to admit that the interpretation made by the seventy elders who were with Ptolemy [king] of the

Egyptians is a correct one; and they attempt to frame another. And I wish you to observe, that they have altogether taken away many Scriptures from the translations effected by those seventy elders who were with Ptolemy, and by which this very man who was crucified is proved to have been set forth expressly as God, and man, and as being crucified, and as dying; but since I am aware that this is denied by all of your nation, I do not address myself to these points, but I proceed to carry on my discussions by means of those passages which are still admitted by you. For you assent to those which I have brought before your attention, except that you contradict the statement, 'Behold, the virgin shall conceive,' and say it ought to be read, 'Behold, the young woman shall conceive.' And I promised to prove that the prophecy referred, not, as you were taught, to Hezekiah, but to this Christ of mine: and now I shall go to the proof."

Here Trypho remarked, "We ask you first of all to tell us some of the Scriptures which you allege have been completely cancelled."

And I said, "I shall do as you please. From the statements, then, which Esdras made in reference to the law of the passover, they have taken away the following: 'And Esdras said to the people, This passover is our Saviour and our refuge. And if you have understood, and your heart has taken it in, that we shall humble Him on a standard, and thereafter hope in Him, then this place shall not be forsaken for ever, says the God of hosts. But if you will not believe Him, and will not listen to His declaration, you shall be a laughing-stock to the nations.' And from the sayings of Jeremiah they have cut out the following: 'I [was] like a lamb that is brought to the slaughter: they devised a device against me, saying, Come, let us lay on wood on His bread, and let us blot Him out from the land of the living; and His name shall no more be remembered.' And since this passage from the sayings of Jeremiah is still written in some copies [of the Scriptures] in the synagogues of the Jews (for it is only a short time since they were cut out), and since from these words it is demonstrated that the Jews deliberated about the Christ Himself, to crucify and put Him to death, He Himself is both declared to be led as a sheep to the slaughter, as was predicted by Isaiah, and is here represented as a harmless lamb; but being in a difficulty about them, they give themselves over to blasphemy. And again, from the sayings of the same Jeremiah these have been cut out: 'The Lord God remembered His dead people of Israel who lay in the graves; and He descended to preach to them His own salvation.'

"And from the ninety-fifth (ninety-sixth) Psalm they have taken away this short saying of the words of David: 'From the wood.' For when the passage said, 'Tell ye among the nations, the Lord hath reigned from the wood,' they have left, 'Tell ye among the nations, the Lord hath reigned.' Now no one of your people has ever been said to have reigned as God and Lord among the nations, with the exception of Him only who was crucified, of whom also the Holy Spirit affirms in the same Psalm that He was raised again, and freed from [the grave], declaring that there is none like Him among the gods of the nations: for they are idols of demons. But I shall repeat the whole Psalm to you, that you may perceive what has been said. It is thus: 'Sing unto the Lord a new song; sing unto the Lord, all the earth. Sing unto the Lord, and bless His name; show forth His salvation from day to day. Declare His glory among the nations, His wonders among all people. For the Lord is great, and greatly to be praised: He is to be feared above all the gods. For all the gods of the nations are demons but the Lord made the heavens. Confession and beauty are in His presence; holiness and magnificence are in His sanctuary. Bring to the Lord, O ye countries of the nations, bring to the Lord glory and honour, bring to the Lord glory in His name. Take sacrifices, and go into His courts; worship the Lord in His holy temple. Let the whole earth be moved before Him: tell ye among the nations, the Lord hath reigned. For He hath established the world, which shall not be moved; He shall judge the nations with equity. Let the heavens rejoice, and the earth be glad; let the sea and its fulness shake. Let the fields and all therein be joyful. Let all the trees of the wood be glad before the lord: for He comes, for He comes to judge the earth. He shall judge the world with righteousness, and the people with His truth.'"

Here Trypho remarked, "Whether [or not] the rulers of the people have erased any portion of the Scriptures, as you affirm, God knows; but it seems incredible."

"Assuredly," said I, "it does seem incredible. For it is more horrible than the calf which they made, when satisfied with manna on the earth; or than the sacrifice of children to demons; or than the slaying of the prophets. But," said I, "you appear to me not to have heard the Scriptures which I said they had stolen away. For such as have been quoted are more than enough to prove the points in dispute, besides those which are retained by us, and shall yet be brought forward."

(Source: Alexander Roberts and James Donaldson, editors, *The Ante-Nicene Fathers*, volume I: *The Apostolic Fathers: Justin Martyr and Irenaeus*, Charles Scribners Sons, New York: 1899 reprint of 1885 edition, pages 234–235.)

III. *Post-Septuagint Translations*

8. JEROME ON THE TRANSLATION STYLES OF AQUILA, SYMMACHUS, AND THEODOTION

Sorting out the facts concerning these three post–Septuagint translators of the Old Testament is extremely difficult. They were either Jews, proselytes to Judaism, apostates from Christianity, or members of a Judeo-Christian sect called the Ebionites — depending upon what source is consulted. Due to the inconsistencies there appears to have been a mingling of biographical data among these three individuals.

The evidence is considerably clearer in regard to the translations they produced. Aquila, for example, was so literalistic that he carried over the Hebrew sentence structures even when doing so reduced the readability and comprehensibility of the Greek. He was at special pains to element the Messianic implications that Christians found in certain Septuagint texts.

In contrast, Theodotion's work is known for two somewhat paradoxical characteristics: On the one hand it tended to be somewhat "freer" than Aquila's, while on the other hand it frequently resorted to transliteration rather than translation. At least parts of his translation found great favor among Jews and Christians alike. It is certain that his version of Daniel replaced that of the LXX in common usage. It is possible that the same is true in regard to Ezra and Nehemiah.

In the following extract from the introduction to Jerome's *Chronicle of Eusebius* (382 A.D.), the translator of the Vulgate discusses some of the differences in style among these three individuals and the disgruntlement with the Septuagint that led to their efforts:

Jerome to his friends Vincentius and Gallienus, Greeting:
1. It has long been the practice of learned men to exercise their minds by rendering into Latin the works of Greek writers, and, what is more difficult, to translate the poems of illustrious authors though trammelled by the farther requirements of verse. It was thus that our Tully literally translated whole books of Plato; and after publishing an edition of Aratus (who may now be considered a Roman) in hexameter verse, he amused himself with the economics of Xenophon. In this latter work the golden river of eloquence again and again meets with obstacles, around which its waters break and foam to such an extent that persons unacquainted with the original would not believe they were reading Cicero's words. And no wonder! It is hard to follow another man's lines and everywhere keep within bounds. It is an arduous task to preserve felicity and grace unimpaired in a translation. Some word has forcibly expressed a given thought; I have no word of my own to convey the meaning: and while I am seeking to satisfy the sense I may go a long way round and accomplish but a small distance of my journey. Then we must take into account the ins and outs of transposition, the variations in cases, the diversity of figures, and, lastly, the peculiar, and, so to speak, the native idiom of the language. A literal translation sounds absurd: if, on the other hand, I am obliged to change either the order or the words themselves, I shall appear to have forsaken the duty of a translator.
2. So, my dear Vincentius, and you, Gallienus, whom I love as my own soul, I beseech you, whatever may be the value of this hurried piece of work, to read it with the feelings of a friend rather than with those of a critic. And I ask this all the more earnestly because, as you know, I dictated with great rapidity to my amanuensis; and how difficult the task is, the sacred records testify; for the old flavour is not preserved in the Greek version by the Seventy. It was this that stimulated Aquila, Symmachus, and Theodotion; and the result of their labors was to impart a totally different character to one and the same work; one strove to give word for word, another the general meaning, while the third desired to avoid any great divergency from the ancients. A fifth, sixth, and seventh edition, though no one knows to what authors they are to be attributed, exhibit so pleasing a variety of their own that, in spite of their being anonymous, they have won an authoritative position. Hence, some go so far as to consider the sacred writings somewhat harsh and grating to the ear; which arises from the fact that the persons of whom I speak are not aware that the writings in question are a translation from the Hebrew, and therefore, looking at the surface not at the substance, they shudder at the squalid dress before they discover the fair body which the language clothes.

(Source: Philip Schaff and Henry Wace, editors, *The Nicene and Post-Nicene Fathers*, volume VI, Christian Literature Company, New York: 1893, pages 483–484.)

9. CHRYSOSTOM ON THE DANGER OF DOCTRINAL BIAS IN POST-SEPTUAGINT TRANSLATIONS

In his *Homilies on Saint Matthew* (V. 2), Chrysostom raises the question of which translation should be trusted when there is a difference in rendering. Chrysostom speaks out in favor of the Septuagint. He is impressed by the fact that it was undertaken by a large group rather than an individual. Even more important to him is the fact that the accusation of doctrinal bias cannot be lodged against it.

But if, when their mouths are stopped on this point, they should seek another, namely, what is said touching Mary's virginity, and should object to us other translators, saying, that they used not the term "virgin," but "young woman"; in the first place we will say this, that the Seventy were justly entitled to confidence above all the others. For these made their translation after Christ's coming, continuing to be Jews, and may justly be suspected as having spoken rather in enmity, and as darkening the prophecies on purpose; but the Seventy, as having entered upon this work an hundred years or more before the coming of Christ, stand clear from all such suspicion, and on account of the date, and of their number, and of their agreement, would have a better right to be trusted.

(Source: Philip Schaff, editor, *Nicene and Post-Nicene Fathers*; volume X: *Saint Chrysostom: Homilies on the Gospel of Matthew*, New York: Christian Literature Company, 1888.)

10. JEROME'S COMPARISON OF MESSIANIC TEXTS IN THE HEBREW AND IN AQUILA'S TRANSLATION

Jerome was sufficiently concerned with the accusation of doctrinal bias to carefully compare Aquila's rendering with that of the Hebrew. In Letter 32, to Marcella (384 A.D.), he shares the conclusions he had reached.

There are two reasons for the shortness of this letter, one that its bearer is impatient to start, and the other that I am too busy to waste time on trifles. You ask what business can be so urgent as to stop me from a chat on paper. Let me tell you, then, that for some time past I have been comparing Aquila's version of the Old Testament with the scrolls of the Hebrew, to see if from hatred to Christ the synagogue has changed the text; and — to speak frankly to a friend — I have found several variations which confirm our faith. After having exactly revised the prophets, Solomon, the psalter, and the books of Kings, I am now engaged on Exodus (called by the Jews, from its opening words, Eleh shêmoth), and when I have finished this I shall go on to Leviticus. Now you see why I can let no claim for a letter withdraw me from my work. However, as I do not wish my friend Currentius to run altogether in vain, I have tacked on to this little talk two letters which I am sending to your sister Paula, and to her dear child Eustochium. Read these, and if you find them instructive or pleasant, take what I have said to them as meant for you also.

(Source: Philip Schaff and Henry Wace, editors, *The Nicene and Post-Nicene Fathers*, volume VI, Christian Literature Company, New York: 1893, pages 45–46.)

11. JEROME ON DIFFERENCES BETWEEN THE HEBREW BOOK OF DANIEL AND THEODOTION'S BOOK OF DANIEL

Jerome had no convincing explanation of how Theodotion's Greek Daniel had come to take the place of the LXX's version of the book. But of one thing he was certain: Because of additions to the text it contained incidents that were completely unknown to the Hebrew version. At length, he points out how learned Jews could, and did, mock these additions. Writing in the preface to his own translation of Daniel (about 392 A.D.), Jerome said:

The Septuagint version of Daniel the prophet is not read by the Churches of our Lord and Saviour. They use Theodotion's version, but how this came to pass I cannot tell. Whether it be that the language is Chaldee, which differs in certain peculiarities from our speech, and the Seventy were unwilling to follow those deviations in a translation; or that the book was published in the name of the Seventy, by some one or other not familiar with Chaldee, or if there be some other reason, I know not; this one thing I can affirm—that it differs widely from the original, and is rightly rejected. For we must bear in mind that Daniel and Ezra, the former especially, were written in Hebrew letters, but in the Chaldee language, as was one section of Jeremiah; and, further, that Job has much affinity with Arabic. As for myself, when, in my youth, after reading the flowery rhetoric of Quintilian and Tully, I entered on the vigorous study of this language, the expenditure of much time and energy barely enabled me to utter the puffing and hissing words; I seemed to be walking in a sort of underground chamber with a few scattered rays of light shining down upon me; and when at last I met with Daniel, such a sense of weariness came over me that, in a fit of despair, I could have counted all my former toil as useless. But there was a certain Hebrew who encouraged me, and was forever quoting for my benefit the saying that "Persistent labour conquers all things"; and so, conscious that among Hebrews I was only a smatterer, I once more began to study Chaldee. And, to confess the truth, to this day I can read and understand Chaldee better than I can pronounce it. I say this to show you how hard it is to master the book of Daniel, which in Hebrew contains neither the history of Susanna, nor the hymn of the three youths, nor the fables of Bel and the Dragon; because, however, they are to be found everywhere, we have formed them into an appendix, prefixing to them an obelus, and thus making an end of them, so as not to seem to the uninformed to have cut off a large portion of the volume. I heard a certain Jewish teacher, when mocking at the history of Susanna, and saying that it was the fiction of some Greek or other, raise the same objection which Africanus brought against Origen—that these etymologies of σχίσαι from σχῖνος, and πρίσαι from πρῖνος, are to be traced to the Greek. To make the point clear to Latin readers: It is as if he were to say, playing upon the word *ilex, illico pereas*; or upon *lentiscus*, may the angel make a *lentil* of you, or may you perish *non lente*, or may you *lentus* (that is pliant or compliant) be led to death, or anything else suiting the name of the tree. Then he would captiously maintain that the three youths in the furnace of raging fire had leisure enough to amuse themselves with making poetry, and to summon all the elements in turn to praise God. Or what was there miraculous, he would say, or what indication of divine inspiration, in the slaying of the dragon with a lump of pitch, or in frustrating the schemes of the priests of Bel? Such deeds were more the results of an able man's forethought than of a prophetic spirit. But when he came to Habakkuk and read that he was carried from Judaea into Chaldaea to bring a dish of food to Daniel, he asked where we found an instance in the whole of the Old Testament of any saint with an ordinary body flying through the air, and in a quarter of an hour traversing vast tracts of country. And when one of us who was rather too ready to speak adduced the instance of Ezekiel, and said that he was transported from Chaldaea into Judaea, he derided the man and proved from the book itself that Ezekiel, in spirit, saw himself carried over. And he argued that even our own Apostle, being an accomplished man and one who had been taught the law by Hebrews, had not dared to affirm that he was bodily rapt away, but had said: "Whether in the body, or out of the body, I know not; God knoweth." By these and similar arguments he used to refute the apocryphal fables in the Church's book. Leaving this for the reader to pronounce upon as he may think fit, I give warning that Daniel in Hebrew is not found among the prophets, but amongst the writers of the Hagiographa; for all Scripture is by them divided into three parts: the law, the Prophets, and the Hagiographa, which have respectively five, eight, and eleven books, a point which we cannot now discuss. But as to the objections which Porphyry raises against this prophet, or rather brings against the book, Methodius, Eusebius, and Apollinaris may be cited as witnesses, for they replied to his folly in many thousand lines of writing, whether with satisfaction to the curious reader I know not. Therefore, I beseech you, Paula and Eustochium, to pour out your supplications for me to the Lord, that so long as I am in this poor body, I may write something pleasing to you, useful to the Church, worthy of posterity. As for my contemporaries, I am indifferent to their opinions, for they pass from side to side as they are moved by love or hatred.

(Source: Philip Schaff and Henry Wace, editors, *The Nicene and Post-Nicene Fathers*, volume VI, Christian Literature Company, New York: 1893, pages 492–493.)

12. EUSEBIUS ON THE ORIGIN OF THE HEXAPLA

Origen was an intellect of no minor greatness. Combining deep acquaintance with the evolving Catholicism of the early third century with his education in Greek thought, he created his own distinctive theology — so distinctive that his "orthodoxy" was challenged in many quarters.

In the scriptures he always sought for a hidden "mystical" sense. Perhaps because of his intellectual background, this approach to biblical analysis functioned not as an impediment to scholarly studies of the accuracy of the existing text but as a spur to prolonged additional research. The result was his famous Hexapla — the entire Old Testament in Hebrew with several Greek translations in parallel columns.

Writing in his *Ecclesiastical History* (VI. xiv–xvi), Eusebius provides this account of the origin of the Hexapla:

Now Adamantius (for this also was Origen's name), when Zephyrinus was at that time ruling the church of the Romans, himself states in writing somewhere that he stayed at Rome. His words are: "Desiring to see the most ancient church of the Romans."

After spending a short time there, he returned to Alexandria, and indeed continued to fulfil in that city his customary work of instruction with all zeal, Demetrius, the bishop of the people there, still exhorting and wellnigh entreating him to ply diligently his task of usefulness for the brethren.

XV. But when he saw that he was becoming unable for the deeper study of divine things, namely, the examination and translation of the sacred writings, and in addition for the instruction of those who were coming to him and did not give him time to breathe (for one batch of pupils after another kept frequenting from morn to night his lecture-room), he made a division of the numbers. Selecting Heraclas from among his pupils, a man who was zealous of divine things, and, as well, a very learned person and no tyro in philosophy, he gave him a share in the task of instruction, assigning to him the preliminary studies of those who were just learning their elements, and reserving for himself the teaching of the experienced pupils.

XVI. And so accurate was the examination that Origen brought to bear upon the divine books, that he even made a thorough study of the Hebrew tongue, and got into his own possession the original writings in the actual Hebrew characters, which were extant among the Jews. Thus, too, he traced the editions of the other translators of the sacred writings besides the Seventy; and besides the beaten track of translations, that of Aquila and Symmachus and Theodotion, he discovered certain others, which were used in turn, which, after lying hidden for a long time, he traced and brought to light, I know not from what recesses. With regard to these, on account of their obscurity (not knowing whose in the world they were) he merely indicated this: that the one he found at Nicopolis, near Actium, and the other in such another place. At any rate, in the Hexapla of the Psalms, after the four well-known editions, he placed beside them not only a fifth but also a sixth and a seventh translation; and in the case of one of these he has indicated again that it was found at Jericho in a jar in the time of Antoninus the son of Severus. All these he brought together, dividing them into clauses and placing them one over against the other, together with the actual Hebrew text; and so he has left us the copies of the Hexapla, as it is called. He made a further separate arrangement of the edition of Aquila and Symmachus and Theodotion together with that of the Seventy, in the Tetrapla.

(Source: Eusebius: *The Ecclesiastical History*, volume 2, translated by E. L. Oulton and H. J. Lawlor, G. P. Putnam's Sons, New York: MCMXXXII, pages 49, 51, 53.)

TWO

Other Ancient Translations

I. *The Diatessaron of Tatian*

Syriac was a dialect closely related to the Palestinian Aramaic spoken during the first century. Since the area where it was spoken received both orthodox Jewish and Christian missionaries in the first century, it is presumed that at least partial translations of both testaments were undertaken at that time.

Tatian's Diatessaron is of interest as the earliest certain Syriac version of the New Testament. Scholars are still divided as to whether this "harmony of the gospels" into one account (with parts taken from each individual canonical record) was originally prepared in Greek and then translated into Syriac or vice versa.

Tatian was converted in Rome about 150 A.D. and studied under Justin Martyr. After he prepared the Diatessaron (c. 170 A.D.), it spread wide and far. Renditions into Latin and Arabic are certain, and scholars believe they can detect a definite impact from its distinctive renderings on several other versions. Ephraem (second half fourth century A.D.) wrote a commentary in Syriac on it.

Though Tatian embraced nonorthodox convictions after the death of Justin Martyr, this did little to impede the growing popularity of the Diatessaron. Because of its doctrinally oriented deletions and Tatian's personal theology, the rendition gained a bad reputation in many quarters and repeated efforts were made to suppress it. Even laying aside the question of its theology, many feared that its popularity resulted in a lessened use and interest in the four canonical gospels from which it had been compiled. The efforts at suppression were finally successful—to the point where for centuries little more was known about it in the west than the mere fact that it had existed. Translations from non–Syriac versions of the Diatessaron are now available as well as part of Ephraem's commentary on the work.

25

13. FRAGMENTARY REFERENCES IN EUSEBIUS AND EPIPHANIUS

Eusebius (*Ecclesiastical History*, IV.29.6):

The former leader of the Encratites, Tatian, composed somehow a kind of combined and concurrent gospel and called it the Diatessaron, a work which is still circulated in some quarters.

Epiphanius (*Heresies* 46.1; lived 320–402 A.D.):

They say the Diatessaron Gospel owes its origin to Tatian; some people call it the Gospel according to the Hebrews.

(Source: J. Rendel Harris, *The Diatessaron of Tatian: A Preliminary Study*, C. J. Clay and Sons, Cambridge University Warehouse, London: 1890, pages 10 [Eusebius] and 11 [Epiphanius].)

14. THEODORET ON HIS SUPPRESSION OF THE DIATESSARON

In his *De fab. haer.* (c. 453 A.D.) Theodoret provides this account of his activities:

He (Tatian) composed the so-called Diatessaron by cutting out the genealogies and whatever goes to prove the Lord to have been born of the seed of David according to the flesh. And this work was in use not only among his own party but even amongst those who follow the tradition of the Apostles, who used it somewhat too innocently as a compendium of the Gospels, without recognising the craftiness of its composition. I myself found more than 200 copies in reverential use in the churches of my diocese, all of which I removed, replacing them by the Gospels of the four Evangelists.

(Source: J. Rendel Harris, *The Diatessaron of Tatian: A Preliminary Study*, C. J. Clay and Sons, Cambridge University Warehouse, London: 1890, page 13.)

15. DIONSIUS BAR-SALIBI ON WRITERS WHO PREPARED SIMILAR WORKS

In his "Commentary on the Gospels" (12th century A.D.), Dionsius Bar-Salibi wrote:

Tatian, the disciple of Justin the Philosopher and Martyr, selected from the four Gospels and patched up and made a Gospel and called it Diatessaron, that is to say, the Compiled: and this work Mar Ephrem commented on. Elias of Salamia, who is also called Aphtonius, made a Gospel on the mode of the Diatessaron which Ammonius had made, to which Eusebius alludes in the introduction to the

Canons which he gave to the Gospel. But Elias sought for that Diatessaron and could not find it, and so he made another, taking it for his model. And Elias finds fault here and there with the Canons of Eusebius, and points out errors in them, and with good reason. The copy which Elias made is not easy to come at.

(Source: J. Rendel Harris, *The Diatessaron of Tatian: A Preliminary Study*, C. J. Clay and Sons, Cambridge University Warehouse, London: 1890, pages 14–15.)

II. *Jerome's Vulgate*

Sophronius Eusebius Hieronymus (better known to posterity as Saint Jerome) was adviser to Pope Damascus and in 382 A.D. was commissioned by him to revise the current Old Latin version of the New Testament on the basis of the readings found in the Greek. Within a year he had finished the four gospel records and had submitted them to the Pope for his approval. In 384 Damascus died and Jerome saw his own hopes squashed for elevation to the Papacy. He completed a revision of the remainder of the New Testament during the next several years but one not as thorough as his work on the first four books of the New Testament. This difference has caused some to believe that he delegated this later work to others. However, it can more likely be attributed to other factors: external distractions, a psychological backlash caused by his papal hopes being destroyed, and, perhaps, a reaction to the harsh criticism he had received for the degree of change found in his earlier work.

After completing the New Testament, Jerome left for Bethlehem, where he lived out the rest of his life. He studied Hebrew intensely, being convinced that since even the LXX is but a translation of that language, greater accuracy could be assured by reliance upon the Hebrew itself. These studies he freely utilized in his translation of the Old Testament (completed 405 A.D.). Rather than gaining praise for his scholarly labors, he reaped a continuing deluge of criticism, as will be seen in the following extracts.

16. TO TRANSLATE IS TO GUARANTEE CRITICISM (JEROME'S PREFACE TO THE FOUR GOSPELS)

Jerome was keenly aware that by daring to present a revised Latin text he became fair game for anyone and everyone, learned or unlearned. Any change (no matter how justified) would open him to the accusation of "forgery." He takes the opportunity in the following extract to point out a fatal flaw in the reasoning of those who insisted, at all costs, on the supremacy of the Latin text: their inability to agree on *which* Latin text should be accepted as definitive. In his preface to the four gospels (383

A. D.), Jerome proposes a way out of the dilemma: going back to the Greek that existed before the Latin and revising the Latin accordingly.

You urge me to revise the old Latin version, and, as it were, to sit in judgment on the copies of the Scriptures which are now scattered throughout the whole world; and, inasmuch as they differ from one another, you would have me decide which of them agree with the Greek original. The labour is one of love, but at the same time both perilous and presumptuous; for in judging others I must be content to be judged by all; and how can I dare to change the language of the world in its hoary old age, and carry it back to the early days of its infancy? Is there a man, learned or unlearned, who will not, when he takes the volume into his hands, and perceives that what he reads does not suit his settled tastes, break out immediately into violent language, and call me a forger and a profane person for having the audacity to add anything to the ancient books, or to make any changes or corrections therein? Now there are two consoling reflections which enable me to bear the odium—in the first place, the command is given by you who are the supreme bishop; and secondly, even on the showing of those who revile us, readings at variance with the early copies cannot be right. For if we are to pin our faith to the Latin texts, it is for our opponents to tell us *which*; for there are almost as many forms of texts as there are copies. If, on the other hand, we are to glean the truth from a comparison of *many*, why not go back to the original Greek and correct the mistakes introduced by inaccurate translators, and the blundering alterations of confident but ignorant critics, and, further, all that has been inserted or changed by copyists more asleep than awake? I am not discussing the Old Testament, which was turned into Greek by the Seventy elders, and has reached us by a descent of three steps. I do not ask what Aquila and Symmachus think, or why Theodotion takes a middle course between the ancients and the moderns. I am willing to let that be the true translation which had apostolic approval. I am now speaking of the New Testament. This was undoubtedly composed in Greek, with the exception of the work of Matthew the Apostle, who was the first to commit to writing the Gospel of Christ, and who published his work in Judaea in Hebrew characters. We must confess that as we have it in our language it is marked by discrepancies, and now that the stream is distributed into different channels we must go back to the fountainhead. I pass over those manuscripts which are associated with the names of Lucian and Hesychius, and the authority of which is perversely maintained by a handful of disputatious persons. It is obvious that these writers could not amend anything in the Old Testament after the labours of the Seventy; and it was useless to correct the New, for versions of Scripture which already exist in the languages of many nations show that their additions are false. I therefore promise in this short Preface the four Gospels only, which are to be taken in the following order, Matthew, Mark, Luke, John, as they have been revised by a comparison of the Greek manuscripts. Only early ones have been used. But to avoid any great divergences from the Latin which we are accustomed to read, I have used my pen with some restraint, and while I have corrected only such passages as seemed to convey a different meaning, I have allowed the rest to remain as they are.

(Source: Philip Schaff and Henry Wace, editors, *The Nicene and Post-Nicene Fathers*, second series, volume VI, Christian Literature Company, New York: 1893, pages 487–488.)

17. JEROME'S THEORY OF TRANSLATION

In a letter to Pammachius in 395 A.D., Jerome spells out the theory of translation that lay behind his biblical work. He comes out quite strongly in favor of a "free" translation style as opposed to one of slavish literalism. He defends his practice by contending that even the New Testament biblical writers used such a style. So how could he be criticized for doing the same thing? Jerome was not one to demean accuracy in translation, but he was convinced that technical accuracy should never be obtained at the cost of conceptual accuracy.

Terence has translated Menander: Plautus and Caecilius the old comic poets. Do they ever stick at words? Do they not rather in their versions think first of preserving the beauty and charm of their originals? What men like you call fidelity in transcription, the learned term pestilent minuteness. Such were my teachers about twenty years ago: and even then I was the victim of a similar error to that which is now imputed to me, though indeed I never imagined that *you* would charge me with it. In translating the Chronicle of Eusebius of Caesarea into Latin, I made among others the following prefatory observations: "It is difficult in following lines laid down by others not sometimes to diverge from them, and it is hard to preserve in a translation the charm of expressions which in another language are most felicitous. Each particular word conveys a meaning of its own, and possibly I have no equivalent by which to render it, and if I make a circuit to reach my goal, I have to go many miles to cover a short distance. To these difficulties must be added the windings of hyperbata, differences in the use of cases, divergencies of metaphor; and last of all the peculiar and if I may so call it, inbred character of the language. If I render word for word, the result will sound uncouth, and if compelled by necessity I alter anything in the order or wording, I shall seem to have departed from the function of a translator." And after a long discussion which it would be tedious to follow out here, I added what follows: — "If any one imagines that translation does not impair the charm of style, let him render Homer word for word into Latin, nay I will go farther still and say, let him render it into Latin prose, and the result will be that the order of the words will seem ridiculous and the most eloquent of poets scarcely articulate."

6. In quoting my own writings my only object has been to prove that from my youth up I at least have always aimed at rendering sense not words, but if such authority as they supply is deemed insufficient, read and consider the short preface dealing with this matter which occurs in a book narrating the life of the blessed Antony. "A literal translation from one language into another obscures the sense; the exuberance of the growth lessens the yield. For while one's diction is enslaved to cases and metaphors, it has to explain by tedious circumlocutions what a few words would otherwise have sufficed to make plain. I have tried to avoid this error in the translation which at your request I have made of the story of the blessed Antony. My version always preserves the sense although it does not invariably keep the words of the original. Leave others to catch at syllables and letters, do you for your part look for the meaning." Time would fail me were I to unfold the testimonies of all who have translated only according to the sense. It is sufficient for the present to name Hilary the confessor who has turned some homilies on Job and several treatises on the Psalms from Greek into Latin; yet has

not bound himself to the drowsiness of the letter or fettered himself by the stale literalism of inadequate culture. Like a conqueror he has led away captive into his own tongue the meaning of his originals.

7. That secular and church writers should have adopted this line need not surprise us when we consider that the translators of the Septuagint, the evangelists, and the apostles, have done the same in dealing with the sacred writings. We read in Mark of the Lord saying *Talitha cumi* and it is immediately added "which is interpreted, Damsel, I say unto thee, arise." The evangelist may be charged with falsehood for having added the words "I say unto thee" for the Hebrew is only "Damsel arise." . . . In Matthew again we read of the Lord preaching flight to the apostles and confirming His counsel with a passage from Zechariah. "It is written," he says, "I will smite the shepherd, and the sheep of the flock shall be scattered abroad." But in the Septuagint and in the Hebrew it reads differently, for it is not God who speaks, as the evangelist makes out, but the prophet who appeals to God the Father saying: — "Smite the shepherd, and the sheep shall be scattered." In this instance according to my judgment — and I have some careful critics with me — the evangelist is guilty of a fault in presuming to ascribe to God what are the words of the prophet. Again the same evangelist writes that at the warning of an angel Joseph took the young child and his mother and went into Egypt and remained there till the death of Herod; "that it might be fulfilled which was spoken of the Lord by the prophet saying, Out of Egypt have I called my son." The Latin manuscripts do not so give the passage, but in Hosea the true Hebrew text has the following: — "When Israel was a child then I loved him, and called my son out of Egypt." Which the Septuagint renders thus: — "When Israel was a child then I loved him, and called his sons out of Egypt." Are they altogether to be rejected because they have given another turn to a passage which refers primarily to the mystery of Christ? Or should we not rather pardon the shortcomings of the translators on the score of their human frailty according to the saying of James, "In many things we offend all. If any man offend not in word the same is a perfect man and able also to bridle the whole body." Once more it is written in the pages of the same evangelist, "And he came and dwelt in a city called Nazareth: that it might be fulfilled which was spoken by the prophets, He shall be called a Nazarene." Let these word fanciers and nice critics of all composition tell us where they have read the words; and if they cannot, let me tell them that they are in Isaiah. For in the place where we read and translate, "There shall come forth a rod out of the stem of Jesse, and a branch shall grow out of his roots," in the Hebrew idiom it is written thus, "There shall come forth a rod out of the root of Jesse and a Nazarene shall grow from his root." How can the Septuagint leave out the word 'Nazarene,' if it is unlawful to substitute one word for another? It is sacrilege either to conceal or to set at naught a mystery.

8. Let us pass on to other passages, for the brief limits of a letter do not suffer us to dwell too long on any one point. The same Matthew says: — "Now all this was done that it might be fulfilled which was spoken of the Lord by the prophet saying, Behold a virgin shall be with child and shall bring forth a son and they shall call his name Emmanuel." The rendering of the Septuagint is, "Behold a virgin shall receive seed and shall bring forth a son, and ye shall call his name Emmanuel." If people cavil at words, obviously 'to receive seed' is not the exact equivalent of 'to be with child,' and 'ye shall call' differs from 'they shall call.' Moreover in the Hebrew we read thus, "Behold a virgin shall conceive and bear a son and shall call his name Immanuel." Ahaz shall not call him so for he was convicted of want of faith, nor the Jews for they were destined to deny him, but she who is to conceive him and bear him, the virgin herself. In the same evangelist we read that Herod

was troubled at the coming of the Magi and that gathering together the scribes and the priests he demanded of them where Christ should be born and that they answered him, "In Bethlehem of Judaea: for thus it is written by the prophet; And thou Bethlehem in the land of Judah art not the least among the princes of Judah, for out of thee shall come a governour that shall rule my people Israel." In the Vulgate this passage appears as follows:—"And thou Bethlehem, the house of Ephratah, art small to be among the thousands of Judah, yet one shall come out of thee for me to be a prince in Israel." You will be more surprised still at the difference in words and order between Matthew and the Septuagint if you look at the Hebrew which runs thus:—"But thou Bethlehem Ephratah, though thou be little among the thousands of Judah, yet out of thee shall he come forth unto me that is to be ruler in Israel." Consider one by one the words of the evangelist:— "And thou Bethlehem in the land of Judah." For "the land of Judah" the Hebrew has "Ephratah" while the Septuagint gives "the house of Ephratah." The evangelist writes, "art not the least among the princes of Judah." In the Septuagint this is, "art small to be among the thousands of Judah," while the Hebrew gives, "though thou be little among the thousands of Judah." There is a contradiction here—and that not merely verbal—between the evangelist and the prophet; for in this place at any rate both Septuagint and Hebrew agree. The evangelist says that he is not little among the princes of Judah, while the passage from which he quotes says exactly the opposite of this, "Thou art small indeed and little; but yet out of thee, small and little as thou art, there shall come forth for me a leader in Israel," a sentiment in harmony with that of the apostle, "God hath chosen the weak things of the world to confound the things which are mighty." Moreover the last clause "to rule" or "to feed my people Israel" clearly runs differently in the original.

9. I refer to these passages, not to convict the evangelists of falsification—a charge worthy only of impious men like Celsus, Porphyry, and Julian—but to bring home to my critics their own want of knowledge, and to gain from them such consideration that they may concede to me in the case of a simple letter what, whether they like it or not, they will have to concede to the Apostles in the Holy Scriptures.

(Source: Philip Schaff and Henry Wace, editors, *The Nicene and Post-Nicene Fathers*, second series, volume VI, Christian Literature Company, New York: 1893, pages 114–116.)

18. JEROME'S DEFENSE FOR PAYING GREATER ATTENTION TO THE HEBREW THAN TO THE GREEK TRANSLATIONS

In his "Preface to Job," Jerome calls attention to the repeated insults thrown at him and his method of translation. He protests that to establish a better text is in no way an insult to those who translated the Septuagint. Nor are critical apparatuses a radical innovation—for did not Origen use them as well? He sees ignorance and ill will behind the attacks of his critics and strikes out at their inability to comprehend facts that are as clear as day to Jerome himself.

I am compelled at every step in my treatment of the books of Holy Scripture to reply to the abuse of my opponents, who charge my translation with being a censure of the Seventy; as though Aquila among Greek authors, and Symmachus

and Theodotion, had not rendered word for word, or paraphrased, or combined
the two methods in a sort of translation which is neither the one nor the other;
and as though Origen had not marked all the books of the Old Testament with
obeli and asterisks, which he either introduced or adopted from Theodotion, and
inserted in the old translation, thus showing that what he added was deficient in
the older version. My detractors must therefore learn either to receive altogether
what they have in part admitted, or they must erase my translation and at the same
time their own asterisks. For they must allow that those translators, who it is clear
have left out numerous details, have erred in some points; especially in the book
of Job, where, if you withdraw such passages as have been added and marked with
asterisks, the greater part of the book will be cut away. This, at all events, will be
so in Greek. On the other hand, previous to the publication of our recent translation with asterisks and obeli, about seven or eight hundred lines were missing in
the Latin, so that the book, mutilated, torn, and disintegrated, exhibits its deformity
to those who publicly read it. The present translation follows no ancient
translator, but will be found to reproduce now the exact words, now the meaning,
now both together of the original Hebrew, Arabic, and occasionally the Syriac. For
an indirectness and a slipperiness attaches to the whole book, even in the Hebrew;
and, as orators say in Greek, it is tricked out with figures of speech, and while it
says one thing, it does another; just as if you close your hand to hold an eel or a
little muraena, the more you squeeze it, the sooner it escapes. I remember that
in order to understand this volume, I paid a not inconsiderable sum for the services of a teacher, a native of Lydda, who was amongst the Hebrews reckoned to
be in the front rank; whether I profited at all by this teaching, I do not know; of
this one thing I am sure, that I could translate only that which I previously
understood. Well, then, from the beginning of the book to the words of Job, the
Hebrew version is in prose. Further, from the words of Job where he says, "May
the day perish wherein I was born, and the night in which it was said, a man-child
is conceived," to the place where before the close of the book it is written
"Therefore I blame myself and repent in dust and ashes," we have hexameter
verses running in dactyl and spondee: and owing to the idiom of the language
other feet are frequently introduced not containing the same number of syllables,
but the same quantities. Sometimes, also, a sweet and musical rhythm is produced
by the breaking up of the verses in accordance with the laws of metre, a fact better
known to prosodists than to the ordinary reader. But from the aforesaid verse to
the end of the book the small remaining section is a prose composition. And if it
seem incredible to any one that the Hebrews really have metres, and that, whether
we consider the Psalter or the Lamentations of Jeremiah, or almost all the songs
of Scripture, they bear a resemblance to our Flaccus, and the Greek Pindar, and
Alcaeus, and Sappho, let him read Philo, Josephus, Origen, Eusebius of Caesarea,
and with the aid of their testimony he will find that I speak the truth. Wherefore,
let my barking critics listen as I tell them that my motive in toiling at this book
was not to censure the ancient translation, but that those passages in it which are
obscure, or those which have been omitted, or at all events, through the fault of
copyists have been corrupted, might have light thrown upon them by our translation; for we have some slight knowledge of Hebrew, and, as regards Latin, my life,
almost from the cradle, has been spent in the company of grammarians, rhetori-
cians, and philosophers. But if, since the version of the Seventy was published,
and even now, when the Gospel of Christ is beaming forth, the Jewish Aquila,
Symmachus, and Theodotion, judaising heretics, have been welcomed amongst
the Greeks—heretics, who, by their deceitful translation, have concealed many

mysteries of salvation, and yet, in the Hexapla are found in the Churches and are expounded by churchmen; ought not I, a Christian, born of Christian parents, and who carry the standard of the cross on my brow, and am zealous to recover what is lost, to correct what is corrupt, and to disclose in pure and faithful language the mysteries of the Church, ought not I, let me, ask, much more to escape the reprobation of fastidious or malicious readers? Let those who will keep the old books with their gold and silver letters on purple skins, or, to follow the ordinary phrase, in "uncial characters," loads of writing rather than manuscripts, if only they will leave for me and mine, our poor pages and copies which are less remarkable for beauty than for accuracy. I have toiled to translate both the Greek versions of the Seventy, and the Hebrew which is the basis of my own, into Latin. Let every one choose which he likes, and he will find out that what he objects to in me, is the result of sound learning, not of malice.

(Source: Philip Schaff and Henry Wace, editors, *The Nicene and Post-Nicene Fathers*, second series, volume VI, Christian Literature Company, New York: 1893, pages 491–492.)

19. AUGUSTINE'S CHALLENGE: WHAT NEW TRUTH CAN BE GAINED BY A NEW TRANSLATION?

Augustine was displeased with Jerome's plan to translate the Torah and Prophets directly from the Hebrew. In Letter 28 of 394 or 395 A.D., Augustine challenges Jerome as to the need for such an effort. After all, with the Old Testament having been translated upon repeated occasions what could possibly have been missed that a new translation could provide?

CHAP. II.—2. We therefore, and with us all that are devoted to study in the African churches, beseech you not to refuse to devote care and labour to the translation of the books of those who have written in the Greek language most able commentaries on our Scriptures. You may thus put us also in possession of these men, and especially of that one whose name you seem to have singular pleasure in sounding forth in your writings [Origen]. But I beseech you not to devote your labour to the work of translating into Latin the sacred canonical books, unless you follow the method in which you have translated Job, viz. with the addition of notes, to let it be seen plainly what differences there are between this version of yours and that of the LXX., whose authority is worthy of highest esteem. For my own part, I cannot sufficiently express my wonder that anything should at this date be found in the Hebrew MSS. which escaped so many translators perfectly acquainted with the language. I say nothing of the LXX., regarding whose harmony in mind and spirit, surpassing that which is found in even one man, I dare not in any way pronounce a decided opinion, except that in my judgment, beyond question, very high authority must in this work of translation be conceded to them. I am more perplexed by those translators who, though enjoying the advantage of labouring after the LXX. had completed their work, and although well acquainted, as it is reported, with the force of Hebrew words and phrases, and with Hebrew syntax, have not only failed to agree among themselves, but have left many things which, even after so long a time, still remain to be discovered and brought to light. Now these things were either obscure or plain:

if they were obscure, it is believed that you are as likely to have been mistaken as the others; if they were plain, it is not believed that they [the LXX.] could possibly have been mistaken. Having stated the grounds of my perplexity, I appeal to your kindness to give me an answer regarding this matter.

(Source: Philip Schaff and Henry Wace, editors, *The Nicene and Post-Nicene Fathers*, first series, volume I, Christian Literature Company, New York: 1893, page 251.)

20. JEROME'S RESPONSE: WHAT NEW TRUTH CAN BE GAINED BY A NEW COMMENTARY?

In a letter of 404 A.D., Jerome responds at length to various questions that Augustine had raised in previous correspondence. In the following extract, Jerome points out the reason that he omits the "critical" markings found in his earlier work. He also rebuts Augustine's claim that a new translation is not needed because of the excellence of past ones by pointing out that by the same logic Augustine had no business writing his commentaries!

CHAP. V. — 19. In another letter you ask why a former translation which I made of some of the canonical books was carefully marked with asterisks and obelisks, whereas I afterwards published a translation without these. You must pardon my saying that you seem to me not to understand the matter: for the former translation is from the Septuagint; and wherever obelisks are placed, they are designed to indicate that the Seventy have said more than is found in the Hebrew. But the asterisks indicate what has been added by Origen from the version of Theodotion. In that version I was translating from the Greek: but in the later version, translating from the Hebrew itself, I have expressed what I understood it to mean, being careful to preserve rather the exact sense than the order of the words. I am surprised that you do not read the books of the Seventy translators in the genuine form in which they were originally given to the world, but as they have been corrected, or rather corrupted, by Origen, with his obelisks and asterisks; and that you refuse to follow the translation, however feeble, which has been given by a Christian man, especially seeing that Origen borrowed the things which he has added from the edition of a man who, after the passion of Christ, was a Jew and a blasphemer. Do you wish to be a true admirer and partisan of the Seventy translators? Then do not read what you find under the asterisks; rather erase them from the volumes, that you may approve yourself indeed a follower of the ancients. If, however, you do this, you will be compelled to find fault with all the libraries of the Churches; for you will scarcely find more than one MS. here and there which has not these interpolations.

CHAP. VI. — 20. A few words now as to your remark that I ought not to have given a translation, after this had been already done by the ancients; and the novel syllogism which you use: "The passages of which the Seventy have given an interpretation were either obscure or plain. If they were obscure, it is believed that you are as likely to have been mistaken as the others; if they were plain, it is not believed that the Seventy could have been mistaken."

All the commentators who have been our predecessors in the Lord in the work of expounding the Scriptures, have expounded either what was obscure or what was plain. If some passages were obscure, how could you, after them, presume to discuss that which they were not able to explain? If the passages were plain, it was a waste of time for you to have undertaken to treat of that which could not possibly have escaped them. This syllogism applies with peculiar force to the book of Psalms, in the interpretation of which Greek commentators have written many volumes: viz. 1st, Origen: 2d, Eusebius of Caesarea; 3d, Theodorus of Heraclea; 4th, Asterius of Scythopolis; 5th, Apollinaris of Laodicea; and, 6th, Didymus of Alexandria. There are said to be minor works on selections from the Psalms, but I speak at present of the whole book. Moreover, among Latin writers the bishops Hilary of Poitiers, and Eusebius of Verceil, have translated Origen and Eusebius of Caesarea, the former of whom has in some things been followed by our own Ambrose. Now, I put it to your wisdom to answer why you, after all the labours of so many and so competent interpreters, differ from them in your exposition of some passages? If the Psalms are obscure, it must be believed that you are as likely to be mistaken as others; if they are plain, it is incredible that these others could have fallen into mistake. In either case, your exposition has been, by your own showing, an unnecessary labour; and on the same principle, no one would ever venture to speak on any subject after others have pronounced their opinion, and no one would be at liberty to write anything regarding that which another has once handled, however important the matter might be.

It is, however, more in keeping with your enlightened judgment, to grant to all others the liberty which you tolerate in yourself; for in my attempt to translate into Latin, for the benefit of those who speak the same language with myself, the corrected Greek version of the Scriptures, I have laboured not to supersede what has been long esteemed, but only to bring prominently forward those things which have been either omitted or tampered with by the Jews, in order that Latin readers might know what is found in the original Hebrew. If any one is averse to reading it, none compels him against his will. Let him drink with satisfaction the old wine, and despise my new wine, i.e. the sentences which I have published in explanation of former writers, with the design of making more obvious by my remarks what in them seemed to me to be obscure.

(Source: Philip Schaff and Henry Wace, editors, *The Nicene and Post-Nicene Fathers*, first series, volume I, Christian Literature Company, New York: 1893, pages 341–342.)

21. A BISHOP IS ALMOST DEPOSED FOR USING JEROME'S NEW BOOK OF JONAH

In a letter (Number LXXI) of 403 A.D., Augustine renewed his protests against Jerome's translation project. In addition to calling attention to the lack of a "critical" apparatus (responded to in Extract 20, above), the venerable Augustine stresses two additional objections. First, even assuming that Jerome does provide a better rendering of the text, how is he going to convince others they should admit it—especially critical Jews? Second, he points to the danger of internal tumult and turmoil that can be caused by reliance on a modern translation: Witness the bishop whose use of Jerome's Jonah stirred a bitter response in his congregation.

2. As I have sent you two letters already to which I have received no reply, I have resolved to send you at this time copies of both of them, for I suppose that they never reached you. If they did reach you, and your replies have failed, as may be the case, to reach me, send me a second time the same as you sent before, if you have copies of them preserved: if you have not, dictate again what I may read, and do not refuse to send to these former letters the answer for which I have been waiting so long. . . .

CHAP. II. — 3. In this letter I have further to say, that I have since heard that you have translated Job out of the original Hebrew, although in your own translation of the same prophet from the Greek tongue we had already a version of that book. In that earlier version you marked with asterisks the words found in the Hebrew but wanting in the Greek, and with obelisks the words found in the Greek but wanting in the Hebrew; and this was done with such astonishing exactness, that in some places we have every word distinguished by a separate asterisk, as a sign that these words are in the Hebrew, but not in the Greek. Now, however, in this more recent version from the Hebrew, there is not the same scrupulous fidelity as to the words; and it perplexes any thoughtful reader to understand either what was the reason for marking the asterisks in the former version with so much care that they indicate the absence from the Greek version of even the smallest grammatical particles which have not been rendered from the Hebrew, or what is the reason for so much less care having been taken in this recent version from the Hebrew to secure that these same particles be found in their own places. I would have put down here an extract or two in illustration of this criticism; but at present I have not access to the MS. of the translation from the Hebrew. Since, however, your quick discernment anticipates and goes beyond not only what I have said, but also what I meant to say, you already understand, I think, enough to be able, by giving the reason for the plan which you have adopted, to explain what perplexes me.

4. For my part, I would much rather that you would furnish us with a translation of the Greek version of the canonical Scriptures known as the work of the Seventy translators. For if your translation begins to be more generally read in many churches, it will be a grievous thing that, in the reading of Scripture, differences must arise between the Latin Churches and the Greek Churches, especially seeing that the discrepancy is easily condemned in a Latin version by the production of the original in Greek, which is a language very widely known; whereas, if any one has been disturbed by the occurrence of something to which he was not accustomed in the translation taken from the Hebrew, and alleges that the new translation is wrong, it will be found difficult, if not impossible, to get at the Hebrew documents by which the version to which exception is taken may be defended. And when they are obtained, who will submit to have so many Latin and Greek authorities pronounced to be in the wrong? Besides all this, Jews, if consulted as to the meaning of the Hebrew text, may give a different opinion from yours: in which case it will seem as if your presence were indispensable, as being the only one who could refute their view; and it would be a miracle if one could be found capable of acting as arbiter between you and them.

CHAP. III. — 5. A certain bishop, one of our brethren, having introduced in the church over which he presides the reading of your version, came upon a word in the book of the prophet Jonah, of which you have given a very different rendering from that which had been of old familiar to the senses and memory of all the worshippers, and had been chanted for so many generations in the church. Thereupon arose such a tumult in the congregation, especially among the Greeks, correcting what had been read, and denouncing the translation as false, that the bishop was compelled to ask the testimony of the Jewish residents (it was in the town of Oea). These, whether from ignorance or from spite, answered that the words in the Hebrew MSS. were correctly rendered in the Greek version, and in the Latin one taken from it. What further need I say? The man was compelled to correct your version in that passage as if it had been falsely translated, as he desired not to be left without a congregation, — a calamity which he narrowly escaped. From this case we also are led to think that you may be occasionally mistaken. You will also observe how great must have been the difficulty if this had occurred in those writings which cannot be explained by comparing the testimony of languages now in use.

CHAP. IV. — 6. At the same time, we are in no small measure thankful to God for the work in which you have translated the Gospels from the original Greek, because in almost every passage we have found nothing to object to, when we compared it with the Greek Scriptures. By this work, any disputant who supports an old false translation is either convinced or confuted with the utmost ease by the production and collation of MSS. And if, as indeed very rarely happens, something be found to which exception may be taken, who would be so unreasonable as not to excuse it readily in a work so useful that it cannot be too highly praised? I wish you would have the kindness to open up to me what you think to be the reason for the frequent discrepancies between the text supported by the Hebrew codices and the Greek Septuagint version. For the latter has no mean authority, seeing that it has obtained so wide circulation, and was the one which the apostles used, as is not only proved by looking to the text itself, but has also been, as I remember, affirmed by yourself. You would therefore confer upon us a much greater boon if you gave an exact Latin translation of the Greek Septuagint version: for the variations found in the different codices of the Latin text are intolerably numerous; and it is so justly open to suspicion as possibly different from what is to be found in the Greek, that one has no confidence in either quoting it or proving anything by its help.

(Source, Philip Schaff and Henry Wace, editors, *The Nicene and Post-Nicene Fathers*, first series, volume I, Christian Literature Company, New York: 1893, pages 326–327.)

22. JEROME: BUT WHERE IS THE ERROR IN THE NEW BOOK OF JONAH?

In dealing with the poor bishop who was nearly deposed for using his translation, Jerome responds by pointing out that he can hardly defend himself unless he is informed of the wording of the disputed text. He points to some other readings of which he did have personal knowledge as being challenged and provides the reasoning behind them.

As to the principles which ought to be followed in the interpretation of the Sacred Scriptures, they are stated in the book which I have written, and in all the introductions to the divine books which I have in my edition prefixed to each; and to these I think it sufficient to refer the prudent reader. And since you approve of my labours in revising the translation of the New Testament, as you say, — giving me at the same time this as your reason, that very many are acquainted with the Greek language, and are therefore competent judges of my work, — it would have been but fair to have given me credit for the same fidelity in the Old Testament; for I have not followed my own imagination, but have rendered the divine words as I found them understood by those who speak the Hebrew language. If you have any doubt of this in any passage, ask the Jews what is the meaning of the original.

21. Perhaps you will say, "What if the Jews decline to answer, or choose to impose upon us?" Is it conceivable that the whole multitude of Jews will agree together to be silent if asked about my translation, and that none shall be found that has any knowledge of the Hebrew language? Or will they all imitate those Jews whom you mention as having, in some little town, conspired to injure my reputation? For in your letter you put together the following story: — "A certain bishop, one of our brethren, having introduced in the Church over which he presides the reading of your version, came upon a word in the book of the prophet Jonah, of which you have given a very different rendering from that which had been of old familiar to the senses and memory of all the worshippers, and had been chanted for so many generations in the Church. Thereupon arose such a tumult in the congregation, especially among the Greeks, correcting what had been read, and denouncing the translation as false, that the bishop was compelled to ask the testimony of the Jewish residents (it was in the town of Oea). These, whether from ignorance or from spite, answered that the words in the Hebrew MSS. were correctly rendered in the Greek version, and in the Latin one taken from it. What further need I say? The man was compelled to correct your version in that passage as if it had been falsely translated, as he desired not to be left without a congregation, — a calamity which he narrowly escaped. From this case we also are led to think that you may be occasionally mistaken."

CHAP. VII. — 22. You tell me that I have given a wrong translation of some word in Jonah, and that a worthy bishop narrowly escaped losing his charge through the clamorous tumult of his people, which was caused by the different rendering of this one word. At the same time, you withhold from me what the word was which I have mistranslated; thus taking away the possibility of my saying anything in my own vindication, lest my reply should be fatal to your objection. Perhaps it is the old dispute about the gourd which has been revived, after slumbering for many long years since the illustrious man, who in that day combined in his own person the ancestral honours of the Cornelii and of Asinius Pollio, brought against me the charge of giving in my translation the word "ivy" instead of "gourd." I have already given a sufficient answer to this in my commentary on Jonah. At present, I deem it enough to say that in that passage, where the Septuagint has "gourd," and Aquila and the others have rendered the word "ivy" (κισσος), the Hebrew MS. has "ciceion," which is in the Syriac tongue, as now spoken, "ciceia." It is a kind of shrub having large leaves like a vine, and when planted it quickly springs up to the size of a small tree, standing upright by its own stem, without requiring any support of canes or poles, as both gourds and ivy do. If, therefore, in translating word for word, I had put the word "ciceia," no one would know what it meant; if I had used the word "gourd," I would have said what is not found in the Hebrew. I therefore put down "ivy," that I might not differ from all other translators. But if your Jews said, either through malice or ignorance, as you yourself suggest, that the word is in the Hebrew text which is found in the Greek and Latin versions, it is evident that they were either unacquainted with Hebrew, or have been pleased to say what was not true, in order to make sport of the gourd-planters.

(Source: Philip Schaff and Henry Wace, editors, *The Nicene and Post-Nicene Fathers*, first series, volume I, Christian Literature Company, New York: 1893, page 342.)

23. AUGUSTINE CONCEDES THE PROPRIETY OF A HEBREW-BASED TRANSLATION

Augustine gave careful consideration to Jerome's arguments and came to the conclusion that he was right, at least so far as this particular subject went. In Letter LXXXII (405 A.D.) Augustine wrote:

CHAP. V. — 34. As to your translation, you have now convinced me of the benefits to be secured by your proposal to translate the Scriptures from the original Hebrew, in order that you may bring to light those things which have been either omitted or perverted by the Jews. But I beg you to be so good as state by what Jews this has been done, whether by those who before the Lord's advent translated the Old Testament — and if so, by what one or more of them — or by the Jews of later times, who may be supposed to have mutilated or corrupted the Greek MSS., in order to prevent themselves from being unable to answer the evidence given by these concerning the Christian faith. I cannot find any reason which should have prompted the earlier Jewish translators to such unfaithfulness. I beg of you, moreover, to send us your translation of the Septuagint, which I did not know that you had published. I am also longing to read that book of yours which you named *De optimo genere interpretandi*, and to know from it how to adjust the balance between the product of the translator's acquaintance with the original language, and the conjectures of those who are able commentators on the Scripture, who, notwithstanding their common loyalty to the one true faith, must often bring forward various opinions on account of the obscurity of many passages; although this difference of interpretation by no means involves departure from the unity of the faith; just as one commentator may himself give, in harmony with the faith which he holds, two different interpretations of the same passage, because the obscurity of the passage makes both equally admissible.

35. I desire, moreover, your translation of the Septuagint, in order that we may be delivered, so far as is possible, from the consequences of the notable incompetency of those who, whether qualified or not, have attempted a Latin translation; and in order that those who think that I look with jealousy on your useful labours, may at length, if it be possible, perceive that my only reason for objecting to the public reading of your translation from the Hebrew in our churches was, lest, bringing forward anything which was, as it were, new and opposed to the authority of the Septuagint version, we should trouble by serious cause of offence the flocks of Christ, whose ears and hearts have become accustomed to listen to that version to which the seal of approbation was given by the apostles themselves. Wherefore, as to that shrub in the book of Jonah, if in the Hebrew it is neither "gourd" nor "ivy," but something else which stands erect, supported by its own stem without other props, I would prefer to call it "gourd" in all our Latin versions; for I do not think that the Seventy would have rendered it thus at random, had they not known that the plant was something like a gourd.

(Source: Philip Schaff and Henry Wace, editors, *The Nicene and Post-Nicene Fathers*, first series, volume I, Christian Literature Company, New York: 1893, page 361.)

24. THE MAN WHO STOLE JEROME'S BIBLE

A translator's life may be unexciting or it may be full of danger. One of the hindrances we would least expect him to encounter would be the theft of his translation. Yet Jerome was the victim of just such a crime, to which he alludes in a postscript of a letter to Augustine in 416 A.D.,

We suffer in this province from a grievous scarcity of clerks acquainted with the Latin language; this is the reason why we are not able to comply with your instructions, especially in regard to that version of the Septuagint which is furnished with distinctive asterisks and obelisks; for we have lost, through some one's dishonesty, the most of the results of our earlier labour.

(Source: Philip Schaff and Henry Wace, editors, *The Nicene and Post-Nicene Fathers*, first series, volume I, Christian Literature Company, New York: 1893, page 544.)

25. A TRANSLATOR BESIEGED BY ILL HEALTH

During much of his life in the Near East, Jerome suffered from recurring physical ailments. These affected how he went about his translation labors and are referred to in the following extracts.

In the preface to his commentary on Galatians, Jerome writes:

How far I have profited by my unflagging study of Hebrew I leave to others to decide; what I have lost in my own language, I can tell. In addition to this, on account of the weakness of my eyes and bodily infirmity generally, I do not write with my own hand; and I cannot make up for my slowness of utterance by greater pains and diligence, as is said to have been the case with Virgil, of whom it is related that he treated his books as a bear treats her cubs, and licked them into shape. I must summon a secretary, and either say whatever comes uppermost; or, if I wish to think a little and hope to produce something superior, my helper silently reproves me, clenches his fist, wrinkles his brow, and plainly declares by his whole bearing that he has come for nothing.

In the preface to his commentary on Amos, Jerome says:

We have not discussed them in regular sequence from the first to the ninth, as they are read, but as we have been able, and in accordance with requests made to us. Nahum, Micah, Zephaniah, Haggai, I first addressed to Paula and Eustochium, her daughter, who are never weary; I next dedicated two books on Habakkuk to Chromatius, bishop of Aquileia; I then proceeded to explain, at your command, Pammachius, and after a long interval of silence, Obadiah and Jonah. In the present year, which bears in the calendar the name of the sixth consulate of Arcadius Augustus and Anitius Probus, I interpreted Malachi for Exsuperius, bishop of Toulouse, and Minervius and Alexander, monks of that city. Unable to refuse your request I immediately went back to the beginning of the volume, and expounded Hosea, Joel, and Amos. A severe sickness followed, and I showed my rashness in resuming the dictation of this work too hastily; and, whereas others hesitate to write and frequently correct their work, I entrusted mine to the fortune which attends those who employ a secretary, and hazarded my reputation for ability and orthodoxy; for, as I have often testified, I cannot endure the toil of writing with my own hand; and, in expounding the Holy Scriptures, what we want is not a polished style and oratorical flourishes, but learning and simple truth.

(Source: Philip Schaff and Henry Wace, editors, *The Nicene and Post-Nicene Fathers*, second series, volume VI, Christian Literature Company, New York: 1893, pages 497–498 [Galatians] and page 501 [Amos].)

THREE

Reformation-Era
European Translations

I. German-Language Translations

26. A TRANSLATOR'S BITTER ADVERSARY

The genesis of pre–Lutheran German-language Bibles can be traced to a New Testament produced in manuscript form about the year 1400. During the next fifty or so years an unknown number of individuals translated the Old Testament as well. The one translator whose name can be safely attached to at least part of the translation was one John Rellach, a Dominican. It was his intention to translate the entire Bible, but that goal was frustrated, at least in part, by his wide travels preaching a crusade against the Turks.

Of the canonical books, Rellach translated at least Joshua, Judges, and Ruth. In a manuscript introduction (c. 1455) to these books (preserved in several copies), the translator refers to an adversary who had bitterly opposed his translation endeavors:

> This is a foreword against him, who is opposed to the German writing, which is, nevertheless, useful and profitable for men's souls. My enemies have up till now done violence to their own conscience, because they have till now been silent as regards my plan to translate the holy gospel into German. Now however they have taken a different stand, inspired by foolish pride, and they bring forward foolish counsels, and say:
> "But what shall we [clergy] now preach, when [lay] men read and listen to the holy scriptures in the German tongue in their rooms and houses?"
> Him will I answer from holy scripture, until it is again necessary that we should meet. Now mark that they have objected to me with the more pride, because they think that they themselves excel in holy scripture, and have somewhat noised this abroad: and would that their knowledge were less than it is! For no one accuses the perfect of knowledge, and withholds them from preaching, if they read and

strive diligently to strengthen faithful Christians in the word of God. *Woe to you who call good evil, and evil good*: as they do, who in their pride contradict what learned priests and blessed laymen praise and call good. It is through pride that these unlearned philosophers and their followers contradict with their subtlety, and fight against, the righteous truth: that is, they fight against the holy scriptures and hinder the spread of their revealing. . . .

And my proud enemies, set about with highmindedness, have held forth before lords and learned people, desiring to gain their respect: but thus is their deep folly the more fully known to the people, who before knew it not. For while they were wisely silent, they were esteemed prudent and well-learned. . . . And now they hotly attack my fitness to deal with the lore of holy scripture: whereof I have good hope towards God that they shall be confounded and put to silence. And now they suggest from pride that I am too poor a scholar for this matter, because I have not been in great places of learning. And that is true! But the Holy Ghost supplies by His grace what is lacking in me, and it is also well supplied by the help and counsel of learned people. For I have known many a man, who has been at places of learning, and returned as ignorant as he went, unless it be that he has gained patrons, or learned how to find Easter: for the knowledge of holy writ is neglected. For the truly learned willingly hear and diligently learn, and gain true knowledge in their own home, when they ponder what in universities is counted worthless. For it is quite obvious that there are certain simple lay people who thoroughly and perfectly understand holy scripture, in all its parts: even as there are some, who think they know what they have never learned.

In a separate introduction to the book of Joshua in particular, Rellach presumably has the same critic in mind when he writes:

"My enemy," he says, "is an apostate monk, who has gone from one order to another, and now is not living under a rule at all: he has been an Augustinian, . . . a parish priest and a Benedictine: no faith is to be placed in such a man. My lord the bishop of Eichstädt has denounced him, and exhorted him to return to his cloister."

(Source: Margaret Deanesly, *The Lollard Bible and Other Medieval Biblical Versions*, copyrighted 1920 and published by Cambridge University Press. Used by permission.)

27. PREFACE TO THE COLOGNE GERMAN BIBLE OF 1480

The preface to this printing is interesting because it candidly reveals the target audience aimed at by the publisher: relatively uneducated "spiritual and secular . . . religious" who could not read the Latin version. Intentionally or not, this provided a convenient excuse for bringing out a Bible that, by force of numbers alone, was bound to have a wider distribution than that openly avowed.

Yet even here we detect a certain defensiveness, as if even allowing *these* devotees of the Catholic faith an unimpeded access to the sacred text might produce censure in some powerful quarters. Also of interest is that the publisher pointedly disavows any pretense that this is a new translation—again protecting himself from potential censure and ecclesiastical reaction. He goes even further and establishes the de facto orthodoxy of the work by its widespread use (in manuscript form) "in men's and women's convents."

The writer points out that highly educated masters of schools

read and use the translations of S. Jerome, whereas unlearned and simple men, both spiritual and secular, but especially children brought up in monasteries and dedicated to be religious, should use the German translation of the Latin Bible, for the avoiding of idleness, on saints' days, when they have time. Therefore a lover of the salvation of all men, not moved by earthy praise and honour, but by Christian love and virtue, and urged thereto by certain men of good heart: this man, with the help and counsel of many highly-learned men, has had printed at great cost, in the city of Cologne, the German translation of the Latin Bible; which translation was made many years before, and used in manuscripts by many devout men, both in men's and women's convents: and long before this time it has been printed in the Oberland, and in some towns of the Netherlands: and it has spread into many lands, and is bought there with the greatest eagerness at great cost.

(Source: Margaret Deanesly, *The Lollard Bible and Other Medieval Biblical Versions*, copyrighted 1920 and published by Cambridge University Press. Used by permission.)

28. LUTHER'S THEORY OF TRANSLATION

In translating the scriptures, Luther found the New Testament the easier. He completed his translation in less than three months. The Old Testament, however, presented him with far greater difficulties; he labored on it for over a decade. In a letter of 1528, he reveals just how difficult the task was:

We are sweating over the work of putting the Prophets into German. God, how much of it there is, and how hard it is to make these Hebrew writers talk German! They resist us, and do not want to leave their Hebrew and imitate our German barbarisms. It is like making a nightingale leave her own sweet song and imitate the monotonous voice of a cuckoo, which she detests.

(Source: *Luther's Works* (volume 35), edited by E. Theodore Bachmann, copyright 1960 by Fortress Press. Used by permission.)

In 1530 he brought out a pamphlet entitled *On Translating: An Open Letter*. Although part of the work deals with the question of intercessory prayer by the dead on behalf of the living, the first section deals with what the title suggests. Since his addition of "only" to salvation by faith in Romans 3 had been strongly denounced as doctrinal interpolation, Luther's discussion of how a good translator must function is designed with that criticism in mind.

Luther stresses that two key attitudes must always be in the mind of the translator if he is to properly fulfill his function. First, he must be faithful to the intent of the sacred writer even if verbal literalness is sacrificed. Second, he must use language, idioms, and expressions that convey a clear meaning.

We do not have to inquire of the literal Latin, how we are to speak German, as these asses do. Rather we must inquire about this of the mother in the home, the children on the street, the common man in the marketplace. We must be guided by their language, the way they speak, and do our translating accordingly. That way they will understand it and recognize that we are speaking German to them.

For example, Christ says: *Ex abundantia cordis os loquitur* [Matt. 12:34, Luke 6:45]. If I am to follow these asses, they will lay the original before me literally and translate thus: "Out of the abundance of the heart the mouth speaks." Tell me, is that speaking German? What German could understand something like that? What is "the abundance of the heart"? No German can say that; unless, perhaps, he was trying to say that someone was altogether too magnanimous or too courageous, though even that would not yet be correct. For "abundance of the heart" is not German, any more than "abundance of the house," "abundance of the stove," or "abundance of the bench" is German. But the mother in the home and the common man say this, "What fills the heart overflows the mouth." That is speaking good German, the kind that I have tried for—and unfortunately not always reached or hit upon. For the literal Latin is a great hindrance to speaking good German.

So, for example, Judas the traitor says, in Matthew 26[:8], *Ut quid perditio haec?* and in Mark 14[:4], *Ut quid perditio ista unguenti facta est?* If I follow these literalistic asses I would have to translate it thus: "Why has this loss of ointment happened?" But what kind of German is that? What German says, "Loss of the ointment has happened"? If he understands that at all, he thinks that the ointment is lost and must be looked for and found again; though even that is still obscure and uncertain. Now if that is good German, why do they not come out and make us a fine, pretty, new German Testament like that, and let Luther's Testament lie? I think that would really bring their talents to light! But a German would say *Ut quid,* etc., thus: "Why this waste?" Or, "Why this extravagance [*schade*]?" Indeed, "It's a shame about the ointment." That is good German, from which it is understood that Magdalene had wasted the ointment that she poured out and been extravagant. That was what Judas meant, for he thought he could have used it to better advantage.

Again, when the angel greets Mary, he says, "Hail Mary, full of grace, the Lord is with you!" [Luke 1:28]. Up to now that has simply been translated according to the literal Latin. Tell me whether that is also good German! When does a German speak like that, "You are full of grace"? He would have to think of a keg "full of" beer or a purse "full of" money. Therefore I have translated it, "Thou gracious one," so that a German can at least think his way through to what the angel meant by this greeting. Here, however, the papists are going wild about me, because I have corrupted the Angelic Salutation; though I have still not hit upon the best German rendering for it. Suppose I had taken the best German, and translated the salutation thus: "Hello there, Mary"—for that is what the angel wanted to say, and what he would have said, if he had wanted to greet her in German. Suppose I had done that! I believe that they would have hanged themselves out of tremendous fanaticism for the Virgin Mary, because I had thus destroyed the salutation.

But what do I care if they rage or rave? I shall not prevent them from translating as they please. However I shall translate too, not as they please but as I please. Whoever does not like it can just leave it alone and keep his criticism to himself, for I shall neither look at nor listen to it. They do not have to answer for my translation, nor bear any responsibility for it. Listen well to this! I shall say "gracious [holdselige] Mary," and "dear [liebe] Mary," and let them say "Mary full of grace [volgnaden]." Whoever knows German knows very well what a fine, expressive [hertzlich] word that word liebe is: the dear Mary, the dear God, the dear emperor, the dear prince, the dear man, the dear child. I do not know whether this word liebe can be said in Latin or other languages with such fulness of sentiment, so that it pierces and rings through the heart, through all the senses, as it does in our language.

I believe that with the Greek kecharitomene [Luke 1:28] St. Luke, a master of the Hebrew and Greek tongues, wanted to render and clarify the Hebrew word that the angel used. And I think that the angel Gabriel spoke with Mary as he speaks with Daniel, calling him Chamudoth and Ish chamudoth, vir desideriorum, that is, "You dear Daniel"; for that is Gabriel's way of speaking as we see in the book of Daniel. Now if I were to translate the angel's words literally, with the skill of these asses, I should have to say this, "Daniel, thou man of desires." That would be pretty German! A German would hear, of course, that Man, Lueste, and begyrunge are German words — though not altogether pure German words, for lust and begyr would be better. But when the words are thus put together: "thou man of desires," no German would know what is said. He would think, perhaps, that Daniel is full of evil desires. Well that would be fine translating! Therefore I must let the literal words go and try to learn how the German says that which the Hebrew expresses with ish chamudoth. I find then that the German says this, "You dear Daniel," "You dear Mary," or "You gracious maid," "You lovely maiden," "You gentle girl," and the like. For a translator must have a great store of words, so that he can have them on hand in the event that one word does not fit in every context.

And why should I talk so much about translating? If I were to point out the reasons and considerations back of all my words, I should need a year to write on it. I have learned by experience what an art and what a task translating is. Therefore I will tolerate no papal ass or mule to be my judge or critic, for they have never tried it. He who desires none of my translating may let it alone. If anyone dislikes it or criticizes it without my knowledge and consent, the devil repay him! If it is to be criticized, I shall do it myself. If I do not do it, then let them leave my translation in peace. Let each of them make for himself one that suits — what do I care?

This I can testify with a good conscience — I gave it my utmost in care and effort, and I never had any ulterior motives. I have neither taken nor sought a single penny for it, nor made one by it. Neither have I sought my own honor by it; God, my Lord, knows this. Rather I have done it as a service to the dear Christians and to the honor of One who sitteth above, who blesses me so much every hour of my life that if I had translated a thousand times as much or as diligently, I should not for a single hour have deserved to live or to have a sound eye. All that I am and have is of his grace and mercy, indeed of his precious blood and bitter sweat. Therefore, God willing, all of it shall also serve to his honor, joyfully and sincerely. Scribblers and papal asses may blaspheme me, but real Christians — and Christ, their Lord — bless me! And I am more than plentifully repaid, if even a single

Christian acknowledges me as an honest workman. I care nothing for the papal asses; they are not worthy of acknowledging my work, and it would grieve me to the bottom of my heart if they blessed me. Their blasphemy is my highest praise and honor. I shall be a doctor anyway, yes even a distinguished doctor; and that name they shall not take from me till the Last Day, this I know for certain.

On the other hand I have not just gone ahead anyway and disregarded altogether the exact wording of the original. Rather with my helpers I have been very careful to see that where everything turns on a single passage, I have kept to the original quite literally and have not lightly departed from it. For example, in John 6[:27] Christ says, "Him has God the Father sealed [*versiegelt*]." It would have been better German to say, "Him has God the Father signified [*gezeichent*]," or, "He it is whom God the Father means [*meinet*]." But I preferred to do violence to the German language rather than to depart from the word. Ah, translating is not every man's skill as the mad saints imagine. It requires a right, devout, honest, sincere, God-fearing, Christian, trained, informed, and experienced heart. Therefore I hold that no false Christian or factious spirit can be a decent translator. That becomes obvious in the translation of the Prophets made at Worms. It has been carefully done and approaches my German very closely. But Jews had a hand in it, and they do not show much reverence for Christ. Apart from that there is plenty of skill and craftsmanship there. So much for translating and the nature of the languages!

Now I was not relying on and following the nature of the languages alone, however, when, in Roman 3[:28] I inserted the word *solum* (alone). Actually the text itself and the meaning of St. Paul urgently require and demand it. For in that very passage he is dealing with the main point of Christian doctrine, namely, that we are justified by faith in Christ without any works of the law. And Paul cuts away all works so completely, as even to say that the works of the law— though it is God's law and word—do not help us for justification [Rom. 3:20]. He cites Abraham as an example and says that he was justified so entirely without works that even the highest work—which, moreover, had been newly commanded by God, over and above all other works and ordinances, namely circumcision—did not help him for justification; rather he was justified without circumcision and without any works, by faith, as he says in chapter 4[:2], "If Abraham was justified by works, he may boast, but not before God." But when all works are so completely cut away—and that must mean that faith alone justifies—whoever would speak plainly and clearly about this cutting away of works will have to say, "Faith alone justifies us, and not works." The matter itself, as well as the nature of the language, demands it.

(Source: Luther's Works (volume 35), edited by E. Theodore Bachmann, copyright 1960 by Fortress Press. Used by permission of Augsburg Fortress.)

29. EMSER'S NEW TESTAMENT: THE CRITIC AS PLAGIARIST

Jerome Emser was born in March 1477 or 1478. He obtained master's degrees in both theology and arts and for one summer (in 1504) taught at the University of Erfurt. Later he asserted that Luther had been among his students that summer. Be that as it may, after the Leipzig Disputation of mid–1519, an irrevocable theological breach drove Emser and Luther further and further apart. In addition to each regarding the other as a heretic, they engaged in the customary exchange of insults.

The first edition of Luther's translation appeared in 1522, and Emser was commissioned by Duke George to prepare a critique of it, which he proceeded to do with great vigor and enthusiasm. In 1527 Emser published his own New Testament. Luther found that translation hard to criticize since he rightly regarded it as essentially his own, sufficiently catholicized to make it acceptable to the Roman authorities. In contrast, the glosses (annotations) infuriated him since there were numerous allusions critical of both Luther himself and his reform movement.

In his *On Translating: An Open Letter* (1530) he takes this swipe at Emser:

Second you may say that I translated the New Testament conscientiously and to the best of my ability. I have compelled no one to read it, but have left that open, doing the work only as a service to those who could not do it better. No one is forbidden to do a better piece of work. If anyone does not want to read it, he can let it alone. I neither ask anybody to read it nor praise anyone who does so. It is my Testament and my translation, and it shall continue to be mine. If I have made some mistakes in it – though I am not conscious of any and would certainly be most unwilling to give a single letter a wrong translation intentionally – I will not allow the papists [to act] as judges. For their ears are still too long, and their hee-haws too weak, for them to criticize my translating. I know very well – and they know it even less than the miller's beast – how much skill, energy, sense, and brains are required in a good translator. For they have never tried it.

There is a saying, "He who builds along the road has many masters." That is the way it is with me too. Those who have never even been able to speak properly, to say nothing of translating, have all at once become my masters and I must be the pupil of them all. If I were to have asked them how to put into German the first two words of Matthew's Gospel, *Liber Generationis*, none of them would have been able to say Quack! And now they sit in judgment on my whole work! Fine fellows! That is the way it was with St. Jerome too when he translated the Bible. Everybody was his master. He was the only one who was totally incompetent. And people who were not worthy to clean his shoes criticized the good man's work. It takes a great deal of patience to do a good thing publicly, for the world always wants to be Master Know-it-all. It must always be putting the bit under the horse's tail, criticizing everything but doing nothing itself. That is its nature; it cannot get away from it.

I should like to see a papist who would come forward and translate even a single epistle of St. Paul or one of the prophets without making use of Luther's German translation. Then we should see a fine, beautiful, praiseworthy German translation! We have seen the Dresden scribbler who played the master to my New Testament. I shall not mention his name again in my books as he has his Judge now, and is already well known anyway. He admits that my German is sweet and good. He saw that he could not improve on it. But eager to discredit it, he went to work and took my New Testament almost word for word as I had written it. He removed my introductions and explanations, inserted his own, and thus sold my

New Testament under his name. Oh my, dear children, how it hurt me when his prince, in a nasty preface, condemned Luther's New Testament and forbade the reading of it; yet commanded at the same time that the scribbler's New Testament be read, even though it was the very same one that Luther had produced!

That no one may think I am lying, just take the two Testaments, Luther's and the scribbler's, and compare them; you will see who is the translator in both of them. He has patched and altered it in a few places. And though not all of it pleases me, still I can let it go; it does me no particular harm, so far as the text is concerned. For this reason I never intended to write against it either. But I did have to laugh at the great wisdom that so terribly slandered, condemned, and forbade my New Testament, when it was published under my name, but made it required reading when it was published under the name of another. What kind of virtue that is, to heap slander and shame on somebody else's book, then to steal it and publish it under one's own name — thus seeking personal praise and reputation through the slandered work of somebody else — I leave that for his Judge to discover. Meanwhile I am satisfied and glad that my work (as St. Paul also boasts [Phil. 1:18]) must be furthered even by enemies; and that Luther's book, without Luther's name but under that of his enemies, must be read. How could I avenge myself better?

(Source: *Luther's Works*, (volume 35), edited by E. Theodore Bachmann, copyright 1960 by Fortress Press. Used by permission of Augsburg Fortress.)

II. *French-Language Translations*

Although coming chronologically before the Reformation Era, those using the following translations were equally dedicated (albeit with far less success) to the cause of radical change in the Medieval Church. Likewise their opponents would have regarded them as proponents of many of the same "errors" that gained popularity under the leadership of men like Luther and Calvin. Hence it is appropriate to consider these versions in this section on Reformation-Era Translations.

30. PETER WALDO SPONSORS A BIBLE TRANSLATION

In the late twelfth century, a rich merchant in Lyons, France, by the name of Peter Waldo was so intrigued by the gospel as he heard it read, that he paid a priest by the name of Bernardus Ydros to translate the scriptures for him and to dictate the text to another priest whom he also hired. After much study of the biblical record and the lives of the respected saints, Waldo launched a radical reform movement that challenged both the exclusive right of the priesthood to preach and (equally dangerous to the establishment) the accumulation of financial wealth that had swollen its coffers. The movement was called Waldensian (as well as other names), and after not many years it was condemned as heretical.

The translator, Ydros, told the story to his contemporary, Etienne de

Bourbon, who was a Dominican inquisitor and who recorded the following contemporary account in his *Anecdotes Historiques*:

A certain rich man of the city (Lyons), called Waldo, was curious when he heard the gospel read, since he was not much lettered, to know what was said. Wherefore he made a pact with certain priests, the one, that he should translate to him the Bible: the other, that he should write as the first dictated. Which they did; and in like manner many books of the Bible, and many authorities of the saints, which they called *Sentences*. Which when the said citizen had often read and learned by heart, he proposed to observe evangelical perfection as the apostles observed it; and he sold all his goods, and despising the world, he gave all his money to the poor, and usurped the apostolic office by preaching the gospel, and those things which he had learned by heart, in the villages and open places, and by calling to him many men and women to do the same thing, and teaching them the gospel by heart. . . . Who indeed, being simple and illiterate men and women, wandered through villages and entered houses and preached in open places, and even in churches, and provoked others to the same course.

(Source: Margaret Deanesly, *The Lollard Bible and Other Medieval Biblical Versions*, copyrighted 1920 and published by Cambridge University Press. Used by permission.)

31. AN ATTEMPT TO GAIN PAPAL APPROVAL FOR A WALDENSIAN TRANSLATION

Walter Mapp was an Englishman who attended the meetings of the Third Lateran Council in 1179. A delegation of Waldensians presented the Pope with a collection of translations of various parts of the Bible and sought his permission to preach to the public. Mapp spoke with two of the petitioners and quickly became convinced that their theology was heretical and that their translations should be rejected. In his *De Nugis Curialium* (written between 1181 and 1192), he gives this account:

We saw the Waldensians at the council celebrated at Rome under pope Alexander III. They were simple and illiterate men, named after their leader, Waldo, who was a citizen of Lyons on the Rhone: and they presented to the lord pope a book written in the French tongue, in which were contained a text and gloss on the psalter, and on very many other books of both testaments. These besought with great urgency that authority to preach should be confirmed to them, for they thought themselves expert, when they were scarcely learned at all. . . . For in every small point of the sacred page, so many meanings fly on the wings of virtue, such stores of wealth are accumulated, that only he can fully exhaust them whom God has inspired. Shall not therefore the Word given to the unlearned be as *pearls before swine*, when we know them to be fitted neither to receive it, nor to give out what they have received? Away with this idea, and let it be rooted out. *The ointment ran down from the head, even to the skirts of his clothing*: waters flow from the spring, not from the mud of public ways.

(Source: Margaret Deanesly, *The Lollard Bible and Other Medieval Biblical Versions*, copyrighted 1920 and published by Cambridge University Press. Used by permission.)

32. POPE INNOCENT III FEARS THAT VERNACULAR TRANSLATIONS WOULD USURP THE TEACHING FUNCTIONS OF THE CHURCH

Repeated efforts were made to suppress the Waldensian and closely related movements. From about 1180 to 1190 the effort was concentrated around Lyons, France. However, within a few years the Waldensians were again attracting attention, and the Archbishop of Metz wrote to the Pope seeking approval of the repressive measures he had undertaken against those he called the "Vaudois." Their private meetings, in which various members preached, the Pope strongly denounced, encouraging their suppression. As to the translations they were desiring to use, however, the Pope responded cautiously, calling for an investigation into the orthodoxy of the translator.

The verbal neutrality was an inherently untenable position, for if the users were such "heretics" as to be persisting in unauthorized meetings and preaching, how could the translation itself escape the tarnish of heresy? Hence it is no surprise that when in December 1199 the Pontiff sent three Cistercian abbots, they assisted the Archbishop in smothering the movement, and they burnt all biblical manuscripts that they found in the possession of the Vaudois.

The following extract comes from Innocent III's letter of July 1199 to the Archbishop of Metz:

We are completely ignorant of the opinions and way of life of those who have thus translated the holy scriptures, or of those who teach them this translation (neither of which could be done without a knowledge of letters). . . . Warn them to desist from those things which appear blameworthy, and not to claim for themselves the office of others. Enquire diligently, who was the author of this translation; what was his intention: the faith of those who use it: the reason of their teaching: whether they venerate the apostolic see and the catholic Church: so that . . . we may the better understand what ought to be decreed.

(Source: Margaret Deanesly, *The Lollard Bible and Other Medieval Biblical Versions*, copyrighted 1920 and published by Cambridge University Press. Used by permission.)

III. Erasmus' Translation into Latin

There was no way his scholarly reputation could protect him when Erasmus offended a broad spectrum of orthodox Catholic intellectualism through his publication of the *Novuum Instrumentum* in 1516. The effort to establish a "critical" Greek text through the comparison of manuscripts offended a goodly number of readers because of the departures from the wording they were used to. As if that aggravation were insufficient, Erasmus accompanied the critical text with his own revised translation into Latin. As Jerome had discovered a millennium earlier, any departure from the accepted translation guaranteed the unyielding wrath of many.

A year later Erasmus began the publication of his *Paraphrases* of the New Testament books. These were as enthusiastically received as his Greek text and Latin translation were vehemently denounced. He perceived the irony that the strenuous mental labor that went into the critical text should be spurned while the much easier paraphrases were embraced:

> I am especially pleased that men who are so well thought of should think well of my paraphrase; I only wish I had always laboured in that sort of field. I would rather construct a thousand paraphrases than one critical edition.

(Source: R. A. B. Mynors and D. F. S. Thomson, editors, *The Correspondence of Erasmus: Letters 298 to 445 (1514–1516)*, copyright University of Toronto Press, 1976. Reprinted by permission of University of Toronto Press.)

The second edition of his critical text and Latin translation appeared in 1519 under the title *Novuum Testamentum*. Perhaps convinced that there was no way to appease his critics, he abandoned his 1516 Latin translation and substituted the more radical one he had prepared while in England in 1505–1506.

33. WORKING AT THE PRINTER'S SIDE

In the following extract we have Erasmus' first-hand account of how he babied the first edition of his translation through the printer. Revising and expanding the annotations to the volume at the last minute at the printer's plant, he was also burdened by responsibility for other scholarly work being simultaneously set.

> As for the points on which you partly disagree with me, partly agree, and partly suspend judgment and remain doubtful, I could not reply at the moment, being prevented in the first place by lack of time and second by having no text at hand, for before I answer there are some things I must reread. It shall be done on another occasion, and done soon. Meanwhile I will say this much in general: my Budé's opinion carries so much weight with me that if I find he seriously approves of something, I shall have no hesitation in recanting on any subject. Not but what in this work I have done what I usually do elsewhere. I had decided to treat the whole thing lightly, as I was to be concerned with minutiae, and merely to point a finger, as it were, at some passages in passing. Then, when the work was already due to be published, certain people encouraged me to change the Vulgate text by either correcting or explaining it. This additional burden would, I thought, be very light; but in reality I found it by far the heaviest part. Then they pushed me into adding rather fuller annotations; and very soon, as you know, everything had to be done again. And there was a further task: I thought correct copies were available in Basel, and when this hope proved vain, I was obliged to correct in advance the texts which

the compositors were to use. Besides which, two good scholars had been engaged, one a lawyer and the other a theologian who also knows Hebrew, who were to be in charge of correcting proofs; but they had no experience of this and were unable to fulfil their undertaking, so it was necessary for me to take the final checking of the formes, as they call them, upon myself. So the work was edited and printed simultaneously, one ternion (which is the modern word) being printed off every day: nor was I able all this time to devote myself entirely to the task. At the same time they were printing off Jerome, who claimed a large share of me; and I had made up my mind either to work myself to death or to get myself free of that treadmill by Easter. On top of that we made a mistake about the size of the volume. The printer affirmed that it would run to thirty ternions more or less, and it exceeded, if I mistake not, eighty-three. And so the greatest part of my time was spent on things that were not really my business or had been no part of the original plan; and I was already weary and well-nigh exhausted when I came to the annotations. As far as time and my state of health permitted, I did what I could. Some things I even passed over of set purpose; to many I knowingly closed my eyes, and then changed my opinion soon after publication. And so I prepare the second edition, wherein I beg you urgently to help a man who is trying hard. Let people like you rebuke if they must and I shall take it as a friendly act. One thing you must please watch, my excellent 'Budé: do not let the public suspect this, or the copies of this edition will not move from the printing-house.

(Source: R. A. B. Mynors and D. F. S. Thomson, editors, *The Correspondence of Erasmus: Letters 298 to 445 (1514 to 1516), copyright University of Toronto Press, 1976. Reprinted by permission of University of Toronto Press.)*

34. TO THE READER OF THE NOVUUM INSTRUMENTUM

In this introduction (1516), Erasmus summarizes the manuscript evidence he utilized (skimpy by twentieth century standards, of course) and stresses the wide variety of authorities he had consulted in his effort to produce a reliable and authoritative text. He is at great pains to prove to the reader that the textual alterations he has introduced were not manufactured out of whole cloth and an overworked imagination but were due to the actual evidence then available.

ERASMUS OF ROTTERDAM TO THE PIOUS READER GREETING

Although I did do so to the best of my ability at the very outset of this work, yet it may be worth while to warn the reader briefly once again both what he ought to expect from these brief notes and what demands I can reasonably make upon him in return. In the first place, what I have written are short annotations, not a commentary, and they are concerned solely with the integrity of the text; so let no one like a selfish guest demand supper in place of a light luncheon, and expect me to give him something different from what I undertook to produce. This for the moment is the play I have undertaken to perform; and thus, just as I have to keep to my programme, so it is reasonable that the courteous and fair-minded reader, like a friendly spectator, should do his best for the actors and attune himself to the scene before him.

I have taken what they call the New Testament and revised it, with all the diligence I could muster and all the accuracy that was appropriate, checking it in the first instance against the true Greek text. For that is, as it were, the fountainhead to which we are not only encouraged to have recourse in any difficulty by the example of eminent divines, but frequently advised to do so by Jerome and Augustine, and so instructed by the actual decrees of the Roman pontiffs. Second, I checked it against the tradition of very ancient copies of the Latin version, two of which were made available by that distinguished master of the divine philosophy John Colet, dean of St Paul's in London, in such ancient styles of writing that I had to learn to read them from the beginning, and in order to pick up the rudiments I had to become a schoolboy again. A third was provided by the illustrious lady Margaret, aunt of the emperor Charles; its evidence I have frequently cited in this third edition under the name of the Golden Gospels, because it is entirely clad in gold and finely written in gold letters. After that, I was provided with several manuscripts of remarkable antiquity by the equally ancient and celebrated collegiate church of St Donatian at Bruges. Previously the house of Korssendonk had supplied me with a manuscript very neatly corrected, not to mention some lent me by those excellent scholars the brothers Amerbach. It is not therefore that I have made a certain number of corrections dreamed up out of my own head; I have followed the manuscripts listed, and others like them which it is not so important to name. Finally I have checked by the quotations or corrections or explanations of authors who are fully and universally approved—Origen, Chrysostom, Cyril, Jerome, Ambrose, Hilary, Augustine, Theophylact, Basil, Bede—whose evidence I have adduced on many passages with this in mind, that when the intelligent reader has perceived that in certain definite places my correction and their opinion coincide, he may give me his confidence in other places too, in which probably by chance they have neither supplied a note nor supported me in any other way.

I knew however that it is human nature to object to novelty in everything, but especially in the field of learning, and that most people expect to find the old familiar taste and what they call the traditional flavour; and I also reflected how much easier it is, nowadays especially, to corrupt a sound text than to correct a corrupted one. Consequently, after revising the sacred books I added these pointers (so to call them), partly to explain to the reader's satisfaction why each change was made, or at least to pacify him if he has found something he does not like, for men's temperaments and judgments vary; partly in hopes of preserving my work intact, that it might not be so easy in future for anyone to spoil a second time what had once been restored with such great exertions. First then, if I found anything damaged by the carelessness or ignorance of scribes or by the injuries of time, I restored the true reading, not haphazardly but after pursuing every available scent. If anything struck me as obscurely expressed, I threw light on it; if as ambiguous or complicated, I explained it; if differences between the copies or alternative punctuations or simply the ambiguity of the language give rise to several meanings, I laid them open in such a way as to show which seemed to me more acceptable, leaving the final decision to the reader. And although I do not willingly disagree with the translator, whoever he was, because his version is traditional and commonly accepted, yet when the facts proclaim that he nodded or was under a delusion, I did not hesitate to make this also clear to the reader: I have championed the truth, but so as to criticize no man. Blunders that were obvious and unnatural I removed, and I followed the rules of correct writing everywhere so far as it was possible to do so, always provided that there was no loss of simplicity.

Wherever the idiom of the Greek or its peculiar expression has something about it that helps towards the underlying meaning, I was always ready to demonstrate this and make it visible.

Finally I collected and weighed up the Old Testament evidences, not a few of which are cited either from the Septuagint version or from the Hebrew original, if the form in which they are current differs from their Hebrew source; although this I could not do single-handedly 'without my Theseus' as the Greek proverb puts it, for nothing is further from my character and temperament than like Aesop's crow to set myself off with others' plumage. So in this department, when I was first publishing this work, I secured no little help from a man eminent for his knowledge of the three tongues no less than for his piety, which is as much as to say a true theologian, Joannes Oecolampadius of Weinsberg; for I myself had not yet made enough progress in Hebrew to take upon myself the authority to decide.

For my part, I was well aware that these minutiae, these thorny details, promised far more work than reputation, and that this sort of labour does not usually earn its author much gratitude, while the reader gets more benefit than entertainment from it. But if I have gladly endured so much tedious labour in consideration of the general good, it is surely only right that the reader too, for his own good, if for no other reason, should digest a certain amount of what may irk him and contribute for himself and his own advantage the spirit that I have shown in helping others. The points of which I treat are very small, I agree, but their nature is such that almost less effort would be needed to deal with those great problems of which our grand theologians with their lordly manner make such heavy weather, whose swelling cheeks bulge until they crack with pride; what is more, such is their nature that for the sake of these minuscule minutiae one sometimes actually needs to explore those major problems. Minute they may be, but because of these minute points we see even the greatest theologians sometimes make discreditable mistakes and fall into delusions, as I shall indicate in a certain number of places, not for the pleasure of attacking anyone (a disease which ought to be kept poles apart from a Christian's work and indeed from his whole life), but in order to justify my good faith to the reader by a few examples produced without criticizing anyone, so that no one may despise these as worthless trifles; for in reality, as Horace puts it, 'to serious things these trifles lead the way.' Why are we so particular over the serving of our meals, offended by the smallest details of personal attire, ready to think nothing in money matters too small to be taken into account; and in Scripture alone disapprove of thus taking trouble, and prefer neglect? To say nothing for the moment of the majesty of the subject, of which no detail can be so unimportant that a religious man can think it beneath him, so mean that it does not require reverent and devoted treatment. It crawls along the ground, they say; it torments itself over pitiful words and syllables. Why do we regard as beneath our notice a single word uttered by him whom we worship and revere as the Word himself? — all the more so as he tells us himself that one jot or one tittle shall in no wise pass away. It is the least part of Scripture, what they call the letter; but this is the foundation on which rests the mystic meaning. This is only rubble; but rubble that carries the august weight of the whole marvellous edifice.

(Source: R. A. B. Mynors and D. F. S. Thomson, editors, *The Correspondence of Erasmus: Letters 298 to 445 (1514 to 1516)*, copyright University of Toronto Press, 1976. Reprinted by permission of University of Toronto Press.)

35. IS THE LATIN MORE ACCURATE AND RELIABLE THAN THE GREEK? ERASMUS' RESPONSE.

Erasmus' letter to Maarten van Dorp of May 1515 (Letter 337) is a lengthy response to points that van Dorp had raised in earlier correspondence. The following extract comes from the printed edition of the response; it appears that he sent Dorp himself a shorter version of the same material.

Erasmus uses Dorp's preference for the Latin as a springboard to attack this commonly held opinion of his day. He cites Jerome, Augustine, Ambrose, and Hilary as examples of scholars who refused to be so limited. He stresses that the "heretical" nature of Greek theology in their day had not resulted from different readings of the biblical text but had arisen from other sources.

In response to the claim that church councils had endorsed the Latin as authoritative, Jerome replies that there is a world of difference between endorsing the Latin in general and in endorsing a particular version of the Latin. In addition, no council had ever been so bold as to demand that the Latin be left untouched where it had clearly fallen into transmittal error.

Then again what you write in the third part about the New Testament makes me wonder what has happened to you, or what has beguiled for the moment your very clear-sighted mind. You would rather I made no changes, unless the Greek gives the meaning more fully, and you say there are no faults in the version we commonly use. You think it wrong to weaken in any way the hold of something accepted by the agreement of so many centuries and so many synods. I ask you, if what you say is true, my most learned Dorp, why do Jerome and Augustine and Ambrose so often cite a different text from the one we use? Why does Jerome find fault with many things, and correct them explicitly, which corrections are still found in our text? What will you do when there is so much agreement, when the Greek copies are different and Jerome cites the same text as theirs, when the very oldest Latin copies concur, and the sense itself runs much better? Do you intend to overlook all this and follow your own copy, though it was perhaps corrupted by a scribe? For no one asserts that there is any falsehood in Holy Scripture (which you also suggested), nor has the whole question on which Jerome came to grips with Augustine anything at all to do with the matter. But one thing the facts cry out, and it can be clear, as they say, even to a blind man, that often through the translator's clumsiness or inattention the Greek has been wrongly rendered; often the true and genuine reading has been corrupted by ignorant scribes, which we see happen every day, or altered by scribes who are half-taught and half-asleep. Which man encourages falsehood more, he who corrects and restores these passages, or he who would rather see an error added than removed? For it is of the nature of textual corruption that one error should generate another. And the changes I make are usually such as affect the overtones rather than the sense itself; though often the overtones convey a great part of the meaning. But not seldom the text has gone astray entirely. And whenever this happens, where, I ask you, do Augustine and Ambrose and Hilary and Jerome take refuge if not in the Greek original? This is approved also by decrees of the church; and yet you shuffle and try to reject it or rather to worm your way out of it by splitting hairs.

You say that in their day the Greek copies were more correct than the Latin ones, but that now it is the opposite, and we cannot trust the texts of men who have separated from the Roman church. I can hardly persuade myself to believe that you meant this seriously. What? We are not to read the books of renegades from the Christian faith; and how pray do they think Aristotle such an authority, who was a pagan and never had any contact with the faith? The whole Jewish nation turned away from Christ; are we to give no weight to the Psalms and the Prophets, which were written in their language? Now make me a list of all the heads under which the Greeks differ from the orthodox Latins; you will find nothing that arises from the words of the New Testament or has anything to do with this question. The whole controversy relates to the word *hypostasis*, to the procession of the Holy Spirit, to the ceremonies of consecration, to the poverty of the priesthood, to the powers of the Roman pontiff. For none of these questions do they lean on falsified texts. But what will you say when you see their interpretation followed by Origen, Chrysostom, Basil, Jerome? Had somebody falsified the Greek texts as long ago as that? Who has ever detected falsification in the Greek texts even in one passage? And finally, what could be the motive, since they do not defend their particular tenets from this source? Besides which, that in every department of learning the Greek copies have always been more accurate than ours is admitted by no less than Cicero, who is elsewhere so unfair to the Greeks. For the difference between the letters, the accents, and the actual difficulty of writing all mean that they are less easily corrupted and that any corruption is more easily mended.

Again, when you say that one should not depart from a text that enjoys the approval of so many councils, you write like one of our ordinary divines, who habitually attribute anything that has slipped somehow into current usage to the authority of the church. Pray produce me one synod in which this version has been approved. How could it approve a text whose author is unknown? That it is not Jerome's is shown by Jerome's own prefaces. But suppose that some synod has approved it? Was it approved in such terms that it is absolutely forbidden to correct it by the Greek original? Were all the mistakes approved as well, which in various ways may have crept in? Was a decree drawn up by the fathers of the council in some such terms as this? 'This version is of unknown authorship, but none the less we approve it, nor do we wish it to be an objection that the Greek copies have something different, however accurate they may be, or if a different reading is found in Chrysostom or Basil or Athanasius or Jerome, even though it may better suit the meaning of the Gospel, notwithstanding our high approval of these same authorities in other respects. Moreover, whatsoever in future may in any way, whether by men with a little education and rather more self-confidence or by scribes unskilled, drunken, or half-asleep, be corrupted, distorted, added, or omitted, we in virtue of the same authority approve, nor are we willing that any man should have licence to alter what has once been written.' A very comical decree, you say. But it must have been something like this, if you are to frighten me from this kind of work by the authority of a synod.

Finally, what are we to say when we see that even copies of our Vulgate version do not agree? Surely these discrepancies were not approved by a synod, which of course foresaw each change that would be made? I only wish, my dear Dorp, that the Roman pontiffs had sufficient leisure to issue salutary constitutions on these points, which would take care for the restoration of the works of good authors and the preparation and substitution of corrected copies. Yet I would not give any seats on that commission to those most falsely so-called theologians whose one idea is that what they learnt themselves should be the only thing of current value. And what have they learnt that is not utter nonsense and utter confusion? If they once become dictators, farewell to all the best authors! The world will be compelled to accept their brainless rubbish as oracles; and so little sound learning is there in it, that I would rather be a humble cobbler than the best of their tribe, if they can acquire nothing in the way of a liberal education. These are the men who do not like to see a text corrected, for it may look as though there were something they did not know. It is they who try to stop me with the authority of imaginary synods; they who build up this great threat to the Christian faith; they who cry 'the Church is in danger' (and no doubt support her with their own shoulders, which would be better employed in propping a dung-cart) and spread suchlike rumours among the ignorant and superstitious mob; for the said mob takes them for great divines, and they wish to lose none of this reputation. They are afraid that when they misquote Scripture, as they often do, the authority of the Greek or Hebrew text may be cast in their teeth, and it may soon become clear that what used to be quoted as an oracle is all a dream. St Augustine, that very great man and a bishop as well, had no objection to learning from a year-old child. But the kind of people we are dealing with would rather produce utter confusion than risk appearing to be ignorant of any detail that forms part of perfect knowledge, though I see nothing here that much affects the genuineness of our Christian faith. If it were essential to the faith, that would be all the more reason for working hard at it.

Nor can there be any danger that everybody will forthwith abandon Christ if the news happens to get out that some passage has been found in Scripture which an ignorant or sleepy scribe has miscopied or some unknown translator has rendered inadequately. There are other reasons to fear this, of which I prudently say nothing here. How much more truly Christian it would be to have done with quarreling and for each man cheerfully to offer what he can to the common stock and to accept with good will what is offered, so that at the same time you learn in humility what you do not know and teach others ungrudgingly what you do know! If some are so ignorant that they cannot rightly teach anything or so conceited that they are unwilling to learn, let us think no more of them (for they are very few) and concentrate on those who are intelligent or at any rate promising.

(Source: R. A. Mynors and D. F. S. Thomson, editors, *The Correspondence of Erasmus: Letters 298 to 445 (1514 to 1516)*, copyright University of Toronto Press, 1976. Reprinted by permission of University of Toronto Press.)

36. DORP'S RESPONSE TO ERASMUS

In his reply of August 1515, Maarten van Dorp accuses Erasmus of reading into his letter that which he had not claimed. He makes plain that he is far from convinced by Erasmus' counter-arguments and reaffirms the grounds for his own misgivings.

Now I turn to the remainder of your letter. I did not assert, my dear Erasmus, that there are no mistakes in the New Testament, for I knew perfectly well that it had been corrected by Jerome in a number of places; but I affirmed, and it is still my opinion, that it contains no error and no falsehood. You admit this in your letter, but you add that the true reading has been corrupted by the scribes. This is the point where we really disagree. Tell me, which are the copies by which you can judge that it was corrupted, after Jerome had corrected the text against the Greek sources? It was not surprising that they should have been the refuge of Jerome, Ambrose, Augustine, Hilary, the Fathers whom you cite, in their own day, for they were still pure and uncontaminated. But as it is, now that so many heresies have arisen in Greece, and that long schism, how can we be certain that their copies have not been corrupted? You say that what is at issue is the division between words, the accents, and that sort of difficulty; but I am surprised you should use an argument which you turn against yourself; for it is easier to make mistakes when there are many things one has to watch. How easily scribes may have omitted an accent! And this, if I rightly understand you, will make it a corrupted copy. And what is it that does not allow Latin books to be free from error? Is it not the combined carelessness and lack of skill of the printers? Now consider which is the rarer class—those who are equipped to print Greek books, or Latin—and you will know which copies you ought to consider the more correct.

But you do not see what effect this really has on the purity of the faith. This is the thing, my dear Erasmus, that I tried so hard to get from you: that if the translator had nodded anywhere, if his translation was clumsy or did not really give the meaning, you should write a note on this, provided you made no changes, if the Latin copies differed from the Greeks in meaning; for there we must follow the Latin texts. St Jerome admits that, when he was correcting the Gospels after emending them by comparison with the Greek copies, he adopted the principle that he would correct only things that seemed to alter the sense, and let everything else stay as it was. Here is Jerome, restoring whatever had lapsed from the true sense; and anything else, no matter how barbarous or foolish, he allows to stay as it is. If this sort of thing is corrected now, I have no complaints. But if in Jerome's time the Latin copies were corrupted, what reason is there, you will say, why the scribes should not have deviated again from his corrected text during so many centuries? I think the reason is the great care lavished by the holy Fathers on maintaining the integrity of the sacred texts which Jerome had corrected. If they can somehow be shown to be corrupt, I want, and I want badly, to be told why the same reasons have not affected the Greek copies; for the accents and other difficulties, as I said just now, present, rather than remove, the opportunity to make mistakes.

You ask in what council it was that the Vulgate edition, whose author is unknown, was officially approved. I did not say, Erasmus, that it was approved in any one council in particular, but that many councils, when confronted with some knotty problem concerning the faith, took refuge in this edition and no other; as you must know, if you have ever looked into the Decretals. And this, I think, is the reason why it is less elegant and less good Latin, that it answers the Greek more faithfully word for word. For the more you translate word for word, the drier you must become, because many things can be said conveniently in one language which cannot be rendered in another without using many more words or darkening the meaning or being unidiomatic. And so it is probable that of all the translations the church of God and the holy Fathers will have selected this one to be handed down to us, because it is the most faithful. Otherwise what chance would preserve this one out of so many? for Augustine says in the *De doctrina christiana* II 11: 'Those who turned the Scriptures from Hebrew into Greek can be counted, the Latin translators cannot. Any individual in the early days of the Faith who had a Greek codex in his hands and thought he had some skill in the two languages, took it upon himself to translate it.' Thus Augustine. Hence I am induced to believe that, in order that the faithful might not waver when they saw the variations in the texts, all were rejected, and this one alone, which had been corrected by St Jerome, accepted by the church. If you are willing to learn that things happened as I have said (unless you are going to start by saying that there is some reason other than their acceptance by the church of God why these Gospels which we accept are true), listen to Augustine: 'I would not believe the Gospel, unless the authority of the church compelled me to do so.' Tell me then, Erasmus, which edition is the church to approve: the Greek, which it does not use and has not used for centuries, any more than it is in communion with the Greeks themselves, who are schismatics; or the Latin, the only one cited when any definition has to be sought from Holy Scripture, passing over Jerome himself, if he happens to have a different reading, as not seldom happens?

(Source: R. A. Mynors and D. F. S. Thomson, editors, *The Correspondence of Erasmus: Letters 298 to 445 (1514 to 1516)*, copyright University of Toronto Press, 1976. Reprinted by permission of University of Toronto Press.)

37. ERASMUS' REBUTTAL OF EDWARD LEE'S CRITICISMS OF HIS GREEK TEXT AND LATIN TRANSLATION

Edward Lee was an English scholar at Louvain who had prepared an extensive criticism of Erasmus' New Testament. (Unlike Erasmus, Lee had a glowing future ahead of him in the Catholic church; ultimately he became an Archbishop.) A mutual friend obtained a copy of his critique and passed it on to Erasmus for review, reply, and rebuttal. The response is a rather disjointed one, leaving the impression that Erasmus was so indignant that he dictated a response to each individual objection as he encountered it rather than weaving his observations into a more coherent whole.

ERASMUS OF ROTTERDAM TO MAARTEN LIPS, GREETING
Do you not think me exceptionally fortunate? There comes to me unasked a blessing which other men scarcely obtain by great effort and expense: everyone offers to instruct Erasmus. And so of necessity, unless I am a mere blockhead, I must some day make progress. In one point, however, I may be thought somewhat unlucky: most of my would-be teachers play the part of hostile critics rather than instructors. Some of them have as their object not to make me a better scholar or a better man, but by joining battle with me to earn, they hope, some pittance of reputation for themselves. All are furious, none more so than those who can teach me absolutely nothing. They are like some schoolmasters, always shouting and clouting and flogging the boys' skin off their backs, and can teach nothing for all that except bad grammar, which they will soon have to unlearn. The man whose pamphlet you have sent me is one of these; it is so illiterate that I could hardly endure to read it, so comical that I could not fail to, though I kept it for a journey by boat. I should be as mad as he is if I tried to answer such malicious falsehoods. But I will scribble a word of comment on each chapter of his nonsense, in such a way that, if you like, they can actually be numbered. . . .

2. He imagines, and assumes as proved, that I publicly correct and alter the Vulgate text, whereas I leave that intact and untouched and have turned into Latin what is found in the Greek copies, pointing out as I go along the agreements

or disagreements of our own text; not seldom preferring what is in these copies of ours, correcting anything corrupt, explaining ambiguities, elucidating obscurities, and changing anything that is notably barbarous in expression, because I understand that very many people are so disgusted by the prodigious errors (which however are nearly always the translator's work and not the authors') that they cannot bring themselves to read the Scriptures. Nor for that matter have all mortals such an iron digestion that they can endure the style of it. But if we simplify our language for the benefit of ignorant and simple folk, should we not help educated readers too by purifying the language? In any case, if this critic of mine wishes nothing whatever to be published that differs from the Vulgate text in common use, it will not be lawful to publish the New Testament in Greek as the Greeks use it, unless it has first been corrected against our published Vulgate, for fear that someone will detect some disagreement. Who is mad enough to say any such thing? We must do away forthwith with St Ambrose's version or paraphrase, whichever it is, of the Pauline Epistles, which differs extensively from our version; we must do away with Jerome's too, which differs from it in a number of places. And then most of our manuscripts must be done away with, because as a rule they differ among themselves. Observe too the disagreement between your friend and Augustine, whom he seems to think no one else has read. Augustine declares that he has actually been helped by the difference between copies, since what is obscure in one version is more clearly rendered in another; we cannot all do all things. This man supposes that all confidence in Scripture is brought to an end, if the difference in reading is made public, and would rather the most manifest blunders were left in the sacred text than that two or three foolish old men who are hard to please should take offence. Yet St Jerome was not in the least deterred from this line of enquiry by the fact that the change of some small word or other in the prophet Jonah made almost the whole population rebel against their bishop, and pours scorn on those gods so dependent on gourds who are shaken by so small a change, although Augustine had written and told Jerome the story as though it were a serious matter. Why, let that severe critic of yours answer me just this one question: should we wish on behalf of God's church that she should read the books of Holy Scripture in a truly accurate text or no? If he admits that it is desirable, let him tell us whether he admits that sundry errors are imported into those books every day by the ignorance of correctors or the negligence of scribes. If this cannot be denied, why does he not welcome these efforts of mine, which contribute more than anything else to the double object of mending corruptions and preserving from corruption what is correct? For there is no denying that there are corruptions in most of our manuscripts – in fact, in almost all. Then let him tell us whether it is important that the Scriptures should be correctly understood or no. If he thinks it is important, why does he condemn my efforts, which have explained so many passages that even he, learned as he is, never understood before? Let him read my work through and deny if he can that what I say is true.

3. He says that many people have tried to undermine and do away with the Vulgate text, some to add elegance of style, others to exclude error, but that all attempts have failed. Is the man not ashamed of such palpable nonsense? Let him produce one person who has tried this – unless perhaps he will put forward the sole name of Lefèvre. . . .

13. Meanwhile he dreams up the idea that the Latin translator produced what we now have under the inspiration of the Holy Spirit, though Jerome himself in his preface openly testifies that each translator renders to the best of his ability

what he is capable of understanding. Otherwise, Jerome himself would be grossly irreligious, in that he is not afraid to find fault sometimes with what we have in this edition.

14. In order to prove that all eloquence must be sought from Holy Scripture, he produces Jerome as his authority, although Jerome credits some of the prophets with uneducated language and Paul with ignorance of Greek, and that too in more than one passage.

15. We believe that Augustine likewise had the assistance of the Holy Spirit in expounding the books of Scripture; and yet he revises his work and wishes it to be read with a critical eye. . . .

30. He reasons moreover, in his idiot fashion, as follows: 'Hitherto the church has used this version: if the version is done away, the church did not possess the Holy Spirit.' I will now reason in my turn, thus: 'Ambrose did not possess this version: he therefore did not possess the Holy Spirit.'

31. On the contrary, the gift of the Spirit is given more lavishly, the more the church acquires of other good things. In the old days she had no literature and no eloquence, and she lacked wealth and power; now she has both, but it does not follow that Christ has deserted his spouse. . . .

46. He says that the church cannot err. Is the church in error instantly if there is a corruption in your copy of the text? And yet some things can happen to the church of which she has no previous experience. And I maintain, not that in this translation there is anything that can undermine the orthodox faith, but that there are defects which it is worth while to point out. Read my own version, and if you do not find hundreds of passages which you, good scholar as you are, have hitherto misunderstood, have the law on me to your heart's content.

47. 'You are a stumbling-block to the world,' he says, 'with your innovations in things that all accept.' Not at all: all men of the highest station and character are grateful to me, and the dogs who barked to begin with bark no more when they have read my work. A few conceited people take offence, who would not have it thought that there is anything they did not know.

48. 'Granting,' says he, 'that there are errors in the text, it was not right to publish them for ordinary people.' On the contrary, there is every reason to publish things that all men ought to know.

49. 'A private person,' he says, 'without authorization cannot make a new translation or correct an old one.' In the first place, I think that I, like others, have the right, if I have made any progress in theology, to make it publicly known, having been co-opted into a faculty of theology. Secondly, I am not making a new version; I translate the Greek; and so far as I am concerned, the old version is still there for all men's use, as it always was. Last but not least, let us assume that I have no authority: does this mean that, while the ignorant are free to corrupt the sacred text, I may not correct it unless a synod has been summoned first? Suppose I were a bishop or a cardinal, what has that to do with it? The business in hand calls not for a mitre or a red hat, but for skill in the tongues. . . .

51. 'If there is any error in them,' he says, 'it should have been corrected in accordance with the ancient testimony of the Fathers.' And yet what he demands is exactly what I have done; only this has escaped his notice, because he has not glanced at my book. . . .

54. The same wisdom is evident in his remark that the Greeks falsified their texts when they split off from the Roman church. And what, pray, was the reason why they should corrupt them all? Moreover, their separation from the Roman church being quite recent, how comes it that their modern texts and their very

ancient ones are in agreement? How comes it that Origen and Basil and Chyso-stom—and Latin Fathers too, Ambrose, Jerome, Hilary, Cyprian—are in accord with their falsified texts and disagree with ours? Did the Greeks falsify at one stroke the texts used by all these authors?

55. Moreover, where I had objected, following the papal decrees, that the true text of the New Testament ought to be checked against the Greek copies, he admits that in ancient times this was appropriate, but says that nothing could be less so now. And the reason he gives is their separation. As though the revolt of the Greeks had made any difference to their text of the Gospels!

56. But if the fact that the Greeks have split off from the Roman church is a valid reason for mistrusting the Greek text of the Bible, it was equally illicit in Jerome's day to correct the Old Testament out of the Hebrew texts, for the Jewish people had already rebelled, not from the Roman church but from Christ himself, which I consider somewhat more damnable.

57. Last but not least, if we are to put our trust exclusively in the books of Greeks who are not schismatics, it is precisely their texts that I follow for preference; but they do not differ from the schismatics' copies.

58. But his master-stroke of impudence is that, whereas I had written that it is more difficult for a Greek text to be corrupted than for one of ours, he makes out that I said it was impossible for Greek codices to be damaged in any way; and though the reason I adduced was the difficulty of Greek script, which is made up not merely of letters but of ligatures and accents, this liar says the reason I gave was that the Greek language allows no scope for falsehood. What monstrous effrontery—especially as my letter still exists and has been printed more than once!...

61. If, however, he contends that the Greeks did manipulate their texts, at least the passages they corrupted were those which appeared to undermine their schismatic opinions. Then let him produce one single passage which can be suspect on those grounds. In actual fact, if anything can arouse suspicion in the Greek texts, it will be above all the passages which were thought to tell in favour of the Arians or the school of Origen; for the whole of Greece seems to have been united in such hatred or jealousy of them in particular that, although their authors have taken from Origen as their source almost everything they tell us that is worth having, they seem to have had nothing so much at heart, none the less, as the com-plete destruction of everything he wrote—which would have been enough, even in isolation, to give us an understanding of Holy Scripture. I overlook for the mo-ment the way in which he tells me to read Augustine on heresies as though he were the only man who had ever read it, or as though I could not read it unless instructed to by him, or as though I do not in fact cite evidence from that work in several places....

65. He instructs me therefore that I ought to have sent my book to the supreme pontiff for him to decide whether it should be suppressed or published. On that argument every book ought to be sent to the supreme pontiff, for every book might contain matter of offence for someone. But Thomas never did such a thing, nor did Scotus, nor for that matter did Augustine or Jerome. They published first, and the approval followed, and was not asked for. And furthermore, as I do not uproot the old version, but by publishing a revision of it make it easier for us not only to possess it in a purer form but to understand it better, how could I suspect that there would be malignant critics like this man, ready to take offence at a work that would benefit everyone? If anyone had cause to fear a stumbling-block, it was those that are weak; yet on their side no cause of stumbling has arisen. All this

trouble has been stirred up solely by two or three people of the class commonly accounted perfect, who when my book was not yet published poisoned the minds of simple folk everywhere and condemned what as yet they knew nothing of, rousing prejudice against my work before it was known what good it could do. It is their fault, not mine, if any man has been offended. . . .

70. He declares it unlawful for any man to teach without public authorization. Does it not satisfy him that I have the same authorization that Thomas had? (Not that I would compare myself with him.) Does it not satisfy him if I do it at the urgent request of the best of prelates and on encouragement from the pope himself? Though Thomas for that matter is not concerned with publishing texts, but with public sermons or lectures.

71. He maintains that Jerome did not dare undertake a version of Holy Scripture, except on orders from Damasus. What effrontery the man has! On whose authority then did he translate the Pentateuch? At the request of a certain Desiderius, was it not? Was it Damasus put him up to translate the books of Esdras? Read his preface, and let this featherpate blush for his mistakes. And then Tobit: surely he was put up to that by Chromatius and Heliodorus? But why need I refute his falsehoods one by one, seeing that the New Testament was the only thing Jerome revised at the request of Pope Damasus? . . .

You see, my dear Maarten, what a lot of nonsense there is in that small book. Though even so I have noted a few points out of many, and already repent the waste of time. And yet he is so self-confident that he dares to make you the judge whether he has said anything silly, though there are rather more silly things in his book than there are words. Such are the men who set up to teach Erasmus! And yet this is that famous book which he laboriously completed on the basis of those ten conclusions which had passed, he says, through the hands of many men, and which he proposed to dedicate to some outstanding figure; and he tells us to share such valuable material with faithful and right-thinking friends. Then he summons anyone who is willing to take him on into the ring, and demands an antagonist — though we ought to respect the eminent researches of so great a scholar, for they cannot be interrupted without great loss to the world. It would be truer to say that the poor man has a foul itch and wants someone to scratch himself against; and any man of sense will not go near him. I, to be sure, do not yet dislike the man enough to wish to expose him to the jeers of the learned world, though that is what he wants. Pray tell him, my dear Lips, to use his spare time more fruitfully in future. If he is sound at heart, he will accept your warning and amend; if his mind is too far gone, leave him to his distemper. I hope you will devote yourself to reading sacred authors, in preference to wasting your best years on this sort of rubbish.

(Source: R. A. Mynors and D. F. S. Thomson, editors, *The Correspondence of Erasmus, Letters 842 to 992 (1518 to 1519)*, copyright University of Toronto Press, 1979. Reprinted by permission of University of Toronto Press.)

38. "AN EXHORTATION TO THE DILIGENT STUDYE OF SCRIPTURE MADE BY ERASMUS ROTERODAMUS"

While encouraging the study of the New Testament in the original language, Erasmus was also enthusiastic about the study of it in contemporary translations since he knew full well that most Europeans were not able to read it in the Greek. In 1529 his "Exhortation" appeared, which defends not only the propriety but also the moral necessity of Bible reading. The following extract is from the "Inglish" translation of that year.

I would desire that all women should read the gospel and Paul's epistles, and I would to God they were translated into the tongues of all men, so that they might not only be known of the Scots and Irishmen, but also of the Turks and Saracens. . . . I would to God that the ploughman would sing a text of the scripture at his plough-beam; and that the weaver at his loom with this would drive away the tediousness of time. I would the wayfaring man with this pastime would expel the weariness of his journey. And, to be short, I would that all the communication of the Christian should be of the scripture; for in a manner, such are we ourselves, as our daily tales are. . . . Neither truly is it meet . . . sith the reward of immortality pertaineth indifferently unto all men, that only the doctrine should be banished from the secular, and possessed only of a few, whom the commonalty call divines, or religious persons. . . . We cannot call any man a Platonist, unless he have read the works of Plato. Yet call we them Christian, yea and divines, which never have read the scriptures of Christ. . . . If we covet to withdraw our minds from the tedious cares of this life; why had we liefer learn the wisdom of Christ's doctrine out of men's books, than of Christ Himself, which in this scripture doth chiefly perform that thing which He promised unto us, when He said that He would continue with us unto the end of the world? For in this Testament He speaketh, breatheth and liveth among us in a manner more effectually than when His body was presently conversant in this world. The Jews neither saw nor heard so much, as thou mayest daily both hear and see in the scripture of Christ. . . . What a marvellous world is this: we keep the letters which are written from our friends: we kiss them, and bear them about with us; we read them over twice or thrice. And how many thousands are there among the Christian which are esteemed of great literature, and yet have not once in their lives read over the gospels and epistles of the Apostles. . . . They that profess Saint Benedict's rule . . . (observe their example), learn it by heart, and drink it into their hearts. Saint Austin's adherents are not ignorant in their rule. Saint Francis' friars do know, observe, and advance their patron's precepts: . . . Why set they more by their rule which was written of a man, than the whole Christianity by the holy scripture, which Christ did equally preach unto all men? . . . . I would our first and unformed speech should sound of Christ; I would our ignorant childhood should be informed with Christ's evangely. . . . The evangely doth represent and express the quick and living image of His most holy mind, yea, and Christ Himself healing, dying, rising again, and to conclude, all parts of Him, in so much that thou couldst not so plainly and fruitfully see Him, although He were present before thy bodily eyes.

FOUR

Reformation-Era
English Translations

I. Wycliffe

39. SIR THOMAS MORE ON PRE-WYCLIFFE
ENGLISH BIBLES (1528)

Wycliffe's translation is generally regarded as the first English translation of the Bible. Undeniably it was the first one to attract such widespread interest and enthusiasm that even strenuous repression was unable to destroy a large number of its copies. Over 150 partial and complete manuscripts of the two Wycliffe Bibles have survived; how many more survived the persecution but were destroyed by the ravages of age and accident is unknown.

In 1528 Sir Thomas More published his *Dialogue Concerning Heresies*, which strove to oppose the Tyndale translation in particular while upholding the abstract right to translate. More's references to various Bibles he had observed have been used to prove that there were earlier translations than that of Wycliffe, renditions that were translated with the appropriate clerical approvals. However, it should be noted that More assumes that the manuscripts he had seen were pre–Wycliffe on the basis of their approval by "the bishop of the diocese" (perhaps itself an assumption based upon the presence of the Bible in an orthodox home). He seems to be unaware that left with the bare text—stripped of such things as the controversial introductions—there was little to alert the reader to the Wycliffe Bible's "heretical" origin. Hence there would have been no reason to suppress a Wycliffe Bible that was not known to be Wycliffian. Indeed More seems to imply that the standard in deciding whether to confiscate and destroy a Bible lay not in the text itself (assuming nothing transparently heretical was noted), but in its ownership: He admits that Bibles were left in the hands of those known as "good and catholic folk" while "all such as are found in the hands of heretics, they use[d] to take away."

More's fictitious "Messenger" is convinced that Bible translations per se were forbidden, and More is at pains to prove that such is not absolutely the case. The fact that one man (such as More) might see "acceptable" translations but the "Messenger" is unaware of them, strongly argues that if these Bibles were, indeed, non–Wycliffian translations their circulation was extremely limited. More may have had the technicality of law on his side (that translations were permissible), but the "Messenger" not only exhibits popular opinion on the subject but also seems to have a better grasp of the actual situation.

The "Messenger's" summary of popular opinion as to why Wycliffe's translation was suppressed:

And that, for none other intent but for to keep out of the people's hands all knowledge of Christ's gospel, and of God's law, except so much only as the clergy themselves list now and then to tell us. And that, little as it is, and seldom shewed, yet as it is feared, not well and truly told, but watered with false glosses, and altered from the truth of the very words and sentence of scripture, only for the maintenance of their authority. And for the fear lest this thing should evidently appear to the people, if they were suffered to read the scripture themselves in their own tongue, was, (as it is thought), the very cause, not only for which the New Testament translated by Tindale was burned, but also that the clergy of this realm hath before this time by a constitution provincial prohibited any book of scripture to be translated into the English tongue, fearing men with fire as heretics who should so presume to keep them, as though it were heresy for a Christian man to read Christ's gospel. And surely sir, quoth he, some folk that think this dealing of the clergy to be thus, and good men to be mishandled for declaring the truth, and the scripture' self to be pulled out of the people's hands, lest they should perceive the truth, be led in their minds to doubt whether Luther himself, (of whose opinions, or at the least of whose works, all this business began), wrote indeed so evil as he is borne in hand.

More's rebuttal that only unauthorized translations were prohibited:

For ye shall understand that the great arch heretic, Wycliffe, whereas the whole Bible was long before his days by virtuous and well learned men translated into the English tongue, and by good and godly people with devotion and soberness well and reverently read, took upon of a malicious purpose to translate it of new. In which translation he purposely corrupted the holy text, maliciously planting therein such words, as might in the readers' ears serve to the proof of such heresies as he went about to sow: which he not only set forth with his own translation of the Bible, but also with certain prologues and glosses which he made thereon. . . . After that it was perceived what harm the people took by the translation, prologues and glosses of Wycliffe's, and also of some other, that after him holp to set forth his sect: then for that cause, and forasmuch as it is dangerous to translate the text of scripture out of one tongue into another [From this point, More is quoting from the constitutions of Oxford, 1408.], as holy S. Jerome testifieth, forasmuch as in translation it is hard alway to keep the same sentence whole: it was, I say, for these causes at a council holden at Oxford, provided upon great pain, that no man should from thenceforth translate into the English tongue, or any other language, of his own authority, by way of book, libel, or treatise: nor no man openly or secretly any such book, libel or treatise read, newly made in the time of the said John Wycliffe: or that should be made any time after, till the said translation were by the diocesan, or if need should require, by a provincial council approved.... For I trow that in this law ye see nothing unreasonable. For it neither forbiddeth the translations to be read that were already well done of old before Wycliffe's days, nor damneth his because it was new, but because it was naught: nor prohibiteth new to be made, but provideth that they shall not be read if they be mismade, till they be by good examination amended, except they be such translations as Wycliffe made and Tindale, that the malicious mind of the translator had in such wise handled, it were as it were labour lost to go about to mend them.

The "Messenger's" response: More may be right, but his view does not represent the common view on the subject:

"I long by my troth," quoth he, "and even sit on thorns, till I see that constitution. For not myself only, but every man else hath ever taken it for otherwise.... I suppose," quoth he, "that this opinion is rather grown another way, that is to wit, that the clergy, though the law serve them not therefore, do yet in deed take all translations out of every lay man's hand. And sometime, with those that be burned or convicted of heresy, they burn the English Bible without respect, be the translation old or new, bad or good."
"Forsooth," quoth I, "if this were so, then were it, in my mind, not well done. But I believe ye mistake it. Howbeit, what ye have seen I cannot say; but myself have seen, and can shew you, Bibles fair and old written in English, which have been known and seen by the bishop of the diocese, and left in laymen's hands, and women's, to such as he knew for good and catholic folk. But of truth, all such as are found in the hands of heretics, they use to take away."

(Source: Margaret Deanesly, *The Lollard Bible and Other Medieval Biblical Versions*, copyright 1920 and published by Cambridge University Press. Used by permission.)

40. PRINCIPLES OF TRANSLATION BEHIND THE SECOND WYCLIFFE BIBLE

Although it is rightly called the "Wycliffe Bible," the terminology is slightly misleading. Rather than being the translator of the two versions that bear his name, Wycliffe seems to have played the role of intellectual encourager to a circle of friends who did the actual work. Although his followers became known as believers in evangelism for the masses, Wycliffe himself functioned in the academic environment of Oxford, from which he drew those men who carried out the actual translation.

Both versions were based upon the Latin. The first was completed about 1382 and was very literal, one in which the English duplicated the word order of the Latin even at the cost of comprehensibility. One manuscript explicitly labels Nicholas Hereford as the translator of the Old Testament through Baruch 3:20. Since the manuscript involved is written in five different hands, the attribution has been taken in two different senses. Some hold that Hereford was the sole translator and that the different handwriting styles are those of his scribes to whom he dictated the text. The second (and more likely) possibility is that he was in general charge of the effort.

The Second Wycliffe Bible appeared about 1395 and is most likely the work of Wycliffe's secretary and close co-worker, John Puvey (either as sole or primary translator). The "General Prologue," from which the following extract comes, is found only with the Second Wycliffe Bible, never with the First. That it was rarely copied is likely since only ten copies are known to have survived (nine with Bible manuscripts; one in a separate document). Because of the doctrinal views expressed in parts of it, this is hardly surprising. To guarantee the maximum circulation of the sacred text (especially in quarters that would have been hostile to the Wycliffian doctrinal presumptions), the controversial "Prologue" was best left out.

It exhibits a distinct shift in translation theory from the earlier effort. The writer quite explicitly comes out in favor of translating the meaning of "the sentence" even at the cost of strict verbal accuracy; verbal precision that did not adequately communicate the message was firmly rejected.

For though covetous clerks be wooed by simony, heresy, and many other sins to dispise and stop holy writ, as much as they may: yet the lewid people crieth after holy writ, to con it and keep it, with great cost and peril of their life.

For these reasons and other, with common charity to save all men in our realm, which God would have saved, a simple creature hath translated the Bible out of Latin into English. First, this simple creature had much travail, with divers fellows and helpers, to gather many old Bibles, and other doctors, and common glosses, and to make one Latin Bible some deal true; and then to study it of the new, the text with the gloss, and other doctors, as he might get, and specially Lyra on the Old Testament, that helped full much in this work; the third time to counsel with old grammarians and old divines, of hard words, and hard sentences, how they might best be understood, and translated; the fourth time to translate as clearly as he could to the sentence, and to have many good fellows and cunning at the correcting of the translation. First, it is to know, that the best translating is out of Latin into English, to translate after the sentence [meaning], and not only after the words, so that the sentence be as open, or opener, in English as in Latin, and go not far from the letter; and if the letter may not be sued in the translating, let the sentence ever be whole and open, for the words ought to serve to the intent and sentence, and else the words be superfluous or false.... At the beginning I purposed, with God's help, to make the sentence as true and open in English as it is in the Latin, or more true and more open than it is in the Latin; and I pray, for charity and for common profit of Christian souls, that if any wise man find any default of the truth of translation, let him set in the true sentence and open of holy writ, but look that he examine truly his Latin Bible, for no doubt he shall find full many Bibles in Latin full false, if he look, namely, many new; and the common Latin Bibles have more need to be corrected, as many as I have seen in my life, *than hath the English Bible late translated.* . . . And whether I have translated as openly or openlier in English as in Latin, let wise men deem, that know well both languages, and know well the sentence of holy scripture. And whether I have done this or nay, no doubt they that con well the scripture of holy writ and English together, and will travail, with God's grace, thereabouts, may make the Bible as true and open, yea and openlier in English than it is in Latin.

(Source: Margaret Deanesly, *The Lollard Bible and Other Medieval Biblical Versions,* copyrighted 1920 and published by Cambridge University Press.)

II. *Tyndale*

41. HENRY VIII BANS VERNACULAR TRANSLATIONS AND PROMISES AN OFFICIAL VERSION

Henry VIII might break with the Pope in order to gain himself the desired new spouse, but that did not convert the king into a radical. Much as he desired at least a partial reformation of English religion, he was well aware of the danger to political order that could be posed by religious division and the role that vernacular Bible translations could play in promoting such disunity. Hence in June 1530 he issued a proclamation "prohibitinge the hauinge of holy scripture translated into the vulgar tonges." This was specifically aimed at Tyndale's translation but applied equally to any other the people had access to.

In spite of the blanket prohibition, Henry seems well aware that if he wished to successfully ban all "heretical" translations that it would be necessary to provide a reliable one of his own. This he promised to do — on the condition that the English people forsake their "heresies" and existing vernacular translations.

And farthermore, for as moche as it is come to the herynge of our saide soueraigne lorde the kynge, that report is made by diuers and many of his subiectes, that as it were to all men not onely expedyent, but also necessarye, to haue in the englisshe tonge bothe the newe testament and the olde: and that his highnes, his noble men, and prelates were bounden to suffre them so to haue it: His highnes hath therfore semblably there vpon consulted with the sayd primates and vertuous, discrete, and well lerned personages in diuinite forsayde, and by them all it is thought, that it is not necessary, the sayde scripture to be in the englisshe tonge, and in the handes of the commen people: but that the distribution of the sayd scripture, and the permyttyng or denyenge therof, dependeth onely vpon the discretion of the superiours, as they shall thynke it conuenyent. And that hauing respecte to the malignite of this present tyme, with the inclination of people to erronious opinions, the translation of the newe testament and the olde in to the vulgare tonge of englysshe, shulde rather be the occasion of contynuance or increace of errours amonge the sayd people, than any benefyte or commodite towarde the weale of their soules. And that it shall nowe be more conuenient that the same people haue the holy scripture expouned to them, by preachers in their sermons, accordynge as it hath ben of olde tyme accustomed before this tyme. All be it if it shall here after appere to the kynges highnes, that his saide people do vtterly abandon and forsake all peruerse, erronious, and sedicious opinyons, with the newe testament and the olde, corruptly translated in to the englisshe tonge nowe beinge in print: And that the same bokes and all other bokes of heresy, as well in the frenche tonge as in the duche tonge, be clerely extermynate and exiled out of this realme of Englande for euer: his highnes entendeth to prouyde, that the holy scripture shalbe by great lerned and catholyke persones, translated in to the englisshe tonge, if it shall then seme to his grace conuenient so to be.

(Source: David Daiches, *The King James Version of the English Bible: An Account of the Development and Sources of the English Bible of 1611 With Special Reference to the Hebrew Tradition.* Copyrighted 1941; reprinted by Archon Books, 1968, pages 13–14.)

III. *Coverdale's English Translation*

Coverdale was educated at Cambridge and dedicated his life to biblical studies. In his dedication to the 1535 edition, Coverdale refers to his reliance on the work of five earlier efforts, though he does not name them. The two most obvious ones were the English-language Tyndale's and the Latin Vulgate. The latter was used instead of the Hebrew and Greek almost certainly because of Coverdale's lack of knowledge or confidence in handling those languages.

42. THE TRANSLATOR CONCEDES HIS WEAKNESSES

Coverdale was not one to hide his limitations behind a fog of rhetoric. In the prologue to his 1535 Bible he bluntly spells out his own limitations and the translation aids he freely utilized in overcoming them. Indeed he expresses the hope that his own modest effort would serve to goad better qualified men to undertake the task.

"Considering how excellent knowledge and learning an interpreter of scripture ought to have in the tongues, and pondering also mine own insufficiency therein, and how weak I am to perform the office of a translator, I was the more loth to meddle with this work. Notwithstanding when I considered how great pity it was that we should want it so long, and called to my remembrance the adversity of them, which were not only of ripe knowledge, but would also with all their hearts have performed that they began, if they had not had impediment: considering, I say, that by reason of their adversity it could not so soon have been brought to an end, as our most prosperous nation would fain have had it: these and other reasonable causes considered, I was the more bold to take it in hand. And to help me herein, I have had sundry translations, not only in Latin, but also of the Dutch interpreters: whom (because of their singular gifts and special diligence in the bible) I have been the more glad to follow for the most part, according as I was required. But to say the truth before God, it was neither my labour nor desire, to have this work put in my hand: nevertheless it grieved me that other nations should be more plenteously provided for with the scripture in their mother tongue, than we: therefore when I was instantly required, though I could not do so well as I would, I thought it yet my duty to do my best, and that with a good will....

"For the which cause (according as I was desired) I took the more upon me to set forth this special translation, not as a checker, not as a reprover, or despiser of other men's translations (for among many as yet I have found none without occasion of great thanksgiving unto God) but lowly and faithfully have I followed mine interpreters, and that under correction.... And though it be not worthily ministered unto thee in this translation by reason of my rudeness, yet if thou be fervent in thy prayer, God shall not only send it thee in a better shape by the ministration of other that began it afore, but shall also move the hearts of them which as yet meddled not withal, to take it in hand, and to bestow the gift of their understanding thereon, as well in our language as other famous interpreters do in other languages, and I pray God that through my poor ministration herein I may give them that can do better, some occasion so to do."

(Source: J. F. Mozley, *Coverdale and His Bibles,* copyright 1953 by Lutterworth Press. Used by permission.)

43. THE APPEAL FOR ROYAL APPROVAL IN THE DEDICATION OF 1535

Coverdale goes out of his way to stress that in no way, shape, or form is his version intended to be sectarian, i.e., altering or shading the translation in any way in order to maintain the teachings he himself embraces. So convinced is he of the necessity for an authorized English version, that he is even willing to have the king "correct it," "amend it," or "improve it" in order to secure its unfettered circulation. Although he expresses willingness even to have the king "reject it, if your godly wisdom shall think it necessary," this was certainly the one option he was most opposed to.

"Considering now, most gracious prince, the inestimable treasure, fruit and prosperity everlasting that God giveth with his word, and trusting in his infinite goodness that he would bring my simple and rude labour herein to good effect, therefore, as the Holy Ghost moved other men to do the cost hereof, so was I boldened in God to labour in the same. Again, considering your imperial majesty not only to be my natural sovereign liege lord and chief head of the church of England, but also the true defender and maintainer of God's laws, I thought it my duty, and to belong unto my allegiance, when I had translated this bible, not only to dedicate this translation unto your highness, but wholly to commit it unto the same: to the intent that if any thing therein be translated amiss (for in many things we fail, even when we think to be sure) it may stand in your grace's hands, to correct it, to amend it, to improve it, yea and clean to reject it, if your godly wisdom shall think it necessary. And as I do with all humbleness submit mine understanding and my poor translation unto the spirit of truth in your grace, so make I this protestation, having God to record in my conscience, that I have neither wrested nor altered so much as one word for the maintenance of any manner of sect, but have with a clear conscience purely and faithfully translated this out of five sundry interpreters, having only the manifest truth of the scripture before mine eyes."

(Source: J. F. Mozley, *Coverdale and His Bibles*, copyright 1953 by Lutterworth Press. Used by permission.)

44. THE KING APPROVES CIRCULATION OF COVERDALE'S TRANSLATION

William Fulke provides the following recollection of a sermon by Coverdale in which the translator discusses the approval of his translation by the king. The bishops had made the inevitable charge of "faults" in the translation as a means of aborting its approval. The king—exercising astute judgment—refused to be turned aside by that dodge and asked the far more relevant question of whether there were "heresies" taught by it. Forced to answer in the negative, the king allowed it to be freely circulated but did not grant a formal approval to be printed on the title page.

Many writers take this incident to refer to the Great Bible, also a product of the same scholar. They point out that when Fulke refers to Coverdale's Bible he refers to the Great Bible. On the other hand, this extract refers to Coverdale's own words—to Coverdale's usage rather than that of Fulke. Which translation would Coverdale be most likely to refer to as "his" translation? The reference would seem most naturally applied to the 1535 work since that was his private, personal effort, while the Great Bible was undertaken by him on an official government commission.

"I myself, and so did many hundreds beside me hear that reverend father, Master Dr Coverdale, of holy and learned memory, in a sermon at Paul's cross, upon occasion of some slanderous reports that then were raised against his translation, declare his faithful purpose in doing the same: which after it was finished and presented to king Henry VIII, and by him committed to divers bishops of that time to peruse, of which, as I remember, Stephen Gardiner was one; after they had kept it long in their hands, and the king was divers times sued unto for the publication thereof, at the last being called for by the king himself they redelivered the book; and being demanded by the king what was their judgment of the translation they answered that there were many faults therein. 'Well,' said the king, 'but are there any heresies maintained thereby?' They answered there were no heresies that they could find maintained thereby. 'If there be no heresies,' said the king, 'then in God's name let it go abroad among our people.' According to this judgment of the king and the bishops, Mr Coverdale defended his translation, confessing that he did now himself espy some faults which, if he might review it once over again, as he had done twice before, he doubted not but to amend: but for any heresy, he was sure there was none maintained by his translation."

(Source: J. F. Mozley, *Coverdale and His Bibles*, copyright 1953 by Lutterworth Press. Used by permission.)

IV. *Coverdale's Latin-English Diglot of 1538*

Coverdale's bilingual Latin-English New Testament combined a slightly revised text of his English Bible with that of the Vulgate. A potential market clearly existed since the English bishops had instructed the clergy to obtain New Testaments in both of these languages.

For some unknown reason Coverdale did not closely supervise the final stages of the production of the book. When he saw the completed printing he was horrified at the uncorrected errors and the inadequacies in the English prose. He promptly brought out a new edition under closer personal supervision. The repudiated edition was printed in Paris by Francis Regnault. The Nicolson edition, in which Coverdale placed such faith as the rectification of the earlier errors, is itself full of careless mistakes though it did catch and correct many of those fathered by Regnault.

In many copies of the Nicolson edition, the name of Coverdale is missing from the title page. In its place is that of John Hollybush. Hollybush probably had the direct responsibility for overseeing the production of that edition. Some take the presence of his name on the title page as the publisher's way of diverting Coverdale's wrath for the number of remaining errors.

45. DEDICATION TO THE KING (REGNAULT EDITION)

Coverdale has his name printed at the end of this dedication to the king. He clearly takes pleasure at bringing out a Latin Bible to supplement his English one: It powerfully refuted the accusation that he was an enemy of the Latin version.

"Considering how lovingly, how favourably and how tenderly your highness hath taken mine infancy and rudeness in dedicating the whole bible in English to your most noble grace, and having sure experience also how benign and gracious a mind your highness doth ever bear to all them that in their calling are willing to do their best," I am emboldened to dedicate this book also to your majesty. The enemies of God's word slander us, and "affirm that we intend to pervert the scripture and to condemn the common translation in Latin," and "they call your loving and faithful people heretics, newfangled fellows, English biblers, cobblers of divinity, fellows of the new faith &c, with such other ungodly sayings." So far am I from despising the Latin translation that "I have here set it forth and the English also thereof." And I have done this "not so much for the clamorous importunity of evil speakers, as to satisfy the just request of certain your grace's faithful subjects; and specially to induce and instruct such as can but English and are not learned in the Latin, that in comparing these two texts together they may the better understand the one by the other." It may be a help to unlearned clerks, and at least it may lead them to cease their "importune cavillations against us." For inasmuch as "in our other translations we do not follow this old Latin text word for word, they cry out upon us," just as if the scripture were not as valid in other tongues as it is in Latin. The scripture is of like worthiness and authority, "in what language soever the Holy Ghost speaketh it," and I for my part am "always willing and ready to do my best in one translation as in another. . . . To give other men occasion now to do their best, and to express my good will, if I could do better, I have for the causes above rehearsed attempted this small labour," and submit it to your majesty.

(Source: J. F. Mozley, *Coverdale and His Bibles*, copyright 1953 by Lutterworth Press. Used by permission.)

V. Matthew's Bible

This translation has perhaps the unique distinction of having been produced by a man who never lived! The general consensus today is that John Rogers was the actual compiler/translator of this version. The majority of the text is based on Tyndale (including much of Tyndale's previously unpublished Old Testament). As his main secondary source he relies on Coverdale's work. Only as a last resort does he reject both in favor of his own rendering.

Why this deliberate use of a misattribution? The king had officially banned Tyndale's translation less than a decade previously. Hence it would have been embarrassing for the king to officially embrace and endorse the very translator he had previously opposed. This stratagem allowed an essentially Tyndale translation to be published with royal blessing while maintaining the fiction that Tyndale remained under the royal ban. The willingness to tolerate this verbal sleight-of-hand strongly implies a dramatic shift in Henry's attitude.

46. A PRINTER PLEADS FOR ROYAL PROTECTION

The printer for Matthew's Bible was one Richard Grafton. Writing to an influential adviser to the king in late August or early September 1517, he candidly reveals his frustration at unscrupulous competitors who were bringing out unauthorized editions of the Matthew translation. He seeks a royal edict banning the circulation of the competing edition until his own is completely sold out. And to ensure that that goal does not take an inordinate amount of time to accomplish, he suggests that every minister be required to buy one!

RICHARD GRAFTON TO CROMWELL:
According to your lordship's commission, by your servant, I have sent you certain bibles and beg you to accept them as well done. Where I wrote to your lordship for a privy seal as a defence against the enemies of this bible, and you thought

it unnecessary; this work has cost us 500 *l.* and I have printed and booked 1,500 copies, but now others are printing the same work in a lesser letter, intending to sell their little books cheaper than I can sell my great, and so prevent my selling any: Will by this be undone, and so will his creditors who have assisted him. Those who are printing this new copy from his will falsify the text; for they do it not for God's glory but covetousness. Dutchmen dwelling here who can neither write nor speak good English are printing it, and to save 20 *l.* or 40 *l.* to a learned man to oversee it, will issue it full of errors. Desires the King's privilege that none shall print them till these be sold, which shall not be this three year, and will "consider" Cromwell's favour, and doubtless so will my lord of Canterbury and other friends. . . . Desires that, as this goes abroad with the King's licence and is the pure Word of God, Cromwell will command every curate to have one. Every abbey should have six set in different places for the convent and resorters to read. Would have none but the papistical sort compelled to have them, and then there would be enough in my lord of London's diocese "to spend away a great part of them." A very small commission to my lords of Canterbury, Salisbury and Worcester would cause it to be done in their dioceses. It would terminate the schism that is in the realm, some calling themselves of the Old and some of the New; for now we should all follow one God, one book, and one learning. . . .

(Source: David Daiches, *The King James Version of the English Bible*, copyrighted 1941; reprinted by Archon Books, 1968, pages 24–25.)

47. ARCHBISHOP CRANMER'S PLEA FOR ROYAL APPROVAL OF THE MATTHEW BIBLE

On August 4, 1537, Archbishop Cranmer wrote to Cromwell with the request that he forward this new Bible translation to the king. In spite of his disclaimer that there were probably some faults he had missed, Cranmer is convinced that overall it remained the best yet available and, therefore, was deserving of the king's approval.

"You shall receive by the bringer hereof a bible in English, both of a new translation and of a new print, dedicated unto the king's majesty, as farther appeareth by a pistle unto his grace in the beginning of the book, which [i.e. the dedicatory epistle] in mine opinion is very well done, and therefore I pray your lordship to read the same. And as for the translation, so far as I have read thereof, I like it better than any other translation heretofore made, yet not doubting but that there may and will be found some faults therein, as you know no man ever did or can do so well but it may be from time to time amended. And for as much as the book is dedicated unto the king's grace, and also great pains and labour taken in setting forth of the same, I pray you, my lord, that you will exhibit the book unto the king's highness, and to obtain of his grace, if you can, a licence that the same may be sold and read of every person, without danger of any act, proclamation or ordinance heretofore granted to the contrary, until such time that we the bishops shall set forth a better translation, which I think will not be till a day after doomsday."

(Source: J. F. Mozley, *Coverdale and His Bibles*, copyright 1953 by Lutterworth Press. Used by permission.)

48. CRANMER'S ENTHUSIASTIC RESPONSE TO ROYAL APPROVAL

The sought-after approval was granted within less than two weeks. In a letter of August 13, 1537, Cranmer can barely contain his enthusiasm as he pours out praise to an influential advocate of the new translation.

"My lord, for this your pain, taken in this behalf, I give unto you my most hearty thanks, assuring your lordship for the contentation of my mind, you have showed me more pleasure herein than if you had given me a thousand pound: and I doubt not but that hereby such fruit of good knowledge shall ensue, that it shall well appear hereafter, what high and acceptable service you have done unto God and the king, which shall so much redound to your honour that, besides God's reward, you shall obtain perpetual memory for the same within this realm. And as for me, you may reckon me your bondman for the same, and I dare be bold to say, so may ye do my lord of Worcester" [Latimer].

(Source: J. F. Mozley, *Coverdale and His Bibles*, copyright 1953 by Lutterworth Press. Used by permission.)

49. MELANCHTHON'S OPINION OF JOHN ROGERS' CHARACTER AND ATTITUDE

Rogers (the actual translator of the "Matthew" Bible) enjoyed a close relationship with Melanchthon while in Germany. He translated four of the German scholar's books into English, and the respect between the two must have been deep and mutual, as is exhibited in the following letter by Melanchthon recommending Rogers for a pulpit in Germany.

"We have exhorted Master John an Englishman to go to you. This Master John the Englishman is a learned man, sound in the doctrine of Christ's church, and not infected by any evil opinions. And we know that he is gifted with great ability, which he sets off with a noble character; and since he is most anxious to promote the general peace, he will be careful to live in concord with his colleagues. Because of these singular virtues we hope that he will serve well the church of God wherever he preaches. He has just had an invitation in this neighbourhood to the pastorate of a church, but for the sake of peace (*tranquillitatis causa*) he prefers to go to you. At first you will make some allowances for his pronunciation, but that will be corrected by association with the people of your country. By my advice and that of N. [Luther?] he has been induced to undertake the journey; I urged him to it out of a true and sincere zeal for the good of your church. He is an Englishman but he has lived long in Germany, and his integrity, trustworthiness and constancy in every duty make him worthy of the love and support of all good men. Therefore I most earnestly implore you for Christ's sake, the son of God, to give a loving welcome to this stranger, and to commend him to your people so that they may entrust him with the ecclesiastical office. It is of great moment in a church that colleagues should live in concord. Since this John well understands this, and since he is by nature a lover of peace, he will aid you in every way in preserving the general tranquillity; and you should therefore greatly desire to have such a colleague."

(Source: J. F. Mozley, *Coverdale and His Bibles*, copyright 1953 by Lutterworth Press. Used by permission.)

VI. *Great Bible*

The Archbishop of Canterbury wrote the preface to this translation, and through royal endorsement its use quickly spread. In the two years following its initial release, at least seven editions were printed.

Coverdale was the guiding hand behind this version, revising the text of the Matthew Bible in light of the best and most recently available Hebrew (Munster, 1535) and Greek (Erasmus) texts. In the first edition of April 1539, the public was presented with a thoroughly revised New Testament. A similar intensive effort was made on Genesis through Esther. In the second edition of April 1540 — which was the one normally reprinted thereafter with only minor changes — Coverdale treated the remainder of the Old Testament to a similar careful revision. In contrast, the Apocrypha was little touched, retaining the basic text of the Matthew Bible and, hence, being essentially Coverdale's own from years before.

50. HENRY VIII UPHOLDS PUBLICLY AVAILABLE BIBLES FOR CHURCHES

A royal decree of May 1541 made plain that the "abuses" that had arisen out of providing church Bibles for the public to read would not be used as an excuse to remove them. That many a minister was appalled at the result of such easy access to the scriptures can easily be understood: Some people were reading them in a loud voice during services and some were even daring to present their own exposition in competition with the sermon! Though the king demands that such activities be halted (and the violators punished), he refuses to go any further. Indeed, he orders that those churches (presumably a large number) who have not yet obtained a Bible for their place of worship proceed to do so. To guard against price-gouging at this potential bonanza, the king limits how much the publishers can sell their Bibles for.

. . . the Kynges royall maiestye intended, that his louynge subiectes shulde haue and vse the commoditie of the readyng of the sayd Bybles, for the purpose aboue rehersed, humbly, mekely, reuerently and obediently; and not that any of them shulde reade the sayde Bybles, wyth lowde and hyghe voyces, in tyme of the celebracion of the holye Masse and other dyuyne seruyces vsed in the churche, nor that any hys lay subiectes redynge the same, shulde presume to take vpon them, any common dysputacyon, argumente or exposicyon of the mysteries therein conteyned, but that euery suche laye man shulde humbly, mekely and reuerentlye reade the same, for his owne instruction, edificacion, and amendement of hys lyfe, accordynge to goddes holy worde therin mencioned. . . .

And myndynge the execucion of his sayde former, moost godly and gracyous Iniunctions: doeth straytlye charge and commaunde that the Curates and paryshioners of euerye towne and paryshe within thys hys realme of Englande, not hauynge already Bybles prouyded wythin thcyr paryshe churches, shall on thys syde the feaste of Alsayntes next commynge, bye and prouyde Bybles of the largest and greatest volume, and cause the same to be set and fyxed in euery of the sayde paryshe churches, there to be vsed as is aforesayd: accordynge to the sayde former Iniunctions; vpon payne that the Curate and inhabitauntes of the paryshes and townes, shal lose and forfayte to the Kynges maiestye for euery moneth that they shall lacke and want the sayde Bybles, after the same feast of Alsayntes fourty shyllynges. . . . And fynally, the kynges royall maiestie doeth declare and sygnifye to all and syngular his louynge subiectes, that to thentent they maye haue the sayde Bybles of the greatest volume at equall and reasonable pryces, His hyghnes by the aduyse of hys counsayle hath ordeyned and taxed: that the sellers therof, shall not take for any of the sayde Bybles vnbounde, aboue the pryce of ten shyllynges. And for euery of the sayde Bybles well and sufficientlye bounde, trymmed and clasped, not aboue twelue shyllynges, vpon payne, the seller to lose for euerye Byble solde contrary to this his hyghnes proclamacion fourty shyllynges. . . .

(Source: David Daiches, *The King James Version of the English Bible: An Account of the Development and Sources of the English Bible of 1611 With Special Reference to the Hebrew Tradition.* Copyrighted 1941; reprinted by Archon Books, 1968, pages 35–37.)

51. JOHN STANDISH'S TRACT TO PARLIAMENT URGING THE BANNING OF ALL VERNACULAR TRANSLATIONS

With Mary on the throne, determined to reconcile her realm with the Papacy, vernacular translations could be expected to face rough sailing. At first no overt steps were officially taken to suppress the Great Bible and other existing translations. Later a large but uncertain number were destroyed as part of Mary's "reconversion" effort.

In December 1554, John Standish issued a tract for the consideration of Parliament. The following extract comes from this short work of his, entitled *A Discourse Wherein Is Debated Whether It Be Expedient that the Scripture Should Be in English.* His plea fell on deaf ears: The sitting Parliament restored abandoned laws against "Lollardy" but conspicuously refrained from mentioning the suppression of Bible translations.

"Thousands have been brought from the true meaning of God's word through the English bible: therefore away with it; it hath killed too many souls already. . . . Wherefore away with the English damnable translation, and let them learn the mysteries of God reverently by heart. . . . Even the good and catholic people, which would do good and no hurt with the bible in English, yet may not be permitted to keep it in the English tongue. . . . The universal church of Christ did never allow nor approve scripture to be in the vulgar tongue, weighing the manifold inconveniences that have issued thereof; but ever from time to time, among other errors, did tread that down and suppress it. . . . The well must be covered, lest the younglings fall into it and so be drowned. . . . It was never admitted (though sometimes permitted) in any place of Christendom scripture to continue in the vulgar tongue, but only in time of schism or heresy."

(Source: J. F. Mozley, *Coverdale and His Bibles*, copyright 1953 by Lutterworth Press. Used by permission.)

52. FULKE'S DEFENSE OF THE ACCURACY OF EXISTING ENGLISH TRANSLATIONS

The illegality of a translation — the fact that it had not been duly authorized by the appropriate ecclesiastical authorities — may have been sufficient to discourage its use by the more orthodox Catholics. However, this meant little to those who were in rebellion against Catholicism. Hence those who had to defend that church's hostility to translations had to have an argument that even their opponents would respect. Alleged inaccuracies, therefore, became critically important to the Catholic apologist.

Gregory Martin was a well-respected Catholic priest and scholar and a major participant in the translation of the Douay-Rheims New Testament. In the same year that that translation was first printed (1582), Martin unleashed a written broadside against the use of the Protestant English translations used by his fellow countrymen. Although this broadside was written prior to appearance of the King James Version, much of what Martin criticized was continued in that translation as well.

William Fulke was a master at Pembroke College, Cambridge, and took great pleasure in applying his intellectual talents to the religious issues of his day. Being clearly annoyed at Martin's critique, he prepared a prompt rebuttal. It was printed in 1583 under the title *A Defence of the Sincere and True Translations of the Holy Scriptures into the English Tongue Against the Cavils of Gregory Martin*. The volume reprints paragraph by paragraph Martin's attack and Fulke's rebuttal.

In the extracts printed here are reproduced Fulke's comments on four challenged expressions. In two of the cases ("repentance" in place of "penance" and "elders" in place of "priests") the change became standard in later translations. Ironically the King James translators sided with Martin rather than Fulke by using "church" in place of "congregation" and "charity" in place of "love."

The fifth extract deals not with any alleged deficiency in the English but with Luther's addition of "only" to salvation by faith in Romans 3.

The use of "congregation" in place of "church":

Now to answer you, why *ecclesia* was first translated "congregation," and afterward "church"; the reason that moved the first translators, I think, was this: the word *church* of the common people at that time was used ambiguously, both for the assembly of the faithful, and for the place in which they assembled; for the avoiding of which ambiguity they translated *ecclesia* the congregation; and yet in their creed, and in the notes of their bibles, in preaching and writing, they used the word church for the same: the later translators, seeing the people better instructed and able to discern, when they read in the scriptures, the people from the place of their meeting, used the word church in their translations, as they did in their preaching.

The use of "love" in place of "charity":

For all the terms quarrelled at in this section, we have answered before; except perhaps for the term of "love," which is used instead of "charity," expressing what charity is indeed, and not as it is commonly taken of the common people, for an effect of charity, when they call "alms" "charity." No man that patiently could abide the people to be instructed, would cavil at the explication of the word "charity" by "love," when in the English tongue the word "charity" of the common people is either not understood, or taken for another thing than the Latin word *charitas* doth signify.

The use of "repentance" in place of "penance":

If by penance you mean satisfaction for sins by any suffering of ours, we abhor your penance as an horrible blasphemy against the blood of Christ. And for that cause Beza, as hath been shewed before, useth the word *resipiscentia*, rather than *poenitentia*: because the Greek word signifieth not only a sorrow for sin, but also a purpose of amendment of life. We in English use the word "repentance," or "amendment of life"; which word of "repentance" you use also sometimes, when it pleaseth you, or when you cannot for shame use your popish term of "doing penance."

The cause why we never use that word "penance," is, for that you mean not thereby that which the scripture calleth μετανοιαν, but a certain punishment taken upon men for satisfaction of their sins unto God; which is abominable for all christian ears to hear, which acknowledge that "the blood of Christ" only "purgeth us from all sin."

The use of "elders" in place of "priests":

Now you have gotten a fine net to dance naked in, that no ignorant blind buzzard can see you. The masks of your net be the ambiguous and abusive significations of this word "priest"; which indeed, according to the original derivation from *presbyter*, should signify nothing else but an "elder," as we translate it, that is, one appointed to govern the church of God according to his word, but not to offer sacrifice for the quick and the dead. But by usurpation it is commonly taken to signify a sacrificer, such as ιερευς is in Greek, and *sacerdos* in Latin; by which names the ministers of the gospel are never called by the Holy Ghost. After this common acceptation and use of this word "priest," we call the sacrificers of the

Old Testament, and of the gentiles also, because the scripture calleth them by one name, *cohanin*, or ἱερεῖς: but because the scripture calleth the ministers of the New Testament by divers other names, and never by the name of ἱερεῖς, we thought it necessary to observe that distinction which we see the Holy Ghost so precisely hath observed. Therefore, where the scripture calleth them πρεσβυτέρους. we call them, according to the etymology, "elders," and not priests: which word is taken up by common usurpation to signify sacrificers of Jews, gentiles, or papists, or else all Christians in respect of spiritual sacrifices. And although Augustine, and other of the ancient fathers, call the ministers of the New Testament by the name of *sacerdotes*, and ἱερεῖς, which signify the ministers of the Old Testament; yet the authority of the Holy Ghost, making a perfect distinction between these two appellations and functions, ought to be of more estimation with us. The fathers were content to speak in Latin and Greek, as the terms were taken up by the common people newly converted from gentility; but yet they retained the difference of the sacrificing priesthood of the one, and the ministerial office of the other. This may suffice therefore to render a reason, why we use not the word "priest" for "ministers" of the New Testament: not that we refuse it in respect of the etymology, but in respect of the use and common signification thereof.

Defending Luther's addition of "only" to the text of Romans 3:

In the question of justification by faith only, where St James saith no, we say no also; neither can it be proved that we add this word 'only' to the text in any translation of ours. If Luther did in his translation add the word 'only' to the text, it cannot be excused of wrong translation in word, although the sense might well bear it. But seeing Luther doth himself confess it, he may be excused of fraud, though not of lack of judgment. But why should our translation be charged with Luther's corruption? Because "our English protestants honour him as their father." A very lewd slander: for we call no man father upon earth, though you do call the pope your father; albeit in another sense Luther was a reverend father of the church for his time. But as touching the doctrine of only faith justifying, it hath more patrons of the fathers of the ancient primitive church, than Martin can bear their books, though he would break his back, who in the same plain words do affirm it as Luther doth, that only faith doth justify. And the apostle which saith "that a man is justified by faith without the works of the law," speaketh more plainly for justification by faith only (as we do teach it), than if he had said a man is justified by faith only. Which text of Rom. iii., and many other, are as express scripture to prove that we teach and believe, as that St James saith against justification by faith only, where he speaketh of another faith, and of another justification, than St Paul speaketh of, and we understand, when we hold that a man is justified by faith only, or without works of the law, which is all one.

(Source: William Fulke, A *Defence of the Sincere and True Translations of the Holy Scriptures into the English Tongue Against the Cavils of Gregory Martin*. Reprinted by the Parker Society. Printed at the University Press, Cambridge: 1843, pages 90 ["congregation"], 569 ["love"], 429 ["repentance"], 242–243 ["elders"], 121–122 [on Luther].)

VII. *Uncompleted Translations*

53. WILLIAM ROYE'S UNCOMPLETED OLD TESTAMENT

Roye was amanuensis for Tyndale during his translation of the New Testament. However, conflict erupted between them and they parted ways while in Germany in 1526. In 1527 Roye translated a Latin tract into German under the title *A Brief Dialogue Between a Christian Father and His Stubborn Son*. In the extract reprinted below, Roye describes Tonstall's sermon at the public burning of Tyndale's New Testament. He also promises the publication of his own translation of the Old Testament. In 1528 Tyndale predicted that the project would come to nought, saying that Roye "promiseth more a great deal than I fear me he will ever pay." Tyndale was right; the version was never published and quite possibly never completed except in Roye's dreams.

"To the right noble estates and to all other of the town of Calais William Roye desireth grace and peace. . . .This last year the New Testament of our Saviour was delivered unto you through the faithful and diligent study of one of our nation named William Hitchyns, unto whom I was (after the grace given me of the Lord) as helpfellow and partaker of his labours, that every Christian man might thereby hear and understand, at home and in his own house, the spirit of God speaking therein and through his holy apostles. Which our labour and study, specially unto them that presume and think themselves alonely to be apostolical men and spiritual doctors, was most odious: insomuch that without delay, in great hatred and venomous barking, openly at Paul's cross, did that was in them to disannul, forbid and blaspheme the most holiest word of God, food of many a poor soul, long famished with the sour dough of their importable and deceitful traditions. Yea and whereas they had nothing whereon to ground themselves against us, they were not ashamed falsely to defame them which long before that time were dead and rotten, as my father, . . . saying: His father would eat no pork, what fruit can such a tree bring forth? But knowing that the innocency, both of my father and also of me, is not unknown (in that behalf) unto all the nobles of the realm, I little regard their heady undiscretion. Yet it is unto my heart a coresay [i.e. corrosive or grievance] among all other most grievous, to see the price of the precious blood of Christ so despitefully to be trodden under foot by such unclean swine, and the most wholesome doctrine thereof to be forbidden, through the howling and barking of such cruel and infame dogs. Whose cruel tyranny, foxy cavillation and resistance have more inflamed my heart and couraged my mind to go about the translation of holy scripture: insomuch that I have already partly translated certain books of the Old Testament, the which, with the help of God, ere long shall be brought to light."

(Source: J. F. Mozley, *Coverdale and His Bibles*, copyright 1953 by Lutterworth Press. Used by permission.)

54. HOW THE BISHOPS' TRANSLATION OF 1534 WAS ABORTED

Archbishop Cranmer was an outstanding advocate of vernacular translations, often having to do battle with fellow clerics who opposed them. In addition to his efforts to secure royal approval for other translations, he personally pressured the bishops to sponsor a translation of their own, thereby protecting the project from accusations of heresy. In spite of his best efforts, his hopes in this regard were repeatedly frustrated. (It was not until 1568 that a "Bishop's Bible" was finally issued.)

In December 1534 the upper house of the convocation of Canterbury moved to suppress existing translations under the guise of having all copies officially (and hostilely) inspected. However, this was cleverly joined with a proposal to have a new and acceptable translation rendered. In effect Cranmer was head of the revision project. His secretary—one John Fox—tells in the following extract how the project was frustrated by an opponent. Although he refers to only one section not being completed, it is important to remember that he is discussing only the New Testament. How many defaulted in their work on the Old Testament is unknown—as is the answer to whether the project ever reached that stage of translation.

"The like fine answer he made of bishop Stokesley's answer made to my lord of Canterbury his letters requiring his part of the translation of the New Testament.

"My lord Cranmer, minding to have the New Testament thoroughly corrected, divided the same into nine or ten parts, and caused it to be written at large in paper books and sent unto the best learned bishops and other learned men, to the intent they should make a perfect correction thereof, and when they had done, to send them unto him at Lambeth by a day limited for that purpose. It chanced that the Acts of the Apostles were sent to bishop Stokesley to oversee and correct, then bishop of London. When the day came, every man had sent to Lambeth their parts correct; only Stokesley's portion wanted. My lord of Canterbury wrote to the bishop letters for his part, requiring to deliver them unto the bringer thereof, his secretary. Bishop Stokesley being at Fulham received the letters, unto the which he made this answer: I marvel what my lord of Canterbury meaneth, that thus abuseth the people in giving them liberty to read the scriptures, which doth nothing else but infect them with heresies. I have bestowed never an hour upon my portion, nor never will. And therefore my lord shall have his book again, for I will never be guilty to bring the simple people into error.

"My lord of Canterbury's servant took the book, and brought the same to Lambeth unto my lord, declaring my lord of London's answer. When my lord had perceived that the bishop had done nothing therein, I marvel, quod my lord of Canterbury, that my lord of London is so froward, that he will not do as other men do. Mr Lawney stood by, hearing my lord speak so much of the bishop's untowardness, said: I can tell your grace why my lord of London will not bestow any labour or pain this way. Your grace knoweth well (quod Lawney) that his portion is a piece of New Testament. And then he being persuaded that Christ had bequeathed him nothing in his Testament thought it mere madness to bestow any labour or pain where no gain was to be gotten. And besides this, it is the Acts of the Apostles, which were simple poor fellows, and therefore my lord of London disdained to have to do with any of their acts.

"My lord of Canterbury and other that stood by could not forbear from laughter to hear Mr Lawney's acute invention in answering to the bishop of London's froward answer to my lord of Canterbury's letters."

(Source: J. F. Mozley, *Coverdale and His Bibles*, copyright 1953 by Lutterworth Press. Used by permission.)

55. THE KING VETOES A BISHOPS' TRANSLATION

In 1542 Cranmer was able to convince the convocation of Canterbury that the inadequacies of the Great Bible were sufficiently numerous and significant to require a new translation. The majority agreed but required that the revision of the Great Bible be guided by the text of the Vulgate. The New Testament was divided into fifteen sections, a different bishop to oversee each. After the initial work was completed, two revision committees (one for each testament) were to review the work. Since Cranmer's name is not mentioned in regard to any of these committees, it is thought that he himself did the appointing of the committee members.

Although the project had royal backing, the king effectively aborted the effort when he announced that he would prefer to have the revision performed by university scholars rather than by the bishops. The reason for this about-face is uncertain. Was it regal caprice? Was it aggravation (perhaps encouraged by Cranmer himself) at the degree of latinization (transliterating the Latin into English) that was desired by key bishop-translators? Or was it a realization that it was still impossible to secure a translation that would have general, lasting approval among both traditionalist and reform bishops? Whatever the rationale, the project was never brought to completion.

In a letter of 1547 from Gardiner to Cranmer, the former defends his unwillingness to participate in Cranmer's effort to prepare a book of homilies. Gardiner's advice is to let sleeping dogs lie and not stir up a potential hornet's nest as had been done by the Bible revision effort of 1542.

"By occasion hereof I remember what pains was taken by our late sovereign's commandment to correct the translation of the bible sent among the people, and how his highness (God pardon his soul) at a Shrovetide feasted us all, and after dinner told us how gladly he would have that done, and how he would be at the cost to have it printed again. Whereupon there was used a marvellous diligence, and at my cost a bible divided into quires in the convocation house by your grace's direction. The faults were found in a marvellous number and very dangerous, as cannot be denied; so as we know certainly what the fault be, and yet those labours took none effect, which were fruitful if they had had their execution.

"In this matter, if I were now asked whether I would give advice that during the king's majesty's minority those labours should take effect, I would say nay. And yet the people have borne to have God's truth among them so contaminate, sometime (a man might say) with the malice of the translator, as may appear where the words and sense be evidently changed, sometime by ignorance, and sometime by negligence. But omitting to inquire how it came to pass, we all of the convocation confessed it so to be, and agreed to amend it, and yet it is not amended. In which matter if zeal to truth should move us to any labours — but such a zeal were, in the minority of our sovereign lord, clear out of season; for such rumours might arise that we bishops went now about to fashion God's word after our own fancy," while we have no king. In a minority it is one thing to carry things on as they are, and another to make innovations however good they may be.

"And therefore I would not give advice to execute now our late sovereign lord's commandment for correction of the bible: and yet it were best, for God's word would be most pure." In the preface printed in the Great bible under your grace's name there is a misquotation from Gregory Nazianzen, but "I would that rather continued in silence than a wonder to be made in the reformation of it."

(Source: J. F. Mozley, *Coverdale and His Bibles*, copyright 1953 by Lutterworth Press. Used by permission.)

VIII. *King James Version*

James I was far from physically appealing. Intellectually, however, there was no question of his competency. Before reaching ten years of age, he was reputed to have been able to read the Latin Bible and spontaneously translate it into French and then from French into English. By age 20 his tutor had encouraged him to translate some thirty of the Psalms into metrical English and to render for himself a paraphrase of the book of the Revelation. Hence being the spiritual father of a major English translation would have cast him into a most congenial role. Political self-interest — cementing his relationship with the potentially rebellious Puritan faction — reinforced any preexisting predilection in favor of a new translation.

The opportunity to act came during a conference called by James and held at Hampton Court in early 1604. The Puritan representatives were outnumbered nineteen to four by establishment religious and political leaders. The Puritans argued, in effect, that specific biblical authority had to be found for what was done in religion. The majority argued that church tradition was also definitive as long as it was not in conflict with explicit scriptural teaching. At the first session on January 14 the Puritans were totally excluded. At the second meeting, the following day, they were finally admitted to speak their piece.

The Puritans spoke for a deceremonialization of church rite and major changes in the prayer book and ecclesiastical court procedure.

Although minor concessions were granted, there was no question that they had lost the battle. Yet in losing, they set in motion the translation of the Bible that bears King James' name.

On that January 15th of 1604 the Puritan John Rainolds, president of Corpus Christi College, Oxford, requested that His Majesty authorize an improved translation of the Bible that would replace what he considered the inadequate past efforts. Richard Bancroft, Bishop of London, promptly fired a verbal blast at the proposal: "If every man's humor should be followed, there would be no end to the translating."

However, the king felt differently and promptly embraced the proposal with enthusiasm. He ordered that the best competent scholars be chosen from Oxford and Cambridge to do the work. Afterwards it was to be reviewed by the bishops and the Privy Council and then receive the king's blessing (which, contrary to common assumption, it never officially did). He stressed that the doctrinally oriented notes common in previous translations were to be omitted. He described the notes as "partial, untrue, seditious, and savoring of traitorous conceits." In short, they raised inflammatory animosities, dangerous to both the religious and the political order.

At least partially out of self-interest (the desire to be appointed Archbishop of Canterbury), Bishop Bancroft moderated his opposition and then became a supporter of the translation effort. On the king's behalf, he actively promoted it, and — in conformity with James' desires — issued the list of guiding principles which is printed in the following extract.

56. BISHOP BANCROFT'S RULES FOR THE TRANSLATORS

1. The ordinary Bible read in the Church, commonly called the *Bishops Bible*, to be followed, and as little altered as the Truth of the original will permit.

2. The Names of the Prophets, and the Holy Writers, with the other names of the Text, to be retained, as nigh as may be, accordingly as they were vulgarly used.

3. The old Ecclesiastical Words to be kept, *viz.* the Word *Church* not to be translated *Congregation* &c.

4. When a word hath divers Significations, that to be kept which hath been most commonly used by the most of the Ancient Fathers, being agreeable to the Propriety of the Place and the Analogy of the Faith.

5. The Division of the Chapters to be altered, either not at all, or as little as may be, if Necessity so require.

6. No Marginal Notes at all to be affixed, but only for the Explanation of the *Hebrew* or *Greek* Words, which cannot without some circumlocution, so briefly and fitly be expressed in the Text.

7. Such Quotations of Places to be marginally set down as shall serve for the fit Reference of one Scripture to another.

8. Every particular Man of each Company, to take the same Chapter, or Chapters, and having translated or amended them severally by himself, where he

thinketh good, all to meet together, confer what they have done, and agree for their Parts what shall stand.

9. As any one Company hath dispatched any one Book in this Manner they shall send it to the rest, to be considered of seriously and judiciously, for His Majesty is very careful in this Point.

10. If any Company, upon the Review of the Book so sent, doubt or differ upon any Place, to send them Word thereof; note the Place, and withal send the Reasons, to which if they Consent not, the Difference to be compounded at the General Meeting, which is to be of the chief Persons of each Company, at the end of the Work.

11. When any Place of special Obscurity is doubted of Letters to be directed, by Authority, to send to any Learned Man in the Land, for his Judgment of such a Place.

12. Letters to be sent from every Bishop to the rest of his Clergy, admonishing them of this Translation in hand; and to move and charge as many as being skilful in the Tongues; and having taken Pains in that kind, to send his particular Observations to the Company, either at *Westminster, Cambridge* or *Oxford.*

13. The Directors in each Company, to be the Deans of *Westminster* and *Chester* for that Place; and the King's Professors in the *Hebrew* or *Greek* in either University.

14. These translations to be used when they agree better with the Text than the Bishops Bible: *Tindoll's, Matthews, Coverdale's, Whitchurch's, Geneva.*

15. Besides the said Directors before mentioned, three or four of the most Ancient and Grave Divines, in either of the Universities, not employed in Translating, to be assigned by the Vice-Chancellor, upon Conference with the rest of the Heads, to be Overseers of the Translations as well *Hebrew* as *Greek,* for the better Observation of the 4th Rule above specified.

(Source: Olga S. Opfell, *The King James Bible Translators,* McFarland & Company, Jefferson, N.C.: 1982, pages 139–140.)

57. "THE TRANSLATOR TO THE READER"

In their lengthy preface to the King James Version, the translators make three key points that may remain of special interest. Having seen how super-critical had been the reaction to some earlier translations, they carefully put themselves on record warning that such would occur to their translation as well—and that the attacks would be unjustified. They defend the inherent value of vernacular translations and carefully refrain from reproaching earlier efforts by asserting that a new translation should not be interpreted as implying censure of prior labors.

Their response to unjust and excessive anticipated attacks on their translation:

Zeal to promote the common good, whether it be by devising any thing our selves, or revising that which hath been laboured by others, deserveth certainly much respect and esteem, but yet findeth but cold entertainment in the world. It is welcommed with suspicion in stead of love, and with emulation in stead of thanks: and if there be any hole left for cavill to enter, (and cavill, if it do not finde a hole, will make one) it is sure to be misconstrued, and in danger to be condemned. This will easily be granted by as many as know storie, or have any experience. For, was there ever any thing projected, that savoured any way of newnesse or renewing, but the same endured many a storm of gain-saying, or opposition? A man would think that Civility, wholesome laws, learning and eloquence, Synods, and Church-maintenance, (that we speak of no more things of this kinde) should be as safe as a Sanctuary, and out of the danger of the dart, as they say, that no man would lift up the heel, no, nor dogge moove his tongue against the motioners of them. For by the first, we are distinguished from bruit beasts led with sensualitie: By the second, we are bridled and restrained from outragious behaviour, and from doing of injuries, whether by fraud or by violence: by the third, we are enabled to inform and reform others, by the light and feeling that we have attained unto our selves: Briefly, by the fourth being brought together to a parle face to face, we sooner compose our differences then by writings, which are endlesse: And lastly, that the Church be sufficiently provided for, is so agreeable to good reason and conscience, that those mothers are holden to be lesse cruell, that kill their children as soon as they are born, then those nourcing fathers and mothers (wheresoever they be) that withdraw from them who hang upon their breasts (and upon whose breasts again themselves do hang to receive the Spirituall and sincere milk of the word) livelihood and support fit for their estates. Thus it is apparent, that these things which we speak of, are of most necessarie use, and therefore, that none, either without absurdity can speak against them, or without note of wickednesse, can spurn against them.

Their defense of the importance of vernacular translations:

But how shall men meditate in that, which they cannot understand? How shall they understand that, which is kept close in an unknowen tongue? as it is written, *Except I know the power of the voyce, I shall be to him that speaketh, a Barbarian, and he that speaketh, shall be a Barbarian to me.* The Apostle excepteth no tongue; not Hebrew the ancientest, not Greek the most copious, not Latine the finest. Nature taught a naturall man to confesse, that all of us in those tongues which we do not understand, are plainly deaf; we may turn the deaf ear unto them. The *Scythian* counted the *Athenian,* whom he did not understand, barbarous: so the *Romane* did the *Syrian,* and the *Jew,* (even Saint *Hierome* himself calleth the Hebrew tongue barbarous, belike because it was strange to so many) so the Emperour of *Constantinople* called the *Latine* tongue, barbarous, though Pope *Nicolai* do storm at it: so the *Jews* long before *Christ,* called all other nations, *Lognazim,* which is little better than barbarous. Therefore as one complaineth, that alwayes in the Senate of *Rome* there was one or other that called for an interpreter: so lest the Church be driven to the like exigent, it is necessary to have translations in a readinesse. Translation it is that openeth the window, to let in the light; that breaketh the shell, that we may eat the kernell; that putteth aside the curtain, that we may look into the most holy place; that removeth the cover of the well, that we may come by the water, even as *Jacob* rolled away the stone from the mouth of the well, by which means the flocks of *Laban* were watered. Indeed without translation into the vulgar tongue, the unlearned are but like children at *Jacobs* well (which was deep) without a bucket, or something to draw with: or as that person mentioned by *Esay,* to whom when a sealed book was delivered, with this motion. *Read this, I pray thee,* he was fain to make this answer, *I cannot, for it is sealed.*

Their reconciliation of preparing a new translation while retaining respect for previous ones:

Many mens mouthes haue been open a good while, (and yet are not stopped) with speeches about the Translation so long in hand, or rather perusals of Translations made before: and ask what may be the reason, what the necessitie of the employment: Hath the Church been deceived, say they, all this while? Hath her sweet bread been mingled with leaven, her silver with drosse, her wine with water, her milk with lime? (*Lacte gypsum malè miscetur,* said S. *Ireney.*) We hoped that we had been in the right way, that we had had the Oracles of God delivered unto us, and that though all the world had cause to be offended and to complain, yet that we had none. Hath the nurse holden out the breast, and nothing but winde in it? Hath the bread been delivered by the fathers of the Church, and the same proved to be *lapidosus,* as *Seneca* speaketh? What is it to handle the word of God deceitfully, if this be not? Thus certain brethren. Also the adversaries of *Judah* and *Hierusalem,* like *Sanballat* in *Nehemiah,* mock, as we hear, both at the work and workmen, saying; *What do these weak Jews, &c. will they make the stones whole again out of the heaps of dust which are burnt? although they build, yet if a fox go up, he shall even break down their stony wall.* Was their Translation good before? Why do they now mend it? Was it not good? Why then was it obtruded to the people? Yea, why did the Catholicks (meaning Popish *Romanists,*) always go in ieopardie, for refusing to go to heare it? Nay, if it must be translated into English, Catholickes are fittest to do it. They have learning, and they know when a thing is well, they can *manum de tabula.* We will answere them both briefly: and the former, being brethren, thus, with S. *Hierome, Damnamus veteres? minimé, sed post priorum studia in domo Domini, quod possumus laboramus.* That is, *Do we condemn the ancient? In no case: but after the endeuours of them that were before vs, we take the best paines we can in the house of God.* As if he said, Being provoked by the example of the learned that lived before my time, I have thought it my duetie, to assay whether my talent in the knowledge of the tongues, may be profitable in any measure to Gods Church, lest I should seeme to have laboured in them in vain, and lest I should be thought to glory in men, (although ancient,) above that which was in them. Thus S. *Hierome* may be thought to speak.

And to the same effect say we, that we are so farre off from condemning any of their labours that traveiled before us in this kinde, either in this land or beyond sea, either in King *Henries* time, or King *Edwards* (if there were any translation, or correction of a translation in his time) or Queen *Elizabeths* of everrenouned memorie, that we acknowledge them to have been raised up of God, for the building and furnishing of his Church, and that they deserve to be had of us and of posteritie in everlasting remembrance.

(Source: Olga S. Opfell, *The King James Bible Translators,* McFarland & Company, Jefferson, N.C.: 1982, page 143 [anticipated attacks], 147–148 [vernacular translations], 152 [respecting previous translations].)

58. FAMILY TURMOILS IN THE LIFE OF A TRANSLATOR, JOHN BOIS

John Bois might be called the black sheep of the King James translators. He had been a brilliant student at St. John's College, Oxford, and was chief lecturer in Greek there for a decade. Yet when he was appointed to one of the translation committees, there was loud grumbling among the Cambridge scholars: What help did they need from a man who was now a mere "country" minister? One detects in this a certain intellectual snobbery not extinct in our own day and age.

Bois served on the committee that translated the Apocrypha and then on the review committee that examined the preliminary draft and made whatever modifications they deemed necessary. Then the draft was passed on to Bishop Bison (Bishop of Winchester) and Dr. Miles Smith (later Bishop of Gloucester) for a final review and, it appears, a modest number of final revisions.

Although his work as a translator and member of the review committee would automatically make Bois of some interest to us, he is of special significance because he kept a concise chronicle of the deliberations of the review group. After vanishing for over three centuries, a copy of part of that record was uncovered and then reprinted in the late 1960s.

It is sometimes forgotten that even the life of a Bible translator can be full of heartbreak and turmoil. Bois was compelled to sell his library to stay afloat financially; he came close to divorcing his wife; he was (as noted above) the object of scorn from some of his fellow translators. A contemporary of his — one Anthony Walker — wrote a short biography of him. The following extract comes from that biography, which was published along with other similar studies in Francis Peck's *Desiderata Curiosa* (London: 1779). It discusses some of the difficulties and pressures Bois endured.

1. He went not from the universitie when he left Cambridge, only he made his way a little longer to the schooles. For he used constantly to come and hear Mr. Downes and Mr. Lively (those two worthy professors of the Greek and Hebrew tongues) as also divinity acts and lectures. And though he may seem to have lost much time hereby, in riding to and fro so often; yet might he justly stop the mouth of such objectors, with that piece of Erasmus, "ne totum tempus quo equo fuit insidendum 'αμοξοοις et illiteratis fabulis tereretur, malui mecum aliquoties de communibus studiis aliquid agitare, *etc.*" For he used, by the way, to meditate on doubts, wherein he might (propounding them) require satisfaction of his learned friends in Cambridge; witness his *Quaerenda Cantabrigiae*, so frequent in his then pocket-paperbook. And, in his return, to chewe the cud, and lay up his new encrease of knowledge in his safe cabinet, his memory.

2. But, as by this means the scale of his learning was sunk dayly lower by the greatnesse of the weight; so that of his estate was, by the emptynesse, become a very unequall counterpoyse. For (he minding nothing but his book; and his wife, through want of age and experience, not being able sufficiently to manage other things aright) he was, ere he was aware, fallen into debt. The weight whereof (though it were not great) when he began to feel, he, forthwith, parted with his darling (I mean, his library) which he sold (considering what it cost him) I believe, to nigh as much losse as the debt amounted to, for the discharge whereof he sold it. I have heard him say, that "when he left the college, he knew of but

few Greek authors, great or small, extant, which he had not in his own private library."

3. Either upon this, or some other occasion, there grew some discontent betwixt him and his wife; insomuch that I have heard (but never from himself) that he did once intend to travaile beyond the seas. But religion and conscience soon gave those thoughts the check; and made it be with him and his wife, as chirurgeons say, it's with a broken bone; if once well sett, the stronger for a fracture.

4. When he began to be acquainted in the country with his neighbour-ministers, he agreed with, I think, twelve of them, to meet every Friday at one of their houses at dinner, by course; and there to give an account of their studys; and, by joynt help, to discuss and resolve doubts and questions propounded by any one of them, to the publique benefit of them all.

5. He usually kept some young scholler in his house, as well for the instruction of his own children and the poorer sort of the town; as also because many knights and gentlemen of quality did importune him to take their children to board with him, and to take some care in their education, as well for learning as manners.

6. When it pleased God to move King James to that excellent work, the translation of the Bible; when the translators were to be chosen for Cambridge, he was sent for thither by those therein employed, and was chosen one; some university men thereat repining (it may be not more able, yet more ambitious to have born [a] share in that service) disdaining, that it should be thought, they needed any help from the country. — Forgetting that Tully was the same man at Tusculan[um] as he was at Rome. Sure I am, that part of the Apocrypha was allotted to him (for he hath shewed me the very copy he translated by) but, to my grief, I know not which part.

7. All the time he was about his own part, his commons were given him at S. John's; where he abode all the week, till Saturday night; and then home to discharge his cure: returning thence on Monday morning. When he had finished his own part, at the earnest request of him to whom it was assigned, he undertook a second; and then he was in commons in another college: but I forbear to name both the person and the house.

8. Four years were spent in this first service; at the end whereof the whole work being finished, and three copies of the whole Bible sent from Cambridge, Oxford and Westminster, to London; a new choice was to be made of six in all, two out of every company, to review the whole work; and extract one [copy] out of all three, to be committed to the presse.

9. For the dispatch of which businesse Mr. Downes and Mr. Bois were sent for up to London. Where meeting (though Mr. Downes would not go 'till he was either fetcht or threatned with a pursivant) their four fellow-labourers, they went dayly to Stationers Hall, and in three quarters of a year, finished their task. All which time they had from the company of Stationers XXX*s*. [each] *per* week, duly paid them; tho' they had nothing before but, the self-rewarding, ingenious industry. Whilst they were imployed in this last businesse, he, and he only, took notes of their proceedings: which notes he kept till his dying day.

(Source: As reprinted in Ward Allen, *Translating for King James,* Vanderbilt University Press, Kingsport, Tenn.: 1969, pages 138–141.)

FIVE

Major Modern
English Translations

I. *English Revised Version*

No matter how much one may respect individual translations that were made during the nineteenth century, the English Revised Version marked a new era. Unlike private efforts that were viewed as denominational in origin (such as that of the American Bible Union), the ERV consciously set out to expand the borders of its translation committees in both the denominational and geographical senses: It was both interdenominational in origin and international in scholarship.

In spite of these significant breakthroughs, the popularity of the resulting translation was nowhere as lasting as anticipated. Due to the inclusion of distinctive Englishisms and the perceived widespread rejection of the suggested "American" readings, the ERV was quickly rejected as inadequate for an American audience. The original American revision committee decided to continue their efforts and released the results as the American Standard Version in 1901.

In reading the first two of the following extracts, a knowledge of the conflict leaves one puzzled: The alleged "unity" between the American and British committees is so heavily stressed that one wonders whether the writers did not already suspect that the translation would be unacceptable to the American collaborators.

59. THE TRANSLATORS AND THEIR CREDENTIALS

In publishing the initial New Testament section of the ERV, Professor Isaac H. Hall prepared a "History of Revision" which was printed along with the biblical text. He provides the following concise description of the scope of the translation endeavor.

The present revision originated in the convocation, or general assembly of Episcopal clergymen, at Canterbury, England, on May 6th, 1870. Then and there a committee was appointed consisting of eminent Biblical scholars and certain high officials of the Church of England, "with power to revise, for public use, the authorized English versions of 1611, and to associate with them representative Biblical scholars of other Christian denominations using that version."

The movement at its very inception took a form international and inter-denominational. Dr. Philip Schaff pronounces this, "the first effort" of this broad character "in the history of the translation of the Bible"; the present and the older English versions authorized for public use in churches having proceeded from the Church of England, before other evangelical denominations were recognized, or possibly organized, and long before the American people had an independent existence.

The English Committee divided itself into two Companies, one for the work upon the Old Testament, the other for work upon the New. Each Company held regular meetings in the Deanery of Westminister [sic], London.

The American Committee was organized in 1871, on invitation of the British Revisers. It began active work in October, 1872. It was composed of scholars selected from different denominations, and divided into two Companies, which met once a month, in the Bible House, at New York. From their several homes, where they had privately studied over the passages of Scripture under their care, they came together and unitedly toiled for still greater perfection.

From this statement of the case, it is evident that the British and American Committees are virtually one organization, having the same principles and ob-jects, and being in constant correspondence with each other at all stages of their work. It was no purpose of theirs to issue two separate and distinct revisions, but one and the same revision for both nations.

The whole number of scholars who have been connected with this work is one hundred and one. Sixty-seven of these belonged to England, and thirty-four to our own land. Fifteen members of the English Committee have resigned or died, and seven of the American Committee; leaving the combined force as the New Testa-ment work came to completion seventy-nine. Among these are many of the best Biblical scholars of the leading Protestant denominations of Great Britain and the United States. Many of them are well known by their works, both in Europe and America. The American members are nearly all Professors of Hebrew or of Greek in prominent theological institutions. They have been selected with regard to competency and reputation for Biblical scholarship, denominational connection, and local convenience or easy access to New York, where their regular monthly meetings have been held.

(Source: *The Revised New Testament and History of Revision*, Hubbard Brothers, Phila-delphia: 1881, pages 80–81.)

60. THE GOVERNING PRINCIPLES OF THE TRANSLATION

In the preface, the translators reproduce the guidelines that had been given them to govern their work. Note once again the stress on agreement between the American and English translators, an agreement that turned out to be nonexistent.

The fundamental Resolutions adopted by the Convocation of Canterbury on the third and fifth days of May 1870 were as follows:—

'1. That it is desirable that a revision of the Authorised Version of the Holy Scriptures be undertaken.

'2. That the revision be so conducted as to comprise both marginal renderings and such emendations as it may be found necessary to insert in the text of the Authorised Version.

'3. That in the above resolutions we do not contemplate any new translation of the Bible, or any alteration of the language, except where in the judgment of the most competent scholars such change is necessary.

'4. That in such necessary changes, the style of the language employed in the existing version be closely followed.

'5. That it is desirable that Convocation should nominate a body of its own members to undertake the work of revision, who shall be at liberty to invite the co-operation of any eminent for scholarship, to whatever nation or religious body they may belong.'

The Principles and Rules agreed to by the Committee of Convocation on the 25th day of May 1870 were as follows:—

'1. To introduce as few alterations as possible into the Text of the Authorised Version consistently with faithfulness.

'2. To limit, as far as possible, the expression of such alterations to the language of the Authorised and earlier English versions.

'3. Each Company to go twice over the portion to be revised, once provisionally, the second time finally, and on principles of voting as hereinafter is provided.

'4. That the Text to be adopted be that for which the evidence is decidedly preponderating; and that when the Text so adopted differs from that from which the Authorised Version was made, the alteration be indicated in the margin.

'5. To make or retain no change in the Text on the second final revision by each Company, except *two thirds* of those present approve of the same, but on the first revision to decide by simple majorities.

'6. In every case of proposed alteration that may have given rise to discussion, to defer the voting thereupon till the next Meeting, whensoever the same shall be required by one third of those present at the Meeting, such intended vote to be announced in the notice for the next Meeting.

'7. To revise the headings of chapters and pages, paragraphs, italics, and punctuation.

'8. To refer, on the part of each Company, when considered desirable, to Divines, Scholars, and Literary Men, whether at home or abroad, for their opinions.'

These rules it has been our endeavour faithfully and consistently to follow. One only of them we found ourselves unable to observe in all particulars. In accordance with the seventh rule, we have carefully revised the paragraphs, italics, and punctuation. But the revision of the headings of chapters and pages would have involved so much of indirect, and indeed frequently of direct interpretation, that we judged it best to omit them altogether.

Our communications with the American Committee have been of the following nature. We transmitted to them from time to time each several portion of our First Revision, and received from them in return their criticisms and suggestions. These we considered with much care and attention during the time we were engaged on our Second Revision. We then sent over to them the various portions of the Second Revision as they were completed, and received further suggestions, which, like the former, were closely and carefully considered. Last of all, we forwarded to them the Revised Version in its final form; and a list of those passages in which they desire to place on record their preference of other readings and renderings will be found at the end of the volume. We gratefully acknowledge their care, vigilance, and accuracy; and we humbly pray that their labours and our own, thus happily united, may be permitted to bear a blessing to both countries, and to all English-speaking people throughout the world.

The whole time devoted to the work has been ten years and a half. The First Revision occupied about six years; the Second, about two years and a half. The remaining time has been spent in the consideration of the suggestions from America on the Second Revision, and of many details and reserved questions arising out of our own labours. As a rule, a session of four days has been held every month (with the exception of August and September) in each year from the commencement of the work in June 1870. The average attendance for the whole time has been sixteen each day; the whole Company consisting at first of twenty-seven, but for the greater part of the time of twenty-four members, many of them residing at great distances from London. Of the original number four have been removed from us by death.

At an early stage in our labours, we entered into an agreement with the Universities of Oxford and Cambridge for the conveyance to them of our copyright in the work. This arrangement provided for the necessary expenses of the undertaking; and procured for the Revised Version the advantage of being published by Bodies long connected with the publication of the Authorised Version.

(Source: *The Revised New Testament and History of Revision,* Hubbard Brothers, Philadelphia: 1881, pages ix–xii.)

61. HOW THE GREEK TEXT WAS ESTABLISHED

In the preface the translators discuss how they went about establishing their own Greek text rather than relying upon any previously printed one or upon any specific individual manuscript.

A revision of the Greek text was the necessary foundation of our work; but it did not fall within our province to construct a continuous and complete Greek text. In many cases the English rendering was considered to represent correctly either of two competing readings in the Greek, and then the question of the text was usually not raised. A sufficiently laborious task remained in deciding between the rival claims of various readings which might properly affect the translation. When these were adjusted, our deviations from the text presumed to underlie the Authorised Version had next to be indicated, in accordance with the fourth rule; but it proved inconvenient to record them in the margin. A better mode however of giving them publicity has been found, as the University Presses have undertaken to print them in connexion with complete Greek texts of the New Testament.

In regard of the readings thus approved, it may be observed that the fourth rule, by requiring that 'the text to be adopted' should be 'that for which the evidence is decidedly preponderating,' was in effect an instruction to follow the authority of documentary evidence without deference to any printed text of modern times, and therefore to employ the best resources of criticism for estimating the value of evidence. Textual criticism, as applied to the Greek New Testament, forms a special study of much intricacy and difficulty, and even now leaves room for considerable variety of opinion among competent critics. Different schools of criticism have been represented among us, and have together contributed to the final result. In the early part of the work every various reading requiring consideration was discussed and voted on by the Company. After a time the precedents thus established enabled the process to be safely shortened; but it was still at the option of every one to raise a full discussion on any particular reading, and the option was freely used. On the first revision, in accordance with the fifth rule, the decisions were arrived at by simple majorities. On the second revision, at which a majority of two thirds was required to retain or introduce a reading at variance with the reading presumed to underlie the Authorised Version, many readings previously adopted were brought again into debate, and either re-affirmed or set aside.

Many places still remain in which, for the present, it would not be safe to accept one reading to the absolute exclusion of others. In these cases we have given alternative readings in the margin, wherever they seem to be of sufficient importance or interest to deserve notice. In the introductory formula, the phrases 'many ancient authorities,' 'some ancient authorities,' are used with some latitude to denote a greater or lesser proportion of those authorities which have a distinctive right to be called ancient. These ancient authorities comprise not only Greek manuscripts, some of which were written in the fourth and fifth centuries, but versions of a still earlier date in different languages, and also quotations by Christian writers of the second and following centuries.

(Source: *The Revised New Testament and History of Revision,* Hubbard Brothers, Philadelphia: 1881, pages xii–xiii.)

II. American Standard Version

As already noted in our discussion of the ERV, the disagreements between the English and the American translators ultimately led to the publication of the American Standard Version. This translation remains one of the very few accepted in the twentieth century by extremely conservative religious circles as an adequate substitute for the time-honored King James Version.

At the beginning the translation was well received in most quarters, not least of all out of nationalistic motives as the American answer to the earlier British revision. The version earned (and maintained) widespread praise as reliable and accurate in its renderings. Unfortunately for its continued mass usage, this maximization of accuracy was purchased at the price of a perceived lack of readability. For a reference tool, such literalness was quite acceptable, but for a Bible for common everyday reading this proved a considerable drawback.

While the United States translators still considered themselves part of the Anglo-American joint effort, they contributed to a parallel volume intended to demonstrate the need for a new version. Printed "for private circulation," it bore the unpretentious title *Anglo–American Bible Revision*. In its pages (including the extracts printed below) we find the rationale behind all Protestant twentieth century translations. All three writers excerpted were members of the American Revision Committee.

62. DEFENDING THE NEED:
A. INACCURATE OLD TESTAMENT RENDITIONS

In this essay Dr. Joseph Packard lays out a summary of mistranslations found in the KJV Old Testament. It should be stressed that there was not then, nor has there ever been, any assertion that these were conspiratorial in nature. Rather they were the result of a lesser understanding of the Hebrew tongue.

As the more general subjects connected with the Revision of the Authorized Version have been sufficiently discussed, there remains only the more special subject of indisputable errors in our version, which need to be corrected. There is no better argument for revision, than the existence of such errors. If they could not be corrected, it would be unwise and unkind to make them known to those to whom the English Bible, and the English Bible only, is the Word of God. The only course to be pursued would be to hide them reverently, and thus not shake the faith of the unlearned.

We assume that the English translation of the Bible should be as faithful as possible to the inspired original, so that the unlearned reader may be as nearly as possible in the place of the learned one. There are some who practically deny this self-evident proposition. They would have us retain time-hallowed errors in our version; they appeal to popular prejudice. They remind us of the old priest in the reign of Henry VIII., who used to say, *Mumpsimus, Domine*, instead of *Sumpsimus*, and when remonstrated with, replied, "I am not going to change my old *mumpsimus* for your new fangled *sumpsimus*."

While there is a wide spread opinion that our version contains errors, the only way to restore confidence in it is to appoint a committee of investigation to ascertain the exact state of the case. Even when no change is made the fact that examiners, in whom the Church has confidence, have found none necessary, must go far to inspire increased confidence. Isaac Walton tells us, "that Dr. Richard Kilbye, one of the Company of the Translators of the Authorized Version, heard accidentally a young preacher discussing the New Translation, and giving three reasons why a particular word should have been translated differently. The Doctor told him, on meeting him, that he and others had considered the three reasons mentioned, and found thirteen stronger ones for translating it as it was."

We proceed now to give some examples of errors in the English version, which are acknowledged to be such by the almost universal consent of critical commentators. The correction of these errors of translation will affect some texts often preached upon, and upon which a different interpretation has been put by tradition.

In the 24th chapter of Proverbs, 21st verse, we read, "My son, meddle not with them that are given to change." Now it happens that the word *given* belongs entirely to the English version, and is not found in the Hebrew, where the original word is a participial form, and means *changers*, or those *changing*. Matthew Henry says, "He does not say, with *them that change,* for there may be cause to change for the better; but *that are given to change,* that affect it, for change sake."

The English version of the book of Job has always been regarded by the best judges as very unsatisfactory. In Job iii, 3, where Job curses the day of his birth, he represents the night of his birth as saying, with joy, "There is a man child born!" Our version has it, *in which* it was said, thus destroying the poetic figure, which personifies the night. It should have been, Let the night perish, *which said.* In the sublime address of Jehovah to Job, in the 39th and 40th chapters, we find several verses in our version which fail to give the sense of the original. In the description of the war horse, chapter 39th and 24th verse, it is said, "Neither believeth he that it is the sound of the trumpet." If belief can be ascribed to a horse, it is the very thing which he believes, for he has heard the sound of the trumpet often enough before. The primary sense of the verb translated *believeth* is, *to be firm,* and adopting this we have this sense: Neither can he stand still at the sound of the trumpet. Virgil, in describing the war horse, says, "When the arms clash he knows not how to stand still."

In Job xl, 19, in the description of the hippopotamus, it is said in our version, "He that made him can make his sword to approach *unto him.*" The translation now almost universally adopted by the critics is, "His maker gives him his sword," or tusk.

In Job xl, 23, "Behold, he drinketh up a river, and hasteth not; he trusteth that he can draw up Jordan into his mouth." This gives no congruous sense. The translation adopted by Fürst, Conant and others, is—

"Lo a river swells, he is not afraid;
Fearless, though Jordan rushes to his mouth."

In Daniel ii, 5, "The king answered and said to the astrologers, The thing is gone from me." From the heading of the chapter, "Nebuchadnezzar forgetting his dream," etc., we infer that the Authorized Version understood by the *thing,* the dream, and that the king had forgotten his dream; but in that case it would not have troubled him. The true reason of the king's requiring them to tell the dream is given in verse 9th: "Tell me the dream, and I shall know that ye can show me the interpretation thereof." The Chaldee word, translated in our version *thing,* is the same word, translated, verse 9, *word,* and also in chapter iii, 28, *the king's word.* It should then have been translated, The word has gone from me.

In Daniel vii, 9, "I beheld till the thrones were cast down," it should be exactly the reverse—were set up. So Gesenius, Fürst and others, as in Jeremiah i, 15: "They shall set every one his throne," or seat; and in Apocalypse iv, 2, "Behold, a throne was set in heaven."

In 1 Kings x, 28, in our translation it is said, "Solomon had horses brought out of Egypt, and linen yarn: the king's merchants received the linen yarn at a price." The context refers to the manner in which Solomon obtained horses by importation from Egypt. The word translated linen yarn is elsewhere translated gathering together, Gen. i, 10, and is applied in this verse to merchants and to horses. It should be translated, "And the company of the king's merchants fetched each *drove* at a price."

Much of force is lost in our translation by not observing the rule that where the same word occurs in the same context in the original it should be translated by the same word. There are so many cases where this rule is violated in our version that it is difficult to make a selection. In Isaiah xxviii, 15–19, where mention is made of "the overflowing scourge passing through," this is repeated four times in the original, with great emphasis. In our version the word translated pass through in verses 15, 18, is translated *goeth forth* in verse 19, and also *pass over*. The 20th verse would gain much in impression if translated, "As often as it passeth through it shall take you; for morning by morning shall it pass through, by day and by night." In the 17th verse our version makes judgment, or justice, not the measure, but the thing to be measured. The meaning is that God would deal in strict justice. "I will make judgment for a line and righteousness for a plumb line." In the 20th verse the translation might be improved, "For the bed is too short to stretch one's self, and the covering too narrow to wrap one's self."

The translation of the whole chapter is unsatisfactory. To go back to the first verses, the chapter opens with a woe denounced against Samaria, the capital of Ephraim, and alludes to its situation on a hill, at the head of a rich valley. "Woe to the crown of pride of the drunkards of Ephraim, and to the fading flower of his glorious beauty, which is on the head of the fat valley." Verse third: "The crown of pride of the drunkards of Ephraim shall be trodden under foot; and the fading flower of his glorious beauty, which is on the head of the fat valley, shall be as the first ripe fruit before the summer; which he that seeth, while it is yet in his hand, eateth up." If one will take the pains to compare the new translation of the fourth verse with the English version, he will see how much is gained.

In Isaiah vi, 13, our translation mistakes the meaning of the original. It contains a threatening of repeated judgment, but closes with a gracious promise, "And though there be left in it a tenth, it shall again be consumed; as a terebinth, and as an oak, whose trunk remaineth, when they are felled, so its trunk shall be a holy seed."

The space allowed us precludes the specification of any more passages, which might be greatly improved by a reverential and well considered revision, which shall amend the errors and supply the defects of our version. The lack of consistency in it, which cannot fail to strike every one engaged in the laborious yet most interesting task of unifying the translation of the same word in the original, wherever it occurs, and the sense permits it, will, we hope, be remedied by the Committee meeting in the same place. While the received interpretation of some texts may thus have to be given up, other texts, brought out into a new light, will take their place, and the gain will be greater than the loss. No one need fear that "the mingled tenderness and majesty, the Saxon simplicity, the preternatural grandeur" of our Authorized Version will suffer an eclipse in the Revision.

(Source: *Anglo-American Bible Revision*, Bible House, New York: 1879, pages 80–85.)

63. DEFENDING THE NEED: B. THE SOURCE OF INACCURATE NEW TESTAMENT RENDITIONS

Professor Ezra Abbott of Harvard deals with erroneous translations in the New Testament. Although he mentions many minor examples (and some major ones), the main stress of his essay is on the causes for the errors and how the discovery of many new manuscripts had made it possible to obtain a more accurate rendition of the Greek.

It is an unquestionable fact that the Greek text of the New Testament from which our common English version was made contains many hundreds of errors which have affected the translation; and that in some cases whole verses, or even longer passages, in the common English Bible are spurious. This fact alone is sufficient to justify the demand for such a revision of the common version as shall remove these corruptions. Why, when so much pains is taken to obtain as correct a text as possible of ancient classical authors — of Homer, Plato, or Thucydides — should we be content with a text of the New Testament formed from a few modern manuscripts in the infancy of criticism, now that our means of improving it are increased a hundred-fold? Why should the mere mistakes of transcribers still be imposed upon unlearned readers as the words of evangelists and apostles, or even of our Lord himself?

The statements that have just been made require illustration and explanation, in order that the importance of these errors of the received text may not be exaggerated on the one hand or under-estimated on the other. We will consider, then —

I. THE NATURE AND EXTENT OF THE DIFFERENCES OF TEXT IN THE GREEK MANUSCRIPTS OF THE NEW TESTAMENT. — The manuscripts of the New Testament, like those of all other ancient writings, differ from one another in some readings of considerable interest and importance, and in a multitude of unimportant particulars, such as the spelling of certain words; the order of the words; the addition or omission of particles not affecting, or only slightly affecting, the sense; the insertion of words that would otherwise be understood; the substitution of a word or phrase for another synonymous with it; the use of different tenses of the same verb, or different cases of the same noun, where the variation is immaterial; and other points of no more consequence. The various readings which are comparatively important as affecting the sense consist, for the most part: (1) of the *substitution* of one word for another that closely resembles it in spelling or in pronunciation; (2) the *omission* of a clause or longer passage from *homoeoteleuton*, that is, the fact that it ends with the same word or the same series of syllables as the one preceding it; and (3) the *addition* to the text of words which were originally written as a marginal note or gloss, or are supplied from a parallel passage. Ancient scribes, like modern printers, when very knowing, have often made mistakes while they thought they were correcting them; but there is little or no ground for believing that the text of the New Testament has suffered in any place from wilful corruption.

The state of the case will be made plainer by examples. The great majority of questions about the readings, so far as they affect the translation, are such as these: Whether we should read "Jesus Christ" or "Christ Jesus"; "the disciples" or "his disciples"; "and" for "but" or "now," and *vice versa*; "Jesus said" or "he said"; "he said," or "he saith," or "he answered and said"; whether we should add or omit "and," or "but," or "for," or "therefore," the sense not being affected; whether we should read "God," or "Lord," or "Christ," in such phrases as "the word of God," or "of the Lord," or "of Christ"; these three words differing, as abbreviated in the Greek manuscripts, by only a single letter. Of the more important various readings, much the larger part consists of spurious *additions* to the text, not fraudulent, but originally written as marginal or interlinear notes, and afterward taken into the text by a very common and natural mistake. Most of these occur in the Gospels...

The longer passages of which the genuineness is more or less questionable are the doxology in the Lord's Prayer, Matt. vi, 13; Matt. xvi, 2, 3, from "when" to "times" (most critics retain the words); xvii, 21; xviii, 11; xx, 16, last part (genuine in xxii, 14); xxi, 44; xxiii, 14; xxvii, 35 (from "that it might be fulfilled" to "lots"); Mark vi, 11, last sentence; vii, 16; ix, 44, 46; xi, 26; xv, 28; xvi, 9–20 (a peculiar and rather difficult question); Luke ix, 55, 56, from "and said" to "save them"; xvii, 36; xxii, 43, 44 (most critics retain the passage); xxiii, 17, 34, first sentence (most critics retain it); xxiv, 12, 40; John v, 3, 4, from "waiting" to "he had" inclusive (most critics reject this); vii, 53–viii, 11 (also rejected by most critics); xxi, 25 (retained by most critics); Acts viii, 37; ix, 5, 6, from "it is hard" to "unto him" (has no MS. authority; comp. xxvi, 14; xxii, 10); xv, 34; xxiv, 6–8, from "and would" to "unto thee"; xxviii, 29; Rom. xi, 6, second sentence; xvi, 24; 1 John v, 7, 8, from "in heaven" to "in earth," inclusive (the famous text of the Three Heavenly Witnesses, now rejected by common consent of scholars as an interpolation). Most of the questionable additions in the Gospels, it will be seen on examination, are from parallel passages, where the words are genuine; the doxology in the Lord's Prayer probably came in from the ancient liturgies (compare 1 Chron. xxix, 11); the passage about the woman taken in adultery (John vii, 53–viii, 11), and some other additions, especially Luke ix, 55, 56; xxiii, 34 (if this is not genuine), are from early and probably authentic tradition...

I have sufficiently illustrated the nature of the differences in the text of the New Testament manuscripts; we will now consider their extent and importance. The *number* of the "various readings" frightens some innocent people, and figures largely in the writings of the more ignorant disbelievers in Christianity. "One hundred and fifty thousand various readings!" Must not these render the text of the New Testament wholly uncertain, and thus destroy the foundation of our faith?

The true state of the case is something like this. Of the 150,000 various readings, more or less, of the text of the Greek New Testament, we may, as Mr. Norton has remarked, dismiss nineteen-twentieths from consideration at once, as being obviously of such a character, or supported by so little authority, that no critic would regard them as having any claim to reception. This leaves, we will say, 7500. But of these, again, it will appear, on examination, that nineteen out of twenty are of no sort of consequence as affecting the sense; they relate to questions of orthography, or grammatical construction, or the order of words, or such other matters as have been mentioned above, in speaking of unimportant variations. They concern only the form of expression, not the essential meaning. This reduces the number to perhaps 400, which involve a difference of meaning, often very slight, or the omission or addition of a few words, sufficient to render them objects of some curiosity and interest, while a few exceptional cases among them may relatively be called important. But our critical helps are now so abundant, that in a very large majority of these more important questions of reading we are able to determine the true text with a good degree of confidence. What remains doubtful we can afford to leave doubtful. In all ancient writings there are passages in which the text cannot be settled with certainty; and the same is true of the interpretation.

I have referred above to all, or nearly all, of the cases in which the genuineness of a whole verse, or, very rarely, a longer passage, is more or less questionable; and I have given the most remarkable of the other readings of interest which present rival claims to acceptance. Their importance may be somewhat differently estimated by different persons. But it may be safely said that no Christian doctrine or duty rests on those portions of the text which are affected by differences in the manuscripts; still less is anything *essential* in Christianity touched by the various readings. They do, to be sure, affect the bearing of a few passages on the doctrine of the Trinity; but the truth or falsity of the doctrine by no means depends upon the reading of those passages.

The number of the various readings, which have been collected from more than five hundred manuscripts, more than a dozen ancient versions, and from the quotations in the writings of more than a hundred Christian fathers, only attests the abundance of our critical resources, which enable us now to settle the true text of the New Testament with a confidence and precision which are wholly unattainable in the case of the text of any Greek or Latin classical author. I say, enable us *now* to do this; for in the time of our translators of 1611 only a very small portion of our present critical helps was available. This leads us to consider —

II. THE IMPERFECTION OF THE GREEK TEXT ON WHICH OUR COMMON ENGLISH VERSION OF THE NEW TESTAMENT IS FOUNDED. — The principal editions of the Greek Testament which influenced, directly or indirectly, the text of the common version are those of Erasmus, five in number (1516–35); Robert Stephens (Estienne, Stephanus) of Paris and Geneva, four editions (1546–51); Beza, four editions in folio (1565–98), and five smaller editions (1565–1604); and the Complutensian Polyglot (1514, published in 1522). Without entering into minute details, it is enough to say that all these editions were founded on a small number of inferior and comparatively modern manuscripts, very imperfectly collated; and that they consequently contain a multitude of errors, which a comparison with older and better copies has since enabled us to discover and correct. It is true that Erasmus had one valuable manuscript of the Gospels, and Stephens two (D and L); Beza had also D of the Gospels and Acts, and D (the Clermont MS.) of the Pauline Epistles; but they made scarcely any use of them. The text of the common version appears to agree more nearly with that of the later editions of Beza than with any other; but Beza followed very closely Robert Stephens's edition of 1550, and Stephens's again was little more than a reprint of the fourth edition of Erasmus (1527). Erasmus used as the basis of his text in the Gospels an inferior MS. of the fifteenth century, and one of the thirteenth or fourteenth century in the Acts and Epistles. In the Revelation he had only an inaccurate transcript of a mutilated MS. (wanting the last six verses) of little value, the real and supposed defects of which he supplied by *translating* from the Latin Vulgate into Greek. Besides this, he had in all, for his later editions, three MSS. of the Gospels, four of the Acts and Catholic Epistles, and five of the Pauline Epistles, together with the text of the Aldine edition of 1518, and of the Complutensian Polyglot, both of little critical value. In select passages he had also collations of some other manuscripts. The result of the whole is, that in a considerable number of cases, not, to be sure, of great importance, the reading of the common English version is supported by *no known Greek manuscript whatever*, but rests on an error of Erasmus or Beza (*e.g.* Acts ix, 5, 6; Rom. vii, 6; 1 Pet. iii, 20; Rev. i, 9, 11; ii, 3, 20, 24; iii, 2; v, 10, 14; xv, 3; xvi, 5; xvii, 8, 16; xviii, 2, etc); and it is safe to say that in more than a *thousand* instances fidelity to the true text now ascertained requires a change in the common version, though in most cases the change would be slight. But granting that not many of the changes required can be called important, still, in the case of writings so precious as those of the New Testament, every one must feel a strong desire to have the text freed as far as possible from later corruptions, and restored to its primitive purity. Such being the need, we will next consider —

III. OUR PRESENT RESOURCES FOR SETTLING THE TEXT. — Our manuscript materials for the correction of the text are far superior, both in point of number and antiquity, to those which we possess in the case of any ancient Greek classical author, with the exception, as regards antiquity, of a few fragments, as those of Philodemus, preserved in the Herculanean papyri. The cases are very few in which any MSS. of Greek classical authors have been found older than the ninth or tenth century. The oldest manuscript of Aeschylus and Sophocles, that from which all the others are believed to have been copied, directly or indirectly, is of the tenth or eleventh century; the oldest manuscript of Euripides is of the twelfth. For the New Testament, on the other hand, we have manuscripts more or less complete, written in uncial or capital letters, and ranging from the fourth to the tenth century, of the Gospels 27, besides 30 small fragments; of the Acts and Catholic 10, besides 6 small fragments; of the Pauline Epistles11, besides 9 small its; and of the Revelation 5. All of these have been most thoroughly collated, e text of the most important of them has been published. One of these manu- s, the Sinaitic, containing the whole of the New Testament, and another, the an (B), containing much the larger part of it, were written as early probably he middle of the fourth century; two others, the Alexandrine (A) and the hraem (C), belong to about the middle of the fifth; of which date are two more (Q id T), containing considerable portions of the Gospels. A very remarkable manu- cript of the Gospels and Acts, the Cambridge manuscript, or Codex Bezae, belongs to the sixth century, as do E of the Acts and D of the Pauline Epistles, also N, P, R, Z of the Gospels and H of the Epistles (fragmentary). I pass by a number of small but valuable fragments of the fifth and sixth centuries. As to the cursive MSS., ranging from the tenth century to the sixteenth, we have of the Gospels more than 600; of the Acts over 200; of the Pauline Epistles nearly 300; of the Revelation about 100, not reckoning the Lectionaries or MSS. containing the lessons from the Gospels, Acts, and Epistles read in the service of the church, of which there are more than 400. Of these cursive MSS. it is true that the great majority are of comparatively small value; and many have been imperfectly collated or only inspected. Some twenty or thirty of them, however, are of exceptional value—a few of very great value—for their agreement with the most ancient authorities.

(Source: *Anglo-American Bible Revision*, Bible House, New York: 1879, pages 86–96.)

64. DEFENDING THE NEED:
C. ARCHAISMS IN THE KING JAMES VERSION

In this essay, Dr. Howard Crosby, then Chancellor of the University of New York, touches on what is perhaps the most embarrassing aspect of the King James Version to its twentieth century defenders: the question of whether it is any longer in "real English." He does this by, among other things, pointing out words that no longer communicate because of a change in meaning.

The literature of a language serves to check its changes, but not to stop them. A living language must grow, and in the growth new words not only supply new ideas, but become substitutes for old words. The English of the fourteenth century had to be read with a glossary in the sixteenth century; but the three hundred years that have elapsed since Queen Elizabeth have not so altered the language as the preceding two centuries had done. The abundant literature of the latter period accounts for this difference, our English Bible of 1611 having probably had the most influence in this result.

It is not the archaisms of our English Bible which constitute the most important reason for a revised translation. Erroneous or obscure renderings form a far more conspicuous argument. But yet it is very true that there are many words and phrases in the received version which the ordinary reader would be likely to misunderstand, the words themselves having become obsolete, or their significations (or modes of spelling) having undergone a change. We append the following as specimens:

I. CHANGE IN SPELLING. — "The *fats* shall overflow with wine and oil" (Joel ii, 24), for "vats." "Lest he *hale* thee to the judge" (Luke xii, 58), for "haul," and "*hoised* up the mainsail to the wind" (Acts xxvii, 40), for "hoisted." "He overlaid their *chapiters* with gold" (Ex. xxxvi, 38), for "capitals." "And sat down *astonied*" (Ezra ix, 3), for "astonished." "*Or* ever the earth was" (Prov. viii, 23), for "ere." So we find *bewray* (betray), *magnifical* (magnificent), and *delicates* (delicacies). Many of these archaisms in spelling have been omitted in more modern editions of our version, as *leese* for "lose," *sith* for "since," "*cloke* for "cloak." The old plural "hosen," however, still remains, in Dan. iii, 21, for "hose."

II. OBSOLETE WORDS. — "And they shall pass through it, hardly *bestead*" (Isa. viii, 21), for "served." "Besides that which *chapmen* and merchants brought" (2 Chron. ix, 14), for "market-men." "Old shoes and *clouted* upon their feet" (Josh. ix, 5); "took thence old cast *clouts*" (Jer. xxxviii, 11), for "patched" and "patches." "Neither is there any *daysman* betwixt us" (Job ix, 33), for "umpire." "Thou shalt make them to be set in *ouches* of gold" (Ex. xxviii, 11), for "sockets." "Doves *tabering* upon their breasts" (Nahum ii, 7), for "drumming." "The lion filled his dens with *ravin*" (Nahum ii, 12), for "plunder." "He made fifty *taches* of gold" (Ex. xxxvi, 13), for "catches." So *earing* (ploughing), *eschew* (shun), *habergeon* (coat of mail), *hough* (hamstring), *kine* (cows), and *leasing* (lying). We may add to these many of the names of animals, precious stones, etc., as *giereagle*, *ossifrage*, *behemoth*, *leviathan* (these last two being the Hebrew words untranslated), *sardius*, *ligure*, *bdellium*.

III. WORDS OBSOLETE IN THEIR SIGNIFICATIONS. — These are the most numerous and most important of Bible archaisms, because they are likely to be unnoticed, and the reader will thus form a wrong notion of the meaning of a statement. The manifest archaisms will always set one upon his guard, and lead him to investigate; but these words, having a perfectly familiar look, suggest no need of inquiry. Who would imagine that Ezekiel, saying, "as an *adamant*, harder than flint" (Ezek. iii, 9), and Zechariah, saying, "they made their hearts as an *adamant stone*," both referred to a "diamond"? The Hebrew word here translated "adamant" is translated "diamond" in Jer. xvii, 1. The *abjects*, in Ps. xxxv, 15, are the "dregs of the people." The *apothecary*, in Ex. xxx, 25, 35; xxxvii, 29, and Eccl. x, 1, is not our druggist, or preparer of medicines, but simply a "maker of unguents." *Aha*, in Ps. xxxv, 21, and many other places, is not an exclamation of one catching another in evil (as it now is used), but of one exulting over an enemy, and is equivalent to our "hurrah!" *Admired* and *admiration*, in 2 Thess. i, 10, Jude 16, and Rev. xvii, 6, have the old meaning of "wondered at" and "wonder," and not the modern one of delighted appreciation. *Affect*, in Gal. iv, 17; has the signification of "seek after zealously" (the Latin "affectare," rather than "afficere"). The passage means, "They seek after you, but not well; yea, they would shut you out from us, that ye might seek after them; but it is good to be sought after always in a good thing." The Greek verb is ζηλόω, "to desire emulously," "to strive after." [Perhaps the middle sense "to be impelled by zeal" is correct here.] In Judges ix, 53, "*all to* brake his skull" is usually understood as if it were "all to break his skull," *i.e.*, "in order to break," whereas, "all to" is archaic for "thoroughly," or "completely." *Atonement*, in the Old Testament, is the translation of the Hebrew "chopher," a ransom, or a cover for sins. See Ex. xxix, 36, and forty or fifty other places. But it really means "at-one-ment," or "reconciliation," the result of the ransom or cover. In the New Testament the word occurs only once (Rom. v, 11), where it means "reconciliation," (Greek, χαταλλαγην;) but this meaning is now obsolete. The modern *botch* is used exclusively for a clumsy patch or job; but in Deut. xxviii, 27, it means "ulcer." *Bravery*, in Isa. iii, 18, signifies "splendor." Who recognizes in the *camphire* of Solomon's Song i, 14 and iv, 13 (which suggests camphor!) the sweet-smelling "cypress"? and who imagines that the *caterpillar* of the Old Testament is a locust with wings? The *charger*, in Num. vii, 13 and Matt. xiv, 8, is a dish, and not a horse; the *ladder* of Gen. xxviii, 12 is a staircase; the *turtle* of Solomon's Song ii, 12, and Jer. viii, 7, is not a tortoise, but a dove; and the *nephews* of Jud. xii, 14; 1 Tim. v, 4; Job xviii, 19; Isa. xiv, 22, are grandsons. The *pommels* of 2 Chron. iv, 12 have nothing to do with saddles, but are "globes" resting on the summits of the columns. The word "quick" is almost always misunderstood in Ps. cxxiv, 3, "they had swallowed us up *quick*," as if it meant "rapidly." The passage means, "they had swallowed us up alive." *Prevent*, in Scripture means, "not prevent" (*i.e.*, anticipate), and *let* means "not let" (*i.e.*, hinder), so completely have these words turned over in signification. The latter is still used in law phrase as "hinder." *Deal*, in "tenth deal" (Ex. xxix, 40), means "part." *Outlandish*, in Neh. xiii, 26, means simply "foreign." Its modern meaning is "clownish." The *fenced* cities of Num. xxxii, 17, are "walled" cities, and the *hold* of Judges ix, 46; 1 Sam. xxii, 4, is a "stronghold." We use "peep" for the eyes almost altogether; but in Isa. viii, 19; x, 14, it is used of the mouth—"the wizards that *peep*." The same word is translated "chatter" in Isa. xxxviii, 14. *Intreat* (which with us means "beseech") is used for "treat," as in Gen. xii, 16. *Ensue* (French, *ensuivre*) is read in 1 Pet. iii, 11 for "pursue." *Evidently* and *comprehend* are now used of mental conditions, but in the Bible we find them used of physical conditions. "He saw in a vision *evidently*" (*i.e.*, clearly), Acts x, 3; "*comprehended* the dust of the earth in a measure" (*i.e.*, grasped), Isa. xl, 12; so John i, 5.

Conversation, in Scripture, never refers to speech, but always means "manner or course of life." Curious mistakes have been made even in the pulpit, by not observing this. *Comfort*, in the present use, signifies "soothing"; but in old English it had the force of the Latin *confortare*, and meant "strengthening." "Comfort one another with these words," in 1 Thess. iv, 18, is equal to "strengthen one another," etc. *Damn* and *damnation* are simply "condemn" and "condemnation," as in Rom. xiv, 23 and 1 Cor. xi, 29. "They shall *dote*," in Jer. l, 36, is "they shall become foolish." In Zech. i, 21, the carpenters came to *fray* the horns, and the reader supposes that this must mean "to plane" or "to saw"; but it means only "to frighten." *Honest* (Rom. xii, 17) and *honesty* (1 Tim. ii, 2) have not their present meanings, but are equivalent to our "honorable" and "honor." So *modest* (1 Tim. ii, 9) is our "moderate" or "seemly." *Unction*, in 1 John ii, 20, has the meaning of "anointing" (spiritually considered), while our modern use of unction is rather as "earnestness." *Vocation* (Eph. iv, 1) is the "calling" of God to be Christians, and not the trade or the occupation of life. *Go to* (as in James v, 1) is our modern "come," while "we do you to wit" (2 Cor. viii, 1) is the translation of two Greek words meaning, "we certify you." "We do you to wit" is, literally translated into modern English, "We make you to know." We might add another list of words whose signification has undergone a slight shade of change since King James's day, which the reader is almost sure to miss, but we have already surpassed our limits.

Since writing the above, Dr. Ezra Abbot has kindly sent me an additional list of examples, which I append.

1. *Changes in Spelling.*—In the edition of 1611 we find *aliant* or *alient* for *alien*;

clift for *cleft*; *chaws* for *jaws*; *cise* for *size*; *fet* for *fetched* (very often); *flixe* for *flux* (Acts xxviii, 8); *grinne* for *gin*; *moe* for *more* (repeatedly); *ought* for *owed* (Matt. xviii, 24, 28; Luke vii, 41); *price* for *prize* (1 Cor. ix, 24; Phil. iii, 14); *rent* for *rend* (often); *then* for *than* (constantly); *utter* for *outer*.

2. *Obsolete Words.* — *Bolled* = swollen, podded for seed (Exod. ix, 31); *broided* = braided (*not* broidered), (1 Tim. ii, 9); *bruit* = report (Jer. x, 22; Nah. iii, 19); *neese*, *neesing* = sneeze, sneezing (2 Kings iv, 35; Job xli, 18).

3. *Words Obsolete in their Significations.* — *Artillery* = bow and arrows (1 Sam. xx, 40); *by and by* — immediately (Mark vi, 25; xiii, 21; Luke xvii, 7; xxi, 9), *careful* = anxious (Phil. iv, 6); *careless* = free from care (Judges xviii, 7; and so *carelessly*, Isa. xlvii, 8, etc.); *carriage* = baggage (1 Sam. xvii, 22; Isa. x, 28; Acts xxi, 15); *coasts* = borders, territory (very often), to fetch a *compass* (Acts xxviii, 13); set a *compass* (Prov. viii, 27); *convince* convict (John viii, 46; James ii, 9); *desire* = regret (Lat. *desiderare*), (2 Chron. xxi, 20); *discover* = uncover (often); *frankly* freely (Luke vii, 42); *instant* = earnest (often); *frankly* freely (Luke vii, 42); *instant* = earnest and *instantly* = earnestly (Luke vii, 4); *liking* = condition (Job xxxix, 4); *with the manner* = in the act (Num. v, 13); *naughty* = applied to figs (Jer. xxiv, 2); *occupy* = use; deal in trade (Exod. xxxviii, 24; Judg. xvi, 11; Ezek. xxvii, 9, 16, 19, 21, 22; Luke xix, 13); *overrun* = outrun (2 Sam. xviii, 23); *painful*, not "distressing," but *hard*, *difficult* (Ps. lxxiii, 16); *proper* = beautiful, goodly (Heb. xi, 23); *purchase*, not "buy," but *gain*, *acquire* (1 Tim. iii, 13); *having in a readiness* = being ready (2 Cor. x, 6); *road* (make a road) = raid (1 Sam. xxvii, 10); *sometime* or *sometimes* = formerly; *suddenly* = hastily, rashly (1 Tim. v, 22); *take thought* = be anxious (1 Sam. ix, 5; Matt. vi, 25); *uppermost rooms* = highest or most honorable places (Matt. xxiii, 6); *usury* = interest (Matt. xxv, 27); *wealth* — weal, welfare (Ezra ix, 12, Esther x, 3; 1 Cor. x, 24); a *wealthy* place (Ps. lxvi, 12); the *wealthy* nation (Jer. xlix, 31); *worship* = honor (Luke xiv, 10); *witty* = wise, ingenious (Prov. viii, 12); *tree* = beam of wood, applied to a gallows, and especially to the cross. See the article *Tree* in the American edition of Smith's Bible Dictionary.

(Source: *Anglo-American Bible Revision*, Bible House, New York: 1879, pages 144–150.)

65. THE PROCESS OF TRANSLATING THE ASV

The labors of the American Standard Version translators occupied two distinct periods: 1872–1881 (their period of co-labor with the Britishers, culminating in the publication of the ERV) and 1897–1901 (during which the entire text was carefully reconsidered in light of criticisms made of the English Revised Version). In between these two periods, the American translators continued to meet on a yearly basis to lay plans for the eventual publication of their work.

Matthew B. Riddle, the last survivor of the original group of Americans, writes of how the group went about their work:

Three of these, the youngest in years, became the editors of the American Standard Revised New Testament: Drs. Dwight, Thayer and Riddle. Dr. Thayer lived to see the published volume, but died a few months afterward (Nov. 26, 1901). Of the original members the present writer is the sole survivor, though Dr. Dwight was elected very soon after the first meeting.

The sessions were held on the last Friday and Saturday of each month, from September to May. During the summer it was usual to meet once for a longer session, at New Haven or Andover. On Fridays from eight to ten hours were spent in deliberation; on Saturday, the Company adjourned earlier, to enable the members to reach their homes that evening.*

[*It became the habit of four of us to make the home journey together. Dr. Woolsey left us at New Haven, while Drs. Abbot and Thayer parted with the present writer at Hartford. Few memories are more delightful than those connected with these homeward trips. The stress of labor was over, and, while some echoes of the meetings appeared, there was a charming mingling of wit and wisdom in the conversations. All who have known my three companions will understand what a privilege this familiar social intercourse must have been.]

When in session the position about the table was as indicated:

Dr. Schaff, whose private desk was in the room, usually sat there, but joined the group at the table at frequent intervals. While no vice-chairan was ever elected, Dr. Crosby usually presided on the rare occasions when Dr. Woolsey was absent. Professor Short was secretary, but Dr. Thayer was his assistant, and in his hands were the most detailed records of the discussions and decisions.

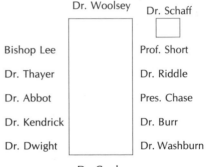

The two Companies in America, unlike those in England, had an organization in common; Dr. Schaff being President, and Dr. George E. Day, Secretary. This proved a great convenience in many ways. No compensation has ever been received by any of the members during the twenty-nine years, from 1872 to 1901. The necessary traveling and incidental expenses were met by contributions from friends of the movement, Mr. Andrew L. Taylor, of the Bible Society, kindly acting as Treasurer. The total amount required during the period of co-operation was nearly $50,000.*

[*At first contributions were solicited by members of the Committee, but afterwards a more convenient way was adopted. To contributors of $10 a presentation copy of the Memorial Volume of the New Testament was offered. The response was gratifying. The Memorial Volume was in the very best style of printing and binding. They were delivered by the University Presses free of charge, and by special Congressional enactment were admitted free of duty. To each of the American Revisers ten copies were allotted; these volumes being the only compensation received. Similar offers were made in regard to the Revised Old Testament.]

The method of co-operation, as finally agreed upon, included: the sending of the first and provisional revision from England to America; then the consideration of this by the American Company, the results being returned to England; then, after careful consideration of the suggestions from America, a second English revision, which was also sent to this country, and the same course pursued in regard to it. Practically a third revision was made in England, in order to secure more uniformity in the renderings. Indeed Bishop Ellicott, in his final report to the Convocation, intimates that there were virtually seven revisions, including the American reviews of the matter sent to this country. Furthermore it was agreed that an appendix should be published with the English Revised Version, containing the more important preferences of the American company. As the Authorized Version of the New Testament was the work of two separate companies, who never discussed their results in common, the superiority of a version resulting from this united and corporate discussion is apparent. It was further stipulated, by the University Presses, who owned the English copyright, that the American Company should not publish an edition of their own for a term of fourteen years.

That the English Revisers gave, as they state in their Preface, "much care and attention" to the American suggestions is shown by the number, either incorporated in the text or added in the margin of the Revision of 1881, probably one thousand in all, as estimated by Bishop Lee. The American Appendix, moreover, formed an essential part of the results of this co-operative labor. In regard to this Appendix further details will be given in a subsequent section.

In the sessions of the American Company the mode of procedure was usually this: A passage was assigned in advance and each member made his individual preparation at home. At the sessions Dr. Woolsey read the passage assigned verse by verse from the English Revision, and was followed by Bishop Lee, who read the corresponding verse from the Authorized Version. Remarks were made by the members, whether in approval or in disapproval of the proposed changes. In many cases little discussion ensued, since the necessity for the emendation was obvious. But frequently a single verse would call for prolonged debate, especially when the change proposed involved a large class of passages. A few of the very important changes called for printed statements, which were transmitted to England.

One of the most important changes urged by the American Company, and finally accepted by the English Company, was the substitution of "Hades" for "hell" in passages where the equivalent Greek term occurs. Where "Gehenna" occurs "hell" was retained, with the margin "Gr. *Gehenna*." The intent was to distinguish between two terms, which are not synonymous. For while "Hades" may include a place of punishment, it usually means the place or state of the dead. "Gehenna" is the place of punishment. Unfortunately this distinction has not been understood, and the substitution of "Hades" has been regarded as an attempt to get rid of the idea of future punishment.

The following extract from Professor Riddle discusses the second intensive phase of translation work (1897–1901):

On the 24th of June, 1897, the formal agreement with Messrs. Thomas Nelson and Sons was consummated in New York, and a contract made between the publishers and the surviving members of the two Companies. The latter agreed to prepare the revised English text, to supply headings and references, to read the proofs. The publishers agreed to bear the necessary incidental expenses, and, in view of the gratuitous services of the revisers, they promised to issue some editions of the book at a price that would put it within the reach of the mass of readers. The first edition was to be in small quarto form, with the marginal readings and renderings on a wide outer margin. Verse numbers were to be inserted in the text. The references were to be placed in a central column. An Appendix was to be prepared, in which should be included all the points of difference between the Revision of 1881-5 and the American Standard edition. The copyright was accorded to the publishers, and a note, signed by the secretaries of the Old and New Testament Companies, was to be printed in every copy, certifying that the editions published by Messrs. Thomas Nelson and Sons "are the only editions authorized by the American Committee of Revision."

That very day the surviving members of the New Testament Company began the work of preparation. The first step was to go over the entire New Testament, as revised in 1881, noting all the suggestions made in the American Company during the years 1872–81. As Professor Thayer had full records of the earlier meetings, often including the suggestions of individual members, even when not adopted by the Company, it was possible to make a review of all the work previously done; and to base the new Version upon the judgment of the entire Company as thus recorded. The three survivors really represented their co- laborers, and the results are in no sense merely the opinions of the trio that remained alive in 1897. The many emendations, forwarded at different times to the English Company, but not accepted by them or included in the Appendix of 1881, were all reconsidered. Not only so, but numerous questions of punctuation, of paragraphing, and of spelling, were discussed. It was, of course, necessary that the three editors should meet several times. As all were actively engaged in teaching, these meetings usually occurred in summer or during the Christmas recess, ordinarily continuing for a week. As the three had been associated so long, it was possible to accomplish a good deal by correspondence, especially as the views of each on important points were already known to the others. In the spring of 1898 this review of the New Testament was completed, and the judgment of the editors put on record. Professor Thayer, according to the usages of the Harvard Divinity School, had a Sabbatical year during 1898 and 1899. He proposed to visit his son-in-law, Professor Caspar René Gregory (the editor of Tischendorf's *Prolegomena*), at Leipsic, Germany, and while there to select the references and headings for the new edition. This exacting work he faithfully and successfully prosecuted. The references in the ordinary editions of the Authorized version are, in many cases, worthless or misleading. The new references were to be more helpful in regard to the use of words, and, by discriminating terms, such as "See," and "Compare," to indicate the bearing of the passages cited upon the place to which the reference was prefixed. Parallel passages were to be distinguished by italics. All this called for minute care as well as wide Scriptural knowledge. The mechanical execution of the plan called for much skill. Professor Thayer sent the "copy," with pasted slips containing the references, to his colleagues by instalments. The other editors examined and verified the lists, occasionally discussing the propriety of using a given passage. All this labor was not without its influence upon the final judgment of the editors.

In the midst of this arduous work something occurred which greatly surprised the American Revisers, and led to a controversy in print, mainly in the columns of The Sunday School Times. It is necessary to allude to this, without reopening the controversy. The University Presses, at the close of the year 1898, just before the expiration of the fourteen years agreed upon, published an edition of the Revised Version, in which the preferences printed in the Appendix of 1881–5 were incorporated in the text and another Appendix substituted, which gave the corresponding readings and renderings of the English Companies. The edition contained an admirable selection of references, and was fairly accurate in its use of the American preferences. But the American Revisers had received no hint of the purpose to publish such an edition, though some years had evidently been required to prepare it for publication. There can be no question that the University Presses had the legal right to issue such a volume. It is altogether probable that it was designed, in some way, to protect the English copyright, of which they were the owners. But the appearance of the book at that time created the impression that this was the American Revised Version which the public had been awaiting for so many years. This impression was furthered by the fact that some booksellers advertised it as "the American Revised Version." The protests from members of the American Companies led to the withdrawal of this title. It was intimated that the Presses were not aware of the purpose of the American Revisers to publish an edition of their own; but this purpose had been frequently announced, and certain facts, presented by Professor Thayer, indicate that the University Presses should have been fully aware of the proposed publication in America. The discussions of 1899, however, made clear the character of this English edition, and while it remains a useful help for the Biblical scholar, it is not "The American Revised Version." It had little or no effect upon the success of the latter, though anticipating it by two years.

On the return of Professor Thayer from Europe in 1899 the editors met for a final review of the entire work. The text, the margins, the headings, the references, the paragraphs, the punctuation, were discussed afresh and in detail. The knowledge that the edition was soon to appear called forth a large number of suggestions from many correspondents. Each of these was duly considered, though very few of them were accepted by the editors, who had already, at some stage of their labors, taken action on the points presented by these correspondents. Arrangements were also made for the Appendix, showing the divergences from the Version of 1881, for the Preface and title-page; and certain details in printing the poetic parts of the Book of Revelation were agreed upon.

The last meeting was held on April 19, 1900, and the "copy" at once placed in the hands of the printers.

The proofreading was exacting work. The proofs were submitted three times to each of the editors, and they interchanged the corrected proofs before returning them to the printer. Every page contained five or six different kinds of type, and the correct position of the reference letters and numbers called for judgment as well as constant care. By June, 1901, the body of the work, the prefaces and title-pages were in press. Drs. Dwight and Thayer then sailed for Europe, leaving the present writer to carry the Appendix through the press. The last proof of the last page was corrected in the room at Castine, Maine, where these lines are penned, and sent off July 15, 1901. Twenty-nine years had well-nigh elapsed since the American Company began its work.

The American Standard Edition of the Revised Version of the Bible was placed on sale August 26, 1901.

(Source: Matthew B. Riddle, *The Story of the Revised New Testament*, Sunday School Times Company, Philadelphia: 1908, pages 20–25 [initial translation effort] and 59–65 [period of 1897–1901].)

66. THE CHOOSING OF A GREEK TEXT

Like most twentieth century translations, the American Standard Version was not based upon a predetermined text. When confronted with a disputed reading the translators made their own independent judgment based upon an evaluation of the evidence. Although every reading could be found somewhere, no one manuscript contained them all. The following extract discusses the method and how the ASV approach differed from that of the English Revised Version.

The chief peculiarity of the Revised New Testament is that it represents a much older, and, in the judgment of all competent scholars, a more accurate Greek text. Naturally this makes it greatly superior to the Authorized Version. The latter was based upon the Greek Testament of Beza, from which it differs in only forty places. Now Beza, while a careful exegete, was not an expert textual critic. In his day the science of textual criticism had not yet been developed. The editors preceding him, Erasmus and Robert Stephen (or, Stephens, as generally printed), had few Greek manuscripts, and no settled critical principles. It is usual to speak of the text of the sixteenth century, on which the Authorized Version is based, as the "Received Text." But this is not strictly correct. The edition which claims to present the Received Text was printed by the Elzevirs, at Leyden, in 1633, twenty-two years after the publication of the Authorized Version. But it differs very slightly from Stephen and Beza. In the discussions between the Roman Catholics and Protestants during the sixteenth century, neither party took the right view of the Greek text. The Roman Catholics accepted the Latin Vulgate as authoritative, while the Protestants contended for the authority of the original Greek (and Hebrew). But the text which the Protestants used was in many cases, it is now acknowledged, less accurate than that represented by the Vulgate. The true position is: that the *original* Greek text is authoritative; not any translation, or any later and possibly impure and inaccurate text. To discover this original Greek text has been the task of textual critics, since the latter part of the eighteenth century. The labors of Bengel, Griesbach, Lachmann, Tischendorf and Tregelles convinced New Testament scholars that the original text had been substantially recovered. While in minor details there was room for discussion, the position of both the English and American New Testament Companies was decidedly in favor of accepting the text resulting from the labors of these critics, in preference to the uncritical text on which the Authorized Version was based. But neither Company attempted "to construct a continuous and complete Greek text," as is stated in the Preface to the Revised New Testament of 1881. So that no edition of the Greek Testament can claim to present "the Revisers' text," since on many passages where there are various readings, different spellings and punctuation, the Revisers passed no judgment. Only upon readings that would affect the English dress was any action taken.

For convenience in England Scrivener's Greek Testament was used to mark the changes in text. This edition has in footnotes the various readings accepted by the principal critical editors, the text itself being that of Stephen. As these notes are numbered, in transmitting the first Revision to America a list of the numbers prefixed to the preferred readings was added. Thus the judgment of the English Revisers was accurately indicated.

It has often been asked: What edition was accepted by the Revisers?

The only answer is, the readings of no one edition were accepted, but each various reading was discussed, first in England and then in America. In England Dr. Scrivener was the main advocate on one side, and Drs. Westcott and Hort on the other. The Greek Testament of the latter had not been published when the work of revision began, but copies of the Gospels were printed and placed in the hands of the English Company. A copy sent to America was entrusted to the present writer, who collated the readings and added notices of them to the footnotes in Scrivener's edition. It was evident that the readings accepted by the English Revisers were quite as frequently those of Tregelles as those of Westcott and Hort. In the American Company the readings were carefully discussed. While in the vast majority of cases the preferences of the English Revisers were approved, this was due to independent judgment. Dr. Ezra Abbot was the foremost textual critic in America, and his opinions usually prevailed when questions of text were debated. It may be said that neither he nor any other member of the Company endorsed the peculiar theory of Westcott and Hort, in regard to what they call the "Neutral" text, a theory which gives to the Codex Vaticanus (designated B) preponderating authority. So also the obvious partiality of Tischendorf for the readings of the Codex Sinaiticus (designated Aleph), which he had discovered, was carefully guarded against.

Another question has frequently been asked: What manuscript or manuscripts did the Revisers follow? The answer again is: No one manuscript. In each case all the leading authorities were recognized, and the judgment based upon evidence, both external and internal. From the results it would appear that the American Company gave more weight to internal evidence, and the English Company to the external evidence. Nearly all the differences between the two Companies, as regards readings, are indicated in the American Appendix published in the Revised New Testament of 1881. In many instances the English Company preferred one reading in the text and another in the margin, while the American Company reversed this position. The marginal notes which refer to alternate readings, that is, to other forms of the Greek text, are carefully worded, and give an estimate of evidence supporting the reading. Usually the formula is: "Some ancient authorities read," etc. Where the reading is more strongly attested, "Many ancient authorities" occurs. In a few special cases the evidence is otherwise indicated: e.g., "Many very ancient authorities," "Very many ancient authorities," "Many authorities, some ancient." Mark 16:9–20, and John 7:53–8:11 required special notes.

As the text of the whole New Testament was discussed during the period of co-operation, when Dr. Abbot's expert knowledge was available, it was not found necessary in the subsequent preparation of the Standard Revised New Testament to modify the judgments rendered by the whole Company. The Appendix of 1881 includes nearly all the readings in regard to which the American Revisers differed from the English. Probably the Greek Testament that most frequently adopts the readings of the Revisers, either those of the text or of the margins, is that of Nestle, the first edition of which was published in 1901. It presents a compromise text, but the readings approved by the Revisers always appear, either in its text or its margins. A student of the Greek Testament can easily determine, from a comparison of the Revised New Testament with this edition, what was the judgment of the Revisers in each case where various readings occur.

(Source: Matthew B. Riddle, *The Story of the Revised New Testament*, Sunday School Times Company, Philadelphia: 1908, pages 27–33.)

67. THE IMMERSION QUESTION

Any translation has a potential use for either upholding or criticizing a wide range of religious doctrine and practice. Although much of the enthusiasm has now gone out of the controversy over the act of baptism (biblically, is it sprinkling, pouring, or strictly immersion?) such was far from the case at the time the ASV appeared. This version did not follow the practice of Alexander Campbell's translation and that of the American Bible Union and render "baptize" as immersion. Instead it endorsed a textual translation that was loudly challenged: In passages such as Matthew 3:11 the ASV rendered "*in* water" while placing in the margin, "or, *with* water." The controversy was sufficiently widespread that one of the translators defended the committee against criticism in his book discussing the translation and how it came about:

But despite the general agreement in regard to the principles that should govern the revision, at every point there was room for discussion. There would be differing views as to the exact sense of a given passage; then, different opinions as to the best mode of expressing the sense. The question often arose whether a rendering should stand in the text or be relegated to the margin. In all these discussions there was manifested the utmost candor. The denominations of Christians represented in the American Company were the Baptist, Congregationalist, Dutch Reformed, Friends, Methodist Episcopal, Presbyterian, Protestant Episcopal, and Unitarian; yet rarely was there what might be termed a "theological" debate.

As an illustration of the candor of the Company, the treatment of the passages referring to baptism may be cited. Since the American Revised Version was published much criticism has been offered on this point. The English Company, in Matthew 3:11 and similar passages, rendered "with water," placing in the margin "Or, *in*," wherever the Greek preposition *en* occurs. The American Company reached this verse in the closing session of 1872. As a class of passages was involved, the discussion was frank and full. It was decided, by a vote of 7 to 3, that the text and margin should exchange places, that "in" should be the rendering in the text, and "Or, *with*" be placed in the margin. That decision was never reversed. It appears in the American Appendix of 1881, and, of course, in the Standard American Version of 1901. Yet it was asserted by some that this action was that of the three editors of the Standard New Testament, also that they were all ecclesiastically Baptists. It is evident that this decision was made at an early, and comparatively full, session of the Company, and that the editors of the American Version simply recorded the action of the whole Company — action taken, moreover, nearly twenty-nine years before.

In 1872, when the vote stood 7 to 3, there were two Baptist members present and voting with the majority. The question was settled by the vote of representatives of other denominations. It was felt that the English reader ought to know where the Greek preposition, usually meaning "in," occurred in connection with baptism. Whether immersion was practised by John the Baptist, or whether it is the proper mode, was not discussed to any great extent. The question simply was, how shall we most fairly present to the English reader the exact force of the original?

(Source: Matthew B. Riddle, *The Story of the Revised New Testament*, Sunday School Times Company, Philadelphia: 1908, pages 37–39.)

III. *Revised Standard Version*

68. THE NEED FOR A BIAS-FREE TRANSLATION

Perhaps in a conscious reaction to the accusation of religious "modernism" in the Revised Standard Version's New Testament section,

III. Revised Standard Version

William A. Irwin (one of the RSV Old Testament translators)
need for a theology-free treatment of the biblical text in the
follows. As a generality few might question this approach; yet it is hig...
questionable whether any translation can truly live up to this claim. For
example, in Isaiah 7:14, should the translator impose the most restricted
Hebrew meaning on *almah* and render it "young woman"? Or should he
take into consideration the fact that an unmarried young woman was expected to be a virgin? And that the Septuagint translates it with the word
"virgin," and the canonical gospels so quote it? In such a case, can one's
judgment be totally free of one's preexisting theological judgments of
truth and falsity? Irwin writes,

The present work likewise is primarily a revision. Its official title declares this:
it is the Revised Standard Version, that is, a revision of the American Standard
Version of 1901, which had its ultimate inception in the official action of the
Church of England in 1870 that authorized a revision of the King James Version.
Through its entire activity the committee for the Revised Standard Version has
been conscious of its role as reviser. The American Standard Version was its basic
English text, and from it deviations were permitted only by majority vote, subject
to final ratification by a two-thirds vote.

A task of revision entails all the problems and difficulties of translation, and in
addition, one that is peculiarly its own: what degree of change from the basic text
is permissible? It is a question of peculiar urgency when the revision concerns the
Bible, for its very words quickly endear themselves to the devout student, so that
any alteration, however slight, can well appear almost a desecration.

But further, any process of translation is in a sense an effort at the impossible.
Languages differ; they are projections of the personalities of those for whom the
speech learned in childhood is as intimate and personal as their native air. From
these, the translators are separated by insuperable psychological barriers. The best
that can be hoped is an approximation to the thought of the original, but its finer
points, its overtones, its allusions, the feeling and atmosphere of its words lie
beyond any process of translation. This is especially true when the task is that of
rendering classics of an ancient language, such as the Old Testament includes, into a modern tongue of far remote genius and relationships. All speech develops
its peculiar expressions that vary from mere slang across a diverse terrain to proverbial sayings at the other end. Colloquialisms soon pass, either into standard
speech, or into desuetude as derelicts of a once pulsing reality; then life moves on
and forgets their occasion and significance. One who works long and seriously
with the Hebrew Old Testament grows steadily more conscious that much of its
allusive and delicate meaning has been for ever lost; the words are known —
generally — but their significance in particular combinations allures, but evades,
the student.

However this may be, the responsibility of the translator is clear. Representing
the best extant understanding of the language with which he deals, he is charged
to tell as accurately as he can in his own language precisely what the original says.
This is of an importance to bear some emphasis. The Bible translator assumes a
strict responsibility to say in English just what the Biblical writers said in Hebrew,
or in Aramaic, or in Greek, as the case may have been. In response to early publicity

about the launching of the Revised Standard project, letters came in to one or another of the committee pointing out their opportunity to deal a blow to certain anti-social views which unfortunately base themselves on this or that Bible passage—the committee should change the offending passage! The only answer that could be given was that the committee did not intend, nor had it any authority, to change the Bible. The purpose was to give a more accurate rendering of what it said, even in these passages. Correction of wrong uses of the Bible, important as this may be, lay entirely outside its responsibility.

Yet this is not all. The danger here is of a subtle sort. A recent speaker has told of a project to issue "a theologically conservative translation of the Bible." Doubtless this is an appealing undertaking in the eyes of many. But the fact must be stressed that there is no place for theology in Bible translation, whether conservative or radical or whatever else. A "theological translation" is not a translation at all, but merely a dogmatic perversion of the Bible. Linguistic science knows no theology; those of most contradictory views can meet on common ground devoid of polemic, agreed that Hebrew words mean such and such, and their inflection and syntactical relations imply this or that. These facts establish an agreed translation. Then, and then only, may the exegete and dogmatist busy himself with theological deductions from the thoughts of the Biblical writers. The Bible translator is not an expositor; however pronounced his views about Biblical doctrines, he has no right whatever to intrude his opinions into the translation, or to permit his dogmatic convictions to qualify or shape its wording. His one responsibility, and it is absolute, is to render the Biblical meaning as accurately and effectively as is possible into appropriate English.

Likewise the translator must be on guard against paraphrase. He must steer between Scylla and Charybdis, and the channel is narrow! Avoiding paraphrastic rendering, it is easy for him to fall into a rigid, mechanical procedure that deprives the result of both life and beauty. No one is a translator who believes that each foreign word has its English equivalent, and that the process of translation is something like shifting pieces in a jigsaw puzzle. A more sinister form of the temptation is to hold that faithfulness binds one to similar sentence structure and, in particular, verbal inflection, and so on. Or again the tempter may come in the cloak of consistency: surely it is necessary that translation reveal the presence of certain great words in the original, or the substitution of some approximate synonym; and can this be done other than by adopting the best available English equivalent for the word or phrase and then using it at every occurrence? While there is much that is sound in this argument, the result can easily run off into a wooden style, that lacks all the beauty and force of the original. Yet to abandon the restraints imposed by these considerations comes close to throwing open the doors to paraphrase. There is a difference, however, which the skilful translator will recognize; indeed his merit not uncommonly is to be gauged by his decisions at these points. He must possess an elasticity of mind and of method that will hold true to the demands of the original and yet will discover a way of rendering it in graceful and forceful English. It is not adequate to define translation as the process of rendering the thought of the original into another language; it is all that, and much more. It should give some feeling of the literary quality of the original writer: his command and use of his language, his mood, his figures of speech, his structure of thought. Yet not least, all must cohere in idiomatic English, that possesses grace and beauty and power.

(Source: "Method and Procedure of the Revision," in Luther A. Weigle, editor, *An Intro-*

duction to the Revised Standard Version of the Old Testament, copyright 1952, reprinted by permission of Thomas Nelson, Inc.)

69. COMPARING THE NUMBER OF WORDS IN THE KJV, ASV, AND RSV

The choice of differing Greek texts and different principles of translation naturally resulted in a different number of words being utilized. In the following extract, Luther A. Weigle provides a comparative listing of representative chapters from the New Testament.

We must speak with caution, for there has been no set purpose to reduce the number of words and no sufficient count has been made. But a count of the words in a few chapters, chosen from various books, shows that the style of the Revised Standard Version is terse. It probably contains fewer words than the former authorized versions, and certainly fewer than other modern versions such as those of Weymouth, Moffatt, and Goodspeed. Here are the figures:

	KJ	ASV	RSV
Matthew 5	1081	1056	1002
Mark 1–2	1654	1618	1534
Luke 8	1431	1431	1367
John 4	1096	1085	1038
Acts 10	1108	1128	1022
Romans 8	904	898	898
1 Cor. 15	1165	1169	1151
Ephesians 3	410	418	405
Philippians 1	632	653	639
Colossians 2	503	515	502

Yet we have not hesitated to use more words than the older versions, if that was necessary to convey the meaning. An interesting example is 1 Cor. 7.19, which starts out with more words in the initial clause, but ends with a total of one less. The verse reads in KJ: "Circumcision is nothing, and uncircumcision is nothing, but the keeping of the commandments of God." This is ambiguous, for "but" may be taken to mean "except." In ASV the wording is unchanged, and the meaning is made to depend upon the punctuation, changing the comma after "nothing" to a semicolon. The RSV reads: "For neither circumcision counts for anything nor uncircumcision, but keeping the commandments of God."

A requirement that has constantly been kept in mind by the present Committee is that the Bible should be translated into language that is euphonious, readable, and suited for use in public and private worship. It must sound well, and be easy to read aloud and in public. The choice of words and ordering of phrases must be such as to avoid harsh collocations of sound, and consonantal juxtapositions over which tongues will trip and lisp — that sentence is an example of what must not be in the English Bible!

(Source: Luther A. Weigle, "The English of the Revised Standard Version," in *An Introduction to the Revised Standard Version of the New Testament,* copyrighted 1946 by International Council of Religious Education. Reprinted by permission of the National Council of the Churches of Christ in the U.S.A.)

70. CHANGING CRITICAL ASSUMPTIONS AND THEIR IMPACT ON THE RSV

Although the English Revised and American Standard versions were affected by the shift in critical analysis of the Greek text pioneered by Westcott and Hort, the consensus had further shifted by the time the RSV revisers did their work. In the following extract Frederick C. Grant summarizes the shift and some of its results.

Even if there had been no other reason for a fresh revision of the New Testament, it would have been required by the discovery of additional manuscripts and the change that has come over textual criticism since 1881, the date of the English revision upon which the American edition of 1901 was based.

1

A mere list of the more important manuscripts and fragments made available to scholars since the last revision is imposing.

One of the most important discoveries has been a manuscript of the Old Syriac version of the Gospels, found in the monastery of St. Catherine on Mt. Sinai by Mrs. Lewis and Mrs. Gibson in 1892. The text of this version is older than the Curetonian Syriac, and probably dates from the second century. Thus it testifies to the state of the Greek text from which it was translated, perhaps around 150 A.D.

Related to this is the remarkable discovery of a fragment of Tatian's *Diatessaron* in Greek, found at Dura on the Euphrates by the Yale Expedition in 1933, and edited by Professor Carl Kraeling.

Another important discovery was the "Washington" manuscript, purchased at Cairo in 1906 by Mr. Charles Freer of Detroit. It contains a mixed text; i.e., some parts were copied from one type of manuscript, others from other types.

Even more important was the discovery in 1931 of fragments of twelve manuscripts (eight Old Testament, three New Testament, and one containing part of Enoch), and their purchase by Mr. A. Chester Beatty, an American living in England. These fragments are of extraordinary importance, as the leading experts agree that they were copied for the most part in the third century—a hundred years, presumably, before Vaticanus and Sinaiticus! The Gospels and Acts probably come from the first half of the third century; the fragments of the Pauline letters are certainly not later than 250 A.D.—which is almost unbelievably early, compared with the "great uncials" upon which Westcott and Hort, and the earlier revisers, had to rely.

These were not the only discoveries, of course; scores of papyrus fragments, and even some vellum codices have continued to turn up. The famous ninth-century Koridethi Gospels were edited by Beermann and Gregory in 1913. Recent American editions include *The Rockefeller McCormick New Testament* (13th century), *The Four Gospels of Karahissar* (13th century), and *The Elizabeth Day McCormick Apocalypse* (17th century). Even these late Byzantine manuscripts are not to be overlooked; once in a while they are of real importance in establishing the earlier text.

In addition to the discovery and publication of Greek and Syriac manuscripts, considerable attention has been given to other versions, such as the Sahidic, Armenian, and above all the Latin, especially the Old Latin, perhaps contemporaneous with the Old Syriac, i.e., around 150 A.D. The result has been a quantity of fresh discoveries and new publications including better editions of manuscripts and versions already known.

All this new material for textual criticism has to be evaluated and assimilated by New Testament scholars. Its influence upon both the editing and the translating of the New Testament is apparent in all the standard editions of its text since 1881, and in many of the newer translations. And it simply demanded a fresh revision of the Revised Version.

2

Now the problem arises, how to make use of these new manuscripts and new editions. Therein lies the whole point of the science of textual criticism. It may be thought that a simple rule would be to count those manuscripts which favor a particular reading; then count up the manuscripts on the other side; or if there are three readings which are competing for recognition, then count up the supporters of all three and choose the reading that has the strongest support in numbers. But such a method would never do, for the reason that the largest number of manuscripts are of a late date; the early manuscripts are more rare. So then another method must be devised. Perhaps this would be to "weight" the manuscripts and give a fifth-century manuscript twice the value of a sixth-century, etc. But the trouble with this scheme is that sometimes a later manuscript turns out to have been copied from a manuscript considerably earlier in date than its immediate rival; in the case just mentioned, the sixth-century manuscript may happen to be copied from a third-century one while the fifth-century manuscript may have been copied from another which was almost contemporary. Hence some better system must be devised for evaluating manuscripts; and when the manuscripts have been evaluated some principles must be set up by which the original text of the autographs may be approximated as closely as possible. This is an indispensable procedure, since we do not possess a single autograph of a New Testament document. As in the case of all other ancient books we have only copies of copies. Our oldest fragment of a New Testament book, the tiny little scrap of papyrus giving a few words from the Gospel of John, is not earlier than a little before 150 A.D. That fragment is now in the John Rylands Library at the University of Manchester in England.

As a result of approximately two hundred and fifty years of modern textual criticism, scholars have come to the conclusion that there existed at the end of the second century five main types of text, that is, all existing manuscripts of the New Testament go back to ancestors that belonged to one or another of these groups. As stated by Sir Frederic Kenyon in his recent books, *The Text of the Greek Bible, The Story of the Bible* and *Our Bible and the Ancient Manuscripts*, these were as follows:

(1) Western, represented by Codex Bezae and the Old Latin version.

(2) Caesarean, represented by the Koridethi Gospels, etc.

(3) Alexandrian, represented by Codex Sinaiticus, Codex Vaticanus, and the Coptic version.

(4) Syriac, represented by the Old Syriac version.

(5) Other, i.e., a classification for readings that do not fall into any of the preceding groups.

This view takes the place of the one which has held the field more or less since Bishop Westcott and Dr. Hort published their Greek New Testament in 1881. Their theory of the "neutral" text has gradually been abandoned even though the manuscripts which they included in that classification are still recognized as of great importance, chiefly Sinaiticus and Vaticanus. There has been a growing recognition among scholars of the importance of the so-called "Western" text. It contains some good readings, and moreover (as Westcott and Hort themselves recognized) it does not include some of the interpolations that got into all other types of text—most of which are found at the end of the Gospel of Luke.

If Kenyon's conclusion is correct—and it is shared by many other experts—the situation is completely changed from that in 1881. Instead of tracing back the text to its original in the autographs by a steady process of convergence following back to a common source the divergent lines of descent, we shall have to stop when we get to the second century; and in place of some rule of preference for one type of text over another, or for their common agreements over their divergences, we shall have to trust a great deal more than heretofore to what is called internal criticism. In fact, this is about the point at which we had arrived anyway: the style of a New Testament author, for example, counts for a great deal more in textual criticism at the present time than it did in the nineteenth century; and Matthew, Luke, and perhaps even John, are pretty good early witnesses to the text of Mark, for example; and so on. But now, with Kenyon's conclusions before us, it is more obvious than ever where our chief problems lie. "In the first two centuries this original text disappeared under a mass of variants, created by errors, by conscious alterations, and by attempts to remedy the uncertainties thus created. Then, as further attempts to recover the lost truth were made, the families of text that we now know took shape. They were, however, nuclei rather than completed forms of text, and did not at once absorb all the atoms that the period of disorder had brought into existence." (*The Text of the Greek Bible*, p. 242.)

I say we have arrived at about this point anyway; for who today would think of applying Gerhard of Maastricht's forty-three "canons of criticism" (A.D. 1711)? Griesbach cut them down to fifteen, at the end of the 18th century, though Bengel in 1734 had already reduced them to one—or perhaps we should say, subsumed them under one: his famous "Let the harder reading prevail." Wordsworth and White, in editing the Vulgate New Testament, reduced them to two: "The shorter reading is the more probable one," and "The true reading wins out in the end"—though both these rules are questionable, the first almost as inevitably as the second. It is now clear that the "shorter reading" canon led directly to Westcott and Hort's preference for Codex Vaticanus. We may venture to state the general situation at present, and the new rules now in force, somewhat as follows:

1. No one type of text is infallible, or to be preferred by virtue of its generally superior authority.

2. Each reading must be examined on its merits, and preference must be given to those readings which are demonstrably in the style of the author under consideration.

3. Readings which explain other variants, but are not contrariwise themselves to be explained by the others, merit our preference; but this is a very subtle process, involving intangible elements, and liable to subjective judgment on the part of the critic.

With the best will in the world, the New Testament translator or reviser of today is forced to adopt the eclectic principle: each variant reading must be studied on its merits, and cannot be adopted or rejected by some rule of thumb, or by adherence to such a theory as that of the "Neutral Text." It is this eclectic principle that has guided us in the present Revision. The Greek text of this Revision is not that of Westcott-Hort, or Nestle, or Souter; though the readings we have adopted will, as a rule, be found either in the text or the margin of the new (17th) edition of Nestle (Stuttgart, 1941).

3

It was a part of our commission to take into account the progress of modern Biblical research. This most certainly includes textual research or criticism. We have endeavored to discharge this part of our commission as faithfully as we could. And it is really extraordinary how often, with the fuller apparatus of variant readings at our disposal, and with the eclectic principle now more widely accepted, we have concurred in following Westcott and Hort. Not that we agreed in advance in favor of Hort — quite the contrary, there was no such unanimity; our agreement is really a tribute to Westcott-Hort, which is still the great classical edition of modern times. I find that we have adopted only one conjectural emendation (in Jude 5, "he who . . ."), and this is one that Hort discussed in his notes, and favored. We have made considerable use of the Chester Beatty fragments; in fact we have consulted them constantly, and have occasionally adopted readings from that source, when supported by others. Usually, the Beatty fragments range themselves with Aleph and B, i.e., Sinaiticus and Vaticanus.

If anyone will take the trouble to go through the footnotes to the new Revision, and list the chief authorities for the reading in the text and for the alternatives cited in the margin, noting especially the passages where we differ from the American Standard Version, he will find that we have followed B-Aleph-Chester Beatty (or some one or two of them) in the following important passages:

Matthew 3.16; 9.14; 12.47; 17.22. Mark 1.1; 7.4; 8.15; 10.24; 15.44; 16.9–20. Luke 2.14; 4.44; 5.17; 12.39; 15.16; 22.16; 23.38. John 3.13; 5.2; 7.53–8.11; 8.16; 8.57; 9.35. Acts 11.20; 18.7; 19.39. Romans 4.1; 5.1; 5.2; 8.28. 1 Corinthians 1.4; 1.14. 2 Corinthians 3.2. Ephesians 1.1. 2 Thessalonians 2.3. Hebrews 3.2; 3.6; 6.2; 6.3; 9.11. 1 Peter 4.1; 5.2. 2 Peter 1.21. 1 John 2.10. 2 John 8. Revelation 21.3; 22.14.

It is unnecessary to list here the changes in the new revision which have resulted from consideration of the textual evidence. The Revised Standard Version of 1946 must itself be read and compared with the American Standard Version of 1901, and the explanation of differences must be sought (1) in a more adequate or a more modern rendering; if this does not explain a change, then (2) recourse should be had to the textual apparatus of the Greek New Testament. This was not the method of the revisers; it is merely a suggestion of a useful method to readers who wish to study the new Revision. As a matter of fact, not a single important variant in the whole New Testament escaped our scrutiny; each was considered, not only once but repeatedly, as our Revision was itself revised in the three or four successive drafts it went through.

It will be obvious to the careful reader that still in 1946, as in 1881 and in 1901, no doctrine of the Christian faith has been affected by the revision, for the simple reason that, out of the thousands of variant readings in the manuscripts, none has turned up thus far that requires a revision of Christian doctrine. At the same time, their variety takes us back to the great days of freedom and of private initiative, when Christians copied out their own Gospels and Epistles, and occasionally made mistakes in doing so, and occasionally also added some words to their copies, for the sake of completeness — days when martyrdom was still common, and a victorious Church was superbly "alive and on the march." May the Book that spoke to these early Christians still speak to us — or rather, the same Lord, speaking through His servants, the apostles and prophets of Jesus Christ.

71. THE PROCESS OF TRANSLATION (OLD TESTAMENT)

Earlier we examined an account of how the translators undertook their labors on the American Standard Version. The following extract comes from one of the RSV translator, William A. Irwin, who discusses how these more recent scholars undertook the task of consultation and revision.

The story of the inception of the revision, of its early activity, which when only well begun was interrupted by the great depression of the 1930's, has been told by Dean Weigle in the *Introduction to the Revised Standard Version of the New Testament*. In 1937 the International Council of Religious Education authorized the revision, and reconstituted the committee to undertake it. The first meeting of the reconstituted committee began at 9 a.m., December 3, 1937, in the Directors' Room of the Union Theological Seminary, New York. It was to prove the only meeting of the full committee; otherwise its work was carried forward in the separate sections for the Old and New Testaments. The concern of this first meeting was the establishment of principles and the setting of modes and procedures for the work.

At this first meeting the six members of the Old Testament section were each allotted fifteen chapters to revise in accordance with established general principles. They were further associated in three pairs, who were each to exchange and discuss their results together before mimeographing them and sending them to the remaining four members for further criticism. Later this pairing was abandoned; it was found most expedient for the individual reviser to send his matured work to Dean Weigle for transmission to the committee. However, six times fifteen, it is apparent, totals ninety; when the Old Testament section convened in Ann Arbor, Michigan, in the following June for its first meeting of work, the entirety of Genesis and Exodus had been revised, a fact which gave basis for a sanguine hope that the work could be quickly pushed through to completion. But such rosy expectations endured less than five days; when the meeting ended, about twenty-seven simple chapters of narrative had been reviewed. The implication became clearer with each meeting. It was relatively easy to secure somewhat large blocks of individual revision; the bottleneck was committee discussion. And if free discussion were throttled in the interest of speed, the result could only be inferior; the wrestle of mind with mind on precise points of the meaning of the original and its most accurate and graceful rendering in English was the one way to the end which all desired. Various efforts were put forth from time to time to expedite progress; in the end nothing was found better than an efficient leadership of the committee to concentrate debate on the matter in hand, and then as soon as practicable to crystallize it in a vote.

Apart from the meeting in Ann Arbor, the section held its sessions in the east, commonly alternating between the Union Theological Seminary and the Divinity School of Yale University. A few subsidiary meetings of the eastern members were held in New York, and of the western in Ann Arbor. Later the section held summer meetings in the chateau of Hotel Northfield, at East Northfield, Massachusetts.

The procedure of a meeting quickly assumed an accustomed form — it had one main thing to do. The meeting opened with a brief prayer. The chairman commonly had a few announcements to present. And then the work began. Seated about a long table, with the chairman at one end, mimeographed copies of a revision draft before them, and surrounded with Hebrew Bibles and an assortment of versions, ancient and modern, and with commentaries and other help near at hand — not least in importance, an unabridged English Dictionary — the members set themselves to the course of debate, which on point after point was to continue eight or nine hours a day through the next week or two. The agendum of the meeting was well known; not infrequently it had been decided at the previous meeting six months before. Mimeographed copies of the revision were in hand, and also an assortment of mimeographed comments by most of the members of the section. And so attention was directed to verse one; there would be a little pause: the committee had not yet warmed up to debating mood; then a member would cautiously venture the opinion such a word was not the best; he proposed another. This might then entail a lengthy discussion of the original Hebrew word and citation of grammar or syntax; perhaps commentaries would be invoked or other translations, and soon or late someone would find it relevant to cross to the English dictionary on its desk nearby and provide authoritative opinion on the usage under discussion. Thus the meeting went on, hour after hour, and day after day. No one could anticipate the course of events; sometimes an apparently innocent passage occupied an hour or more; occasionally considerable departure from the traditional wording was accepted with little demur; sometimes the committee ordered, instead, a return to the American Standard or to the King James. The alignment of the committee was in constant flux, members who had stood shoulder to shoulder on one issue would find themselves completely opposed on the next. There were no cliques or special interests. Old friends not uncommonly were leaders of opposing views that engaged in mortal combat. Then happily, a few moments later when the session had adjourned, all would be found in happy converse, a true symbol and expression of the deep personal friendship that developed through these years, if it had not already been long in existence.

Three times in the course of the years the committee was saddened by the passing of one of its members. President John R. Sampey, of Southern Baptist Theological Seminary, Louisville, Kentucky, constituted one of the links binding together the two periods of the committee's work. He had participated in it from the beginning in 1930; he was present at the reorganization in New York in 1937 and resumed his official relationship as chairman of the Old Testament section. But soon after he decided it was expedient for him to resign in favor of his colleague Professor Kyle M. Yates. Though his association with its later work was thus brief, his death on August 18, 1946, was a real loss to the committee, depriving it of his sane counsel and understanding. Professor James Moffatt died June 27, 1944. He had served as executive secretary from the reorganization in 1937, in this capacity being closely associated with the Old Testament section as well as with the New, where his major specialization belonged. His charming personality had endeared him to all his associates, and his feeling for the nuances of English words and his fine sense of style had been a rich resource whenever debate arrived at the question of the best wording for an idea already hammered out in discussion. Principal William R. Taylor's great contribution to the revision lay in the Psalter. He had served notably since the early days of the committee; his wide and solid scholarship was of incalculable worth in all the detailed mass of questions and problems that arose through the course of the years. But when in the course of allocation of work he was asked to prepare the initial revision of the Psalms, he poured into the task the resources of a lifetime of special study of these incomparable classics of the inner life. When death came to him in the morning of February 24, 1951, he had seen his work carried through the committee almost to its final form.

In 1945 the committee was enlarged by the election of five Old Testament scholars, and one more was added in 1947; for the last few years of its task the Old Testament section had a membership of fifteen. When the section had labored through its first revision of the entire Old Testament, it turned about and went through it all again, reconsidering, and sometimes altering its actions which in some cases lay ten years in the past. This second revision was more expeditious. Members of the entire committee were requested to send in lists of their corrections, and similar suggestions from members of the Advisory Board, to whom drafts had been sent, were welcomed. The procedure now was consideration of these lists and action upon them in book after book of the Old Testament. In the first revision decision was by majority vote; but in this final re-examination a two-thirds vote of the entire committee was required for every departure from the basic text, the votes of the New Testament members being recorded by mail. At the conclusion of this task, the results were submitted to a small subcommittee of the members, to take final action on punctuation, form of notes, consistency, and the like, and then to see the text through the press. This work alone consumed the full time of some of the subcommittee for more than a year.

The revision is issued with no sense of finality. Those who have labored over it for these fifteen years are far more painfully conscious of its shortcomings than others can possibly be. For many of the issues raised in the translation of the Old Testament there is simply no answer; the committee could only do the best possible, knowing full well that such best was inadequate. Further, any committee action is a compromise; no one is satisfied with all the revision; but at the worst a compromise has distinct advantages against the oversights and errors from which no individual translation can possibly be exempt. Yet the committee realize fully that a perfect translation of the Bible is, in the nature of the case, for ever an impossibility; we must be content with merely good and better translations, and may for a short time possess a best one. But the growth of living language entails that presently that best fades into eclipse. No one supposes or hopes that this version will serve for centuries to come. Its time is now. The committee has without stint poured its labor into it through these many years, sustained only by the faith that in the Bible God speaks to each succeeding age, and that our troubled time stands in dire need of clear utterance of the word of God.

(Source: William A. Irwin, "Method and Procedure of the Revision," in Luther A Weigle, editor, *An Introduction to the Revised Standard Version of the Old Testament*, copyright 1952. Reprinted by permission of Thomas Nelson, Inc.)

72. BANISHED WORDS: AN INDICATION OF THEOLOGICAL BIAS AND PRUDISHNESS?

In an earlier extract we saw the assertion that the translators of the RSV aimed at a theologically neutral translation. Many more conservative religionists remain convinced that it is a notable failure when judged by this standard. One of the more interesting charges of bias rests not so much on what the translation *says* but on renderings that it seems to *carefully avoid.* In the following extract William C. Taylor points to some of these as evidence of doctrinal bias and (ironically) as examples of a strange and unexpected prudishness as well.

"NO DOCTRINE OF THE CHRISTIAN FAITH HAS BEEN AFFECTED by the revision," says Professor F. C. Grant (Introduction Booklet on the RSV New Testament, p. 42). That is a matter of opinion. To my mind, many of the most vital doctrines have been fearfully affected. Saying a thing is so doesn't make it so. Such an affirmation or such a denial must be judged by the facts assembled. To write *son* and *spirit,* instead of *Son* and *Spirit* affects doctrinal teaching, in the passages where this occurs, as to two persons of the Trinity, just as would the change of *Our Father* to *our father.* Doctrines are dependent on words for their literary revelation. Can you think of any way truth can be conveyed in writing except in words? What happens, then, when a lot of the key words of revelation are thrown overboard, some entirely, others to a large degree? In this study we shall see the utter abandonment of great key words of the Scripture, in which much of its most vital truth is expressed, and later we shall note other ways in which vital doctrines are altered, revoked, corrupted, confused, enlarged, or diminished. Speaking in the same booklet (p. 59) of the responsibilities of translators, Walter Russell Bowie says: "That responsibility in the first place is to truth."

"CONVERT" A BANISHED VERB

Two verbs are several times, and in great key Scriptures, translated *convert* and *be converted* in the New Testament—but not in the RSV. In it the translators utterly banished the verb *convert,* though by a strange inconsistency they preserve *conversion* once (Acts 15:3.) The Nelson revisers have banished from their Bible *being converted.* Older versions, and many just as modern, used the word *turn* for the translation when physical acts are concerned, but *convert* when the soul turns to God and the right-about-face is inward and spiritual. They certainly are two very different senses of the verb and merit different translations. Other verbs obey this criterion. Why not the verb *convert? Turn* states a physical act. It might, in the process of time, be given great moral, revolutionary meaning. But it has not that meaning now, in itself. Here is a word that has been at the very forefront of conversion theology and evangelism. Now that is banished. We are given what very much looks like an anticonversion Bible . . .

REMISSION

Nine times we read in our King James Version of the "remission of sins." But the word is banished from the new Bible. No converting experience for man; no remission from God. "Remission of sins," for our translators, is taboo. Thayer gives this definition: "forgiveness, pardon of sins (properly, *the letting them go, as if they had not been committed*), remission of their penalty." Now that has been a part of our Christianity for centuries. Is it suddenly to be banished, as it were, by an all-powerful politburo? There is a vast difference between the forgiveness of sins and the remission of sins, in many cases. Forgiveness, for example, for the faithful child of God, may have to do merely with the renewing of fellowship, interrupted by the offense of sin, or the initiation of such fellowship for the forgiven sinner who for the first time enters into it. That is one thing. It is quite another thing to cancel the whole record and all its effects from consideration by divine justice, just as if the sins had never existed. This comes into view in the great experience of conversion, now also banished from the new Bible. Remission of sins links up with the great once-for-all aspects of salvation. It solves the sin problem in its judicial and eternal aspects. The modernist does not believe in those aspects. So he shut out of his new Bible the remission of sins. Only subjectivism is left to salvation. In many Scriptures, however, there is a finality about the divine decision that inevitably means far more than a decision about the fellowship involved. It is a judicial cancellation, not a fatherly forbearance and yearning alone. This is based on that. Think of Hebrews 10:18; "Now where *remission* of these is, there is no more offering for sin." In such contexts, a stronger translation than *forgiveness* is welcome, to give this eternal, final tone. The KJ translators might even have added Colossians 1:14 to the verses having *remission* in the translation; for there *remission* is the equivalent of the whole "redemption"—"redemption (through his blood)" the Berkeley Version has. The RSV never even notices the Textus Receptus reading here, though so eager, at times, to put in the margin trifling variants, when they detract from the critical text. In the new Bible, instead of the canceling of our sins, according to this great doctrine, we merely have the arbitrary cancellation of the word that sets forth the doctrine.

PROPITIATION

The banishment of this great gospel word is another attack on the objective aspects of redemption. Paul represents the Lord Jesus, set forth on Calvary in his blood, as a propitiation, and declares it available through faith. Then he shows the bearing of this on salvation of the saints who lived before Christ. And he gives this blessed declaration of the divine purpose in it all: "that he might be just and the justifier of him which believeth in Jesus" (Rom. 3:25, 26). That is the language of the temple sacrifices, and has a similar meaning. It joins the gospel of the Old Testament figurative ritual with the clear testimony of Paul's greatest literary exposition of his gospel, to the Romans. It is not easy for a just judge to forgive. The whole Bible witnesses to the objective need and the value before God of substitution by a sin-bearing sacrifice. It is folly and gross irreverence to try to make this aspect of divine justice degenerate into the false conception that God had to be made willing to save. God, out of his eternal willingness and the necessities of his universe as a reign of law in the moral realm, always felt the love that planned Calvary and accepted it, from the foundation of the world, as having atoning value, and so acted in view of its timeless meaning. All the Bible is eloquent with tribute to the eternal Father's love. He planned, prophesied, and executed all the sacrifice of the Son, to make possible a just remission of sins. Yet now, for the new Bible readers, both the propitiation of Christ and its remission of sins are gone. And that majestic purpose, "that he might be just and the justifier of him which believeth in Jesus," is queered, too, in the new Bible. It is watered down into a mere accessory statement: "it was to prove that he himself is righteous and that he justifies him who has faith in Jesus." That is a false translation, guts the gospel. It may be said that "expiation," the word used instead of what the Greek means, has a similar idea. Maybe so. But it may take a generation or two for it to soak in on the popular mind. And you never know what any word means to a modernist who cares to twist it...

CALVARY

Professor Craig boasts that the RSV has banished "Calvary" from the New Testament. Doubtful honor. I always remind my students: "You are not Adam."

Someone might well have said to these translators that they are not Adams, at the beginning of all translations. Some translations have created the English geographical names of sacred places. Calvary is now the English name of the place of the crucifixion. "In Luke 23:33, the 1611 Bible kept the word 'Calvary' which had been used since Tyndale for the place which is called a Skull" (Introduction booklet on the New Testament, p. 18). Tyndale died four centuries ago. If Calvary has been the English name of that lonely hill that long, these new translators will never be able to banish it. Did it occur to you, gentle reader, that these translators seem to be men who never sing? Have they never sung about Calvary? The Berkeley Version puts the word in parentheses, by the translation. The ASV says in the margin: "According to the Latin, *Calvary*, which has the same meaning.". . .

ADOPTION

This is a sore word for modernists. If all men, by nature, are the children of God, in any other sense than being created in his image, then how can they be adopted into his family? That, of course, is another judicial—"forensic," if I may use a hated and blessed word—word. It is vinegar in the nostrils of those who believe only in a subjective salvation, if any. Now the word *adoption* is found only five times in true translations of the New Testament. But in the new Bible the word has been banished from a majority of the passages where it occurs in the Greek, and it has been queered, as far as possible, in the substitute translation. (See Rom. 8:15, 23; 9:4; Gal. 4:5; Eph. 1:5.) Yet John Calvin made this one of the major truths he bore witness to as his hope, in his last will and testament. . .

CONFESS

It seems to me utterly meaningless to change Matthew 10:32 to "So every one who acknowledges me before men, I also will acknowledge. . .", and so in Luke 12:8. Now the same Greek verb, in Romans 14:11, is translated, "every tongue shall give praise to God"; but in Philippians 2:11, "every tongue confess." Both passages are cited in the margin as quoting Isaiah 45:23, which is translated, however, "To me . . . every tongue shall swear." How does one *swear to* a superior being? Once more, as so often, the Old Testament committee contradicted the New, whose translators contradicted each other. *Confess* is banished also from the wording of Romans 15:9. . .

SANHEDRIN

This is the great Jewish supreme court and senate. It is banished from the RSV, following the example of the KJ again. But it is retained even in the Basic Bible, at the cost of using another word, because it is essential as the name of an institution. There is no more excuse for calling the Jewish Sanhedrin merely "the council" than there is for calling the United States Senate that. The great, historic body is as much entitled to its name as you are to your name, or I to mine.

HADES

This word is banished from the translation of that key promise of our Lord, rendered merely "the powers of death shall not prevail against it." This is not translation. It tampers with the most important of all Scriptures in the meeting ground between Catholics and Protestants. Why have *Hades* everywhere else, if the word is incomprehensible, and then "liquidate" it here?

EARNEST

Next in the list of the banished is the noun *earnest*. It is a good word and not at all obsolete, according to the dictionary. But it is banished from the doctrine of the Holy Spirit, in which it played a notable part. An "earnest" is a partial payment, made in advance, sealing a contract to pay the whole. We receive now the Holy Spirit, a present "earnest," which both gives us in him, in advance, part of our heavenly inheritance, and seals the eternal covenant of grace. The Spirit, not any sacrament, is the seal of our covenant relation with God, and is the down payment of the spiritual riches promised us in salvation. In the place of this meaningful doctrinal word, arbitrarily banished from the new Bible vocabulary, we have only the word *guarantee*, in II Corinthians 1:22; 5:5, and Ephesians 1:14. Something like the theft of a jewel has been perpetrated. Its removal from the possession of the heirs of salvation, to whom it belongs, is a sin against them and against the Holy Spirit, whose revelation of himself is thereby impoverished . . .

VIRGIN

This sore subject so centers attention on the virgin birth of our Lord that many minor offenses, caused by prejudice against the word *virgin*, are overlooked. Take Acts 21:9. "Philip the evangelist . . . had four unmarried daughters, who prophesied." Luke did not say that. He said more: they were virgins. But the RSV translators banish that word, where they can do it without its being noticed, as the good housewife banishes cockroaches. Yet they are inconsistent, retaining the word when the NT cites Isaiah's great prophecy, but not in translating the prophecy. Banished is the classical parable title, "The Ten Virgins." When the next generation of students reads that in literature, they won't know what the author is talking about, provided this version also banishes the "virgin" versions. Inconsistent? Yes. They keep the abstract noun *virginity* (Luke 2:36). And they show what they think the word means when they use it of men. There they translate it "chaste" (Rev. 14:4). Well, if it means "unmarried," plus "chaste," isn't that *virgin*? II Corinthians 11:2 shows how hardheaded this fixed idea is. There they have rendered the word "bride." The whole emphasis of Paul is on the tempted, but unseduced, virginity of the Corinthian church. It is hardly that he is taking John the Baptist's place in a spiritual wedding as best man, "the friend of the bridegroom." Haven't the translators rather rushed things, confusing the betrothal and the wedding? They certainly overtranslated the word, in any case, out of stark prejudice, trying to banish a great word of revelation. The Psalms translator, where nothing is at stake, gives us the phrase "her virgin companions" (Psalm 45:14). While there was no celibacy in either Judaism or Christianity, it seems to me there must have been a gentle connotation of dedication to a career, on a voluntary basis, when Luke comments on a great evangelist's daughters, four of them, being "virgins," in their dedication to their prophesying. But you can't say that, brother Luke, not in the RSV. That is a banished word, so far as the RSV translators dared.

ONLY BEGOTTEN

This time the banishing has been eager. The word *begat* is so sexual. We must not have it in our Bible, no matter what the Bible itself says about it. So out it goes.

And even John 3:16 is a bit mutilated, to speed the banishing process. One of the beloved titles of the Son of God is lost in the shuffle. To me, he is not just "a son of God" (Mark 15:39). His sonship is set off from ours, in part, by his very title, *only begotten.* Yet, strangely, the antimessianic campaign against Psalm 2 has left the objectionable phrase "today have I begotten you." No earthly father ever could say that to his child. But the eternal Father said that and far more to Lord Messiah. Now the translators are great on fine points. They raise the doubt as to that being the real meaning of the word, and plump for *only.* Yet they know that the word *only,* in Greek as in English, is a very common word, and not a compound word. We have the simple word *only* forty-seven times in the New Testament. Once more, in John 3:16, would have made an even four dozen. But John did not want to say the simple word *only.* Why will the translators force him to? We have, in Greek, another compound word with *only — only-eyed, one-eyed.* Would they translate that *only?* No, they wouldn't dare. How dare they do this, then, to Jesus? Abbott-Smith says that the word is used in LXX and NT of both sons and daughters. The translators have never cared to say "only begotten daughter," "only begotten child" (Luke 8:42; 9:38). But I have no doubt that it is what the Jewish parents thought, with deep tenderness . . .

SEED

There is a lot of twisting and turning in trying to find some way to translate this seminal word of revelation and yet banish it from the translation. "The seed of the woman," in the proto-evangel, keeps the word (Gen. 3:15). From there on the mental gymnastics begin, to say it and not to say it. Any user of the RSV must feel an utter frustration in trying to follow the unity of messianic prophecy and its progressive revelation in the Scriptures. Here we are in a day of stark nakedness on the beaches, which is now transferred to home and streets. Never was there a time of such utter frankness of speech about all private matters of the world of youth. Courses are given in our universities concerning things only doctors used to talk about in private. Films and magazine articles blazon abroad the most intimate sex matters. Nothing is held back in conversation. And behold. A lot of university professors, in translating the Bible, the frankest of all books, act like a set of Victorian old maids and, with eyes averted, banish from the Bible some of its key words of revelation, because of what Dorothy Thompson calls their "prissiness." Radio and television can shout and sing the "Ave Maria," with its incessant tribute to "the fruit of thy womb," but in the RSV the very God of heaven cannot give the simplest revelation about the holy Seed of his promise. Nor can we who believe any longer "remember Christ Jesus, of the *seed* of David." That shocks our old-maidish translators beyond endurance. But I still wonder why they could use the word in Genesis 3:15, if they cannot bear it in the rest of the Bible. Is it all right to be immodest, if it only occurs one time? Professor Millar Burrows says (Introduction booklet on NT, p. 29): "The word 'seed' becomes in our revision 'children' (Mark 12:19–22 and parallels, Rom 9:29), 'offspring' (Gal. 3:16, 19, 29; Rev. 12:17), 'descendants' (John 8:33, 37; Rom. 4:13, 16, 18; 9:7–8; 11:1; II Cor. 11:22; Heb. 2:16), or 'posterity' (Luke 1:55; Acts 7:5–6; 13:23; Heb. 11:18); elsewhere, as the context allows, it is paraphrased by a different construction (Rom. 1:3; II Tim. 2:8), or omitted (Heb. 11:14), or retained (I Pet. 1:23)." Of course, this squeamish makeshift for a translation utterly wrecks all sense of many of these passages. What is given as the translation is *not* the translation and either makes no sense or a false sense. If words could have a Siberia, the RSV must have an icy habitat to which Bible words have been banished, and with sheer arbitrariness. And the version is in the "Authorized" succession, so you have no option but to abandon great Bible words of truth or abandon the RSV.

FORNICATION

It is typical of "a wicked and adulterous generation"—and that describes all generations—that the very wickedness it glories in, in practice, it seeks to make unmentionable in preaching, or even conversation of a moral nature. So we find a queer squirming and twisting as to the matter of the use or nonuse of the word above.

Fifty-five times, the noun and verb that state this sin occur in the New Testament. Yet the translators play hide-and-seek with its translation or banish it from their Bible. We read of "fornication" in Revelation 21:8; 22:15. Elsewhere, such sinners are just "immoral." Now there is a vast lot of "immorality" that is not fornication. Such old-maidish subterfuges are a flight from reason and truth, and about elemental morality. . . . But the Christian conscience will not abdicate. It will demand that we at least stand back and let God condemn fornication, and not a mere vague and nameless "immorality." In the RSV, the word that means fornication, every time, wobbles back and forth between translations and refusals to translate: "unchastity" in Matthew 5:32; "fornication" in Matthew 15:19; "immorality" in I Corinthians 5:1; "impure passion" in Revelation 14:8. Each of these translations takes its turn. How can a group of men retain their self-respect and be so fickle and unstable in their thinking and speech? . . .

SLAVES

This version is superior to many in giving, in some places, the word *slave* or *slaves* as it is in the Greek. There is a vast difference between *slave* and *servant*, and the facts ought to appear in the translation, either in the text or in a marginal note. It alleviates the contrast between those times and ours, if we know that in Matthew 18:23 the case is that of slaves. Naturally they could be sold for debt or treated as no hired servant could. What possible objection can there be to translating the facts? Doesn't everybody know that slavery was one of the evils of Bible times? Just so, in John 18:18, the abjectness of Peter's fall is seen in his companionship of slaves. Why not let the Bible say, *every time*, not just occasionally, its witness to the contemporary facts of life?

FLESH, CARNAL

Arbitrarily, unpardonably, frequently has the RSV substituted *body* for *flesh* and various adjectives for *carnal*. Ugly facts of human depravity and sin need the revealed vocabulary of their guilt and seriousness. Don't banish the vocabulary of evil. That doesn't get rid of the evil. We study some of these passages in other connections. One passage will illustrate both this term and *slaves*: "your earthly masters" (Eph. 6:5). The Greek has *your lords according to the flesh*. There is the contrast, between the lordship of Christ and the lordship that exists only according to the standards of the flesh. This both condemns slavery as a carnal regime and limits its sway to the physical. Translating the phrase as "earthly" loses the suggestiveness of the comparison. The point is, the Christian slave is free, in his inner being, *now* to have Christ as Lord. It isn't a question of a fully comprehensive lord-

he owner of the slave in this earthly regime or hope of a better regime
ty. Here and now the Christian slave is, in the inner realm, though not
f flesh, under the lordship of Christ. Changing the sentence structure,
ng the connotation of the words, and banishing *slave* from the transla-
e times it occurs (including the verb form once), even in this passage,
how slavish the RSV is to the KJ, even at this point, and to the hesitations
that cowed the KJ translators and later ones. There is an unholy trinity: "the world,
the flesh and the devil," and you don't make moral gains by denying the reality of
the triple evil.

(Source: William C. Taylor, *The New Bible: Pro and Con,* Vintage Press, New York: 1955,
pages 50–65, 69–70.)

IV. New Revised Standard Version

73. A PRELIMINARY REVIEW

Having examined elsewhere in this volume the theoretical case for
gender-neutral translations, the question naturally arises of how effectively
the theory can be implemented into practice. Although the New Revised
Standard Version of 1990 was the first major American translation to
openly embrace the approach, even it backed off from eliminating traditional "male" terms such as "He" and "Him" as descriptions of the Deity.
In regard to descriptions of *human beings,* however, it made a good faith
and thorough-going effort to comprehensively eliminate all such
language. Hence it can serve as a useful test case by which to judge the
actual effects of implementing such a translation theory.

In the following extract (written within a few months of the NRSV's
first appeareance) we find a "conservative" or "evangelical" critique which
lays heavy emphasis on the translation's alleged failure to "play fair" with
the original wording of the biblical text. It also points out that the alleged
theological modernism for which the original RSV was widely criticized is
even more inflammatorily present in its planned replacement. Both of
these themes are likely to become standard criticisms of the NRSV and to
minimize its use in the same quarters that rebelled at the Revised Standard
Version throughout its four decades of popularity.

The New Revised Standard Version was officially published in May, 1990. It was
issued in anticipation of it replacing its predecessor, the Revised Standard Version, which was first published in the late Forties and early Fifties, with minor
periodic "mini-revisions" since then.

This study was completed in the first month and a half after publication and
therefore will not be able to take advantage of prior work by others. Since the New
RSV is intended as the replacement of the original RSV, it is only fair to make the
standard of comparison these two versions. Hence the reader can take for granted

that any wording quoted for comparison is from the earlier RSV. (The use of any renderings from different translations will be specifically noted.)

There are a number of general patterns that characterize the New RSV New Testament. These include:

1. In descriptions of Jesus as "Christ" it prefers "Messiah," presumably on the grounds that the substitute wording is more understandable to the modern readers. Representative examples of this change include: Matthew 2:4; 11:2; 16:16, 20; 22:41; Mark 8:29; 13:21; 14:9; Luke 2:26; 3:15; 9:20; Acts 2:31, 36; 3:18; 7:31 (twice); etc.

2. Although the change is far from absolute, the New RSV freely replaces "gospel" with "good news": Matthew 4:23; Mark 1:1, 14–15; 10:29; 13:10; Luke 9:6; Acts 8:25, 40; 16:10; 20:24; 1 Corinthians 15:1; 2 Corinthians 8:18; 10:14. The replacement is even found in Mark 16:15. Technically this is accurate. However, "gospel" suggests a *body of thought,* a *system of thought.* "Good news" stresses the joyfulness that should be produced by it. Indeed our modern world is characterized by seeking the "*joy* of salvation" without any of the *obligations* that go with it. Hence in our day and age the stress on the "good news" being a *system of thought* ("gospel") would seem far more appropriate.

3. The RSV took considerable static for drifting from the Greek word order in its effort to make the translation do maximum service to English readers. When one compares the New RSV with the older one, however, the reader quickly grasps that the more recent effort has gone much, much further in its effort to rearrange sentence structure into a more natural "English speaking" style. Acts 1:20; 11:14; 15:24; 21:35; Rom. 14:1 are representative examples.

4. Modern time replaces that of the Jewish and Roman systems: "one in the afternoon" replaces "seventh hour" (John 4:52); "about noon" takes the place of "about the sixth hour" (John 19:14). Instead of "about the ninth hour of the day" we find "about three o'clock" (Acts 10:2) and for "third hour of the night" we find "nine o'clock tonight" (Acts 23:23).

5. Likewise, translating numbers and distance into modern terminology is of marked advantage to the reader. "Twice ten thousand times ten thousand" (Revelation 9:16) translates into (NRSV) "two hundred million." "One thousand six hundred stadia" will give quite a pause to anyone except an individual well versed in first century culture; the NRSV helps out considerably by rendering it, "about two hundred miles" (Revelation 14:20).

6. When Jewish temple "officers" are mentioned they are called by terms such as "police," "temple police," and "Jewish police": John 7:32, 45, 46; 18:3, 12; Acts 5:22, 26. Although it is likely that they did, indeed, perform police functions there clearly is the danger that we will transpose our *contemporary,* twentieth-century conception of what the word "police" means back into the first century. In our era "police" are representatives of the *state,* of the *government.* These first century "police" were representatives of the Jewish temple. "Temple police" would seem to be the best choice if the word "police" is to be used at all.

7. The New RSV has a liking for "deed(s) of power" as a replacement for "mighty works" (KJV and RSV: Luke 10:13; 19:37) and for "miracle(s)" KJV and RSV: Mark 9:39; Acts 2:22.

8. Many words of condemnation can rightly be laid upon the New RSV because of its partial collapse to militant feminism. However, any one reasonably acquainted with the writings produced by the extremist fringe of feminism is well aware that the homosexual lobby largely *overlaps that fringe.* They aren't identical but you will find few militant feminists who denounce homosexuality and, seemingly, few

gays (and lesbians in particular) who would denounce extreme feminism. Hence it comes as a considerable relief that the New Testament revisers have *not* capitulated to the demands of the homosexual lobby to downgrade the Biblical condemnation of their sin. Indeed, to refer to homosexuality as *"degrading* passions" (rather than "dishonorable passions," Romans 1:26) might indeed be taken as a *strengthening* of the criticism.

EXTREME FEMINISM

The New RSV will be most well known for its attempt to "degenderize" the Biblical text. I cringed at the thought, having had prolonged exposure with the textual mutilation that results in feminist "lectionaries"—collections of scripture reading (available if the reader has a strong stomach). It came as a considerable relief to discover that the process is carried out *only* in terms related to mankind, *not* the Deity. Hence God remains the "Father" and is described as "He." (There are exceptions to this but that's a different story.)

"He" is used in traditional translations (including the original RSV) in three ways: as a description of Deity; as a description of the male gender; as a description of both genders combined. Militant feminists insist that using "he" (and such terms as "man") to *include* the female leaves "many" women with a sense of being excluded. So the RSV purges the Bible of the latter usage and substitutes other terminology. This actually makes the problem worse. *Before* (including in the RSV) "he" included the female. Now it describes ONLY God and the male gender. Does this not give the Deity an even *greater masculine gender slant?* It strikes me that the feminists will have a (legitimate) field day when they criticize the NR3V on this score.

"De-gendering" where the Original is "Gender Free"

Since there is no reason to create needless offense there can be no objection to degenderization IF:

(1) the original wording *does* include both genders;

(2) it is NOT made into an absolute that requires the substitution of awkward, unnatural language or the replacement with non-gender terms NOT found in the original text.

The New King James is a fine example of considerable progress being made by respecting *both* feminist feelings *and* the need for textual integrity. In contrast the New RSV fails on this score. Although it is no where near as awkward as one might expect (since God was eliminated from the degendering process), exalting the principle into an ABSOLUTE one *does* result in ragged sounding language and the forced alteration of the surrounding text to make the process workable.

There can be *no question* that the New RSV has a *multitude* of odd sounding phrases due to its effort to appease the extreme militants. Some feminists insist that "we" (i.e. people at large) will get used to it—and perhaps so. However, *mutilating* the text is something no faithful Christian should *ever* get used to, even when it's in the interest of what he himself believes.

Even when the text is, indeed, "gender free" in the original to make it awkward reading or odd sounding *just to avoid using generic words like "he," "him," and "man"* sacrifices readability for a modern doctrinal orthodoxy. And it is wrong.

Here are a *few* examples that stuck out in my mind:

Text	New RSV	RSV
Matthew 4:19	"I will make you fishers of PEOPLE"	"fishers of men"
Acts 4:12	"There is no other name under heaven given AMONG MORTALS by which we must be saved"	"given AMONG MEN by which we must be saved"
Acts 5:38	"if this plan or this undertaking is of HUMAN ORIGIN, it will fail"	"is of men, it will fail"
Romans 14:18	"The one who thus serves Christ is acceptable to God and has HUMAN APPROVAL"	"and approved BY MEN"
2 Cor. 10:3	"we live as HUMAN BEINGS"	"we live in the world"
	"we do not wage war according to HUMAN STANDARDS"	"we are not carrying on a WORLDLY WAR"
	(cf. several such phrases in verses two to four)	
1 Thess. 2:4	"not to please MORTALS"	"not to please men"
1 Thess. 2:6	"nor did we seek praise from MORTALS"	"from men"
1 Thess. 2:13	"not as a human word"	"the word of men"

In 1 Timothy 2:5–6 we read: "For there is one God; there is also one mediator between God and HUMANKIND, Christ Jesus, HIMSELF HUMAN, who gave himself a ransom for all. . . ." Is this the way *real* people *normally* describe other members of the human species? Or isn't this an arbitrary style of writing adopted solely out of the theological "need" to appease militant feminists?

Additional examples could surely be given if we wished to take the time and the space. The NEW RSV will almost unquestionably be known for the *artificiality of its prose* on matters envolving both genders. Rather than drawing attention *away* from gender differences, the absolute commitment to *avoid* such terminology necessitates speech patterns not found in the real world.

"Degendering" IN SPITE OF the Original

A careful consideration of the New RSV's footnotes will reveal an ongoing pattern of "degenderizing" where faithfulness to the original would require a so-called "male" term. We speak, in particular, of the Greek word which the footnotes concede is "brothers." Yet in spite of this acknowledgment OTHER TERMS are used. "Brothers and sisters" (Romans 1:13; 8:12; etc.) *explains* the translation with nothing in the original to justify it beyond the "necessity" of avoiding any term that might be derided as "solely male." "Neighbor" (Matthew 25:40) etc. are all perfectly good Biblical words—but they are NOT the equivalent of "brethren." Each of these terms carries with it a *different* idea than that of "brethren." The only term that comes close is "comrades" (Revelation 12:10) and *that* carries too heavy an ideological weight to gain popularity.

Furthermore, IF ONE CAN REPLACE "MALE" TERMS THAT ARE IN THE ORIGINAL TEXT WITH "DEGENDERIZED" ONES, BY WHAT STANDARD CAN GOD HIMSELF BE EXEMPTED FROM SUCH TREATMENT? The New RSV refused to apply to God the same course of "degenderized" replacement that was applied to the human race. The ultra feminists will surely rake them over the coals for their inconsistency—and those of us who take the Bible seriously will *also* rake them over the coals, for allowing a modern theology to be more important to them than faithfulness to the original. There are many other things that can be said in regard to the tremendous impact of militant feminism upon the New RSV. Hence what we have covered should—rightly—be judged as just the tip of the iceberg.

DOCTRINAL PASSAGES AND PROOF TEXTS

Almost every major translation has a major rendering or two that scars itself upon the memory of the careful Bible student. The most infamous New Testament rendering of the New RSV will surely be John 1:14:

RSV	New RSV
"And the Word became flesh and dwelt among us, full of grace and truth; we have beheld his glory, glory as of the ONLY SON FROM THE FATHER."	"And the Word became flesh and lived among us, and we have seen his glory, the glory as of A father's only son, full of grace and truth."

WHY would "A father's only son" have unique "glory"? More important note that the reference is *shifted* from the heavenly father to a human father.

If that is difficult to absorb it comes as even a greater shock to discover that only a few verses later (John 1:18), that the testimony to the supernaturalness of Jesus *is strengthened beyond* the traditional reading:

RSV	New RSV
"No one has ever seen God; the only Son, who is in the bosom of the Father, he has made him known."	"No one has ever seen God. It is GOD THE ONLY SON, who is close to the Father's heart, who has made him known."

The proposed change certainly does not read very smoothly and sounds rather disjointed, which immediately makes one suspicious even though the theology is one that we would applaud. Furthermore, if John *did* originally write John 1:18 this way, who can doubt that the "father" in verse 14 *has to be* the *heavenly* Father? Laying aside our firm conviction that John was inspired of God, even an *un*inspired writer could hardly do otherwise if he were to enjoy credibility with his reader.

In its traditional wording, Hebrews 2:6-8 makes an obvious and telling argument for the superiority of Jesus to the angels. In the interest of "degenderizing" the text the wording is so generalized to mankind as a whole that one wonders why the Hebrews writer found it relevant at all. (Which is a good indication that the New RSV is reading it in a dramatically different fashion than the Biblical writer.)

In John 7:39 an assertion that the Holy Spirit had not been given to the apostles is altered into what appears to be a denial that the Spirit was even in existence, "FOR AS YET THERE WAS NO SPIRIT, because Jesus was not yet glorified." Nor can a mental gloss of "given" be inserted after the word Spirit in the contested phrase, for then we would have the reading which a New RSV footnote explicitly rejects.

For some reason in regard to the church contribution in I Corinthians 16 translators have commonly moved in an interpretative direction that could easily imply that the laying by in store was done IN EACH INDIVIDUAL'S PRIVATE HOME rather than in the assembly. Since Paul's purpose in calling for the contributing was to AVOID needing to take up a collection when he arrived, this would have defeated his purpose. The New RSV seems to intend this approach but then adds a new—and startling alteration of the standard of giving ("as he may prosper"): "On the first day of every week, each of you is to put aside and save WHATEVER EXTRA YOU EARN, so that collections need not be taken when I come."

Socialist-type terminology is imposed upon the voluntary communal sharing in the Jerusalem church (Acts 4:32): "Now the whole group of those who believed were of one heart and soul, and no one claimed PRIVATE OWNERSHIP OF ANY POSSESSIONS, but everything they owned was held in common." Peter's rebuke of Ananias included a remark that showed they DID have private property, "While it remained unsold, did it not REMAIN YOUR OWN? And after it was sold, were not the proceeds at YOUR disposal?" (Acts 5:4)

In the New RSV, Acts 15:22 does far more than assert that the entire Jerusalem congregation *agreed* with a letter being sent to the Gentile converts; in this version it sounds as if the church *had the veto power* over the decision. "Then the apostles and the elders, with the *consent* of the whole church, decided to choose men from among their members and to send them to Antioch with Paul and Barnabas. . . ."

Instead of reading that unbelievers "believed" and did such and such, in several places it is rendered "*became* believers AND" did such and such (Acts 11:21 for example).

In certain passages that refer to how unbelievers "believed" we read that they "BECAME believers" (Acts 13:48; 14:1). This shifts the emphasis from what they DID ("believed") to what they BECAME ("*became* believers"). In Acts 18:8 this is taken one step further: "many of the Corinthians who heard Paul BECAME believers AND WERE BAPTIZED." If they were "believers" BEFORE baptism weren't they SAVED *before* baptism? Certainly we can anticipate this construction being put upon it by some defending salvation by faith only. The same odd terminology is found in Acts 11:21: "a greater number BECAME believers AND turned to the Lord." Hence we could use this passage and ask, "Were they saved before they turned to God?"

In the original RSV of Acts 22:16 the connection between baptism and salvation seems clear: "Rise and be baptized, and wash away your sins, calling on his name." The New RSV could be read as diluting this point: "Get up, be baptized, and have your sins washed away, calling on his name." Perhaps this impression is caused by the omission of the first "and," which results in a (verbally) more rigid distinction between the parts of the verse: Get up/be baptized/have your sins washed away . . . as if each is a *distinct* act, with minimum connection with each of the following acts.

In Romans 11:20: (New International Version) we read, "you stand by faith." Essentially the same is asserted in the New American Standard, "you stand by your faith." However both the old and New RSV's seem determined to "bend" the passage in a "faith only" direction. The RSV reads: "stand fast ONLY through faith" while the New RSV seems to inch, verbally, a little further out on that limb: "stand ONLY through faith."

I Timothy 4:1 is always a relevant text in any discussion of the possibility of apostasy, "Now the Spirit expressly says that in later times some will DEPART FROM the faith . . ." (RSV). The New RSV is open to the interpretation that it only pictures a verbal denial of the faith, rather than one affecting the individual's entire lifestyle: "Now the Spirit expressly says that in later times some will DE-NOUNCE the faith . . . ."

In Jude, verse 5, the Old Testament people of God are held up as a warning to Christians. Astoundingly, the New RSV inserts into the text a declaration of their *irrevocable salvation*; "Now I desire to remind you, though you are fully informed, that the Lord, who ONCE FOR ALL SAVED A PEOPLE out of the land of Egypt, afterward destroyed those who did not believe." It does not take a committed atheist to see here a contradiction between the first half of the verse and the concluding words!

An apparent allusion to the name of Christian ("that honorable name by which you are called," James 2:7) is shifted in such a way as to suggest, instead, a priestly-type benediction having been received, "Is it not they who blaspheme the excellent name that was INVOKED OVER YOU?" (cf. similar terminology in Acts 15:17.)

There *are* a *few* good doctrinal readings in this translation. The "first day of EVERY week" (I Corinthians 16:2) is praiseworthy but they've ruined the rest of the verse, even adding their own unique MISconstruction of giving as one has prospered.

In the often misused and misunderstood Pauline prediction of the ending of the miraculous we read, "But when the COMPLETE comes, the partial will come to an end"; I Corinthians 13:10. "Complete" is a definite improvement over "perfect," which is often misinterpreted as a reference to the return of the "perfect," Man, Christ Jesus.

I Peter 3:21 comes through more understandable than in some translations, "And baptism, which this PREFIGURED, now saves you . . ."

The inadequacies are clearly more numerous — and important — than the improvements.

BAD RENDERINGS

There are a number of bad renderings that have nothing to do with what would normally be called "doctrinal" matters. These fall into two categories: (1) inadequate renderings and (2) interpretative renderings.

Inadequate Renderings

To say that "Mary had been ENGAGED to Joseph" (Matthew 1:18) certainly does not carry with it the implications of her being "*betrothed*" to him. How would a divorce have been required if "engagement" was all that was involved?

In Matthew 2:6 the description of Jesus as a "shepherd" does not go well with the idea just mentioned in the verse of His being "a ruler." "Govern" (as in the RSV) fits better.

In a context of the miraculous "Is it lawful to CURE on the sabbath?" (Matthew

12:10) seems inferior to the RSV's "Is it lawful to HEAL on the sabbath?" Although either term could be used of miraculous renewal of health, "cure" seems (at least in my personal judgment) to suggest more of what we get from a doctor rather than that of a miracle.

In the picture of the judgment day found in Matthew 25:32 it is stated that, "He will SEPARATE PEOPLE FROM ONE ANOTHER." The RSV here is both non-gendered AND better, "Before him will be gathered all the nations, and he will separate THEM one from another as a shepherd separates the sheep from the goats."

In the discussion of "unclean" foods, Jesus mentions how the body digests the food and then eliminates it (Mark 7:19, "enter . . . his stomach and so passes on"). The New RSV substitutes, "since it enters, not the heart, but the stomach, and goes out INTO THE SEWER."

In Mark 9:15 we find, "When the whole crowd saw him, they were IMMEDI- ATELY OVERCOME WITH AWE, and they ran forward to greet him." This is certainly a more dramatic reading than "immediately . . . they were greatly amazed" but it introduces a serious problem: If they were "*overcome* with awe" how did they summon the resources to run "forward to greet him"?

As a description of the solemn Passover, "feast" (RSV) is fine but the NRSV's "FESTIVAL," brings to mind visions of Mardi Gras and self-indulgence. (Mark 14:1) At the *minimum* it suggests a time of joy and happiness rather than that of a solemn memorial.

Furthermore since it was "the festival of UNleavened Bread" (Mark 14:1) the pancake like flat sheet of bread was hardly like what we think of when we hear the expression "a LOAF of bread," (Mark 14:22). The RSV wisely left it, simply, as "bread."

A "palace" (RSV) covers a wide variety of expensive and even regal residences, but the NRSV's "castle" would seem to suggest a *medieval* image in particular (Luke 11:21).

In one of Christ's post-resurrection appearances (Luke 24:39), Jesus reassured His apostles, "a SPIRIT has not flesh and bones." In the New RSV this reads, "A GHOST does not have flesh and bones." "Ghost" suggests the image of white sheets and haunted houses. The apostles may well have thought they were beholding a *vision* — but a *ghost*???

Of the immense hostility between Jews and Gentiles we read (John 4:9), "For Jews have NO DEALINGS with Samaritans." The NRSV, rather incredibly, alters this to, "Jews do NOT SHARE THINGS IN COMMON with Samaritans." This substitutes a rather restrained assertion of difference for the candid assertion of hostility.

In Acts 16:17 the gospel preached by Paul is called "THE way of salvation." An infidel could have a field day with the small but significant alterations of this in the NRSV to, "A way of salvation."

In 2 Corinthians 8 and 9 Paul mentions the contribution for the needy brethren back in Palestine. It was for the "relief of the saints" (8:4); it involved an "offering for the saints" (9:1). To change both of these expressions to "ministry to the saints" is needlessly less precise.

In the discussion of the Christian graces in 2 Peter 1, Christians are instructed to "SUPPORT your faith" with these (1:5). In other words BENEATH/UNDER- LYING our faith are these virtues. The RSV (along with other translations) notes that Christians are to "SUPPLEMENT your faith" with these virtues. In other words faith is the *beginning* point rather than the ending. The verse *can* be read as making the virtues the support *beneath* one's faith but our initial impression would seem to be a more natural one.

Interpretative Renderings

These are cases where the text may WELL intend to imply a certain point but rather than leave it to exegesis, the translators *insert it directly into the text itself*. In other cases one (of multiple possibilities) is singled out as *the* meaning rather than leaving the ambiguity found in the actual text. Even though their choice of interpretation may well be right (at least in some cases) this again replaces translation with exegesis. For example:

"I will not SPARE them" (2 Corinthians 13:2) carries with it several applications. The NRSV's "I will not be LENIENT'" covers only one of them.

The fact that God "KEEPS him" who is born of God (1 John 5:18) *includes* the fact that He "PROTECTS them" but is not limited to it.

"To SERVE the living God" (Hebrews 9:14) means that our entire life style is altered. Hence it covers far more territory than merely "to WORSHIP the living God."

A classic interpretation of "husband of one wife" (1 Timothy 3:2; Titus 1:6) is "married only once." Valid or not it places what is only one possible interpretative option into the sacred text itself.

1 Peter 1:13 is guilty of a double offense: "Gird up your minds" *can* mean "prepare your minds for action"; "be sober" *can* mean "discipline yourself." However, both phrases can carry additional implications as well. The instruction to "glorify God on the day of visitation" (1 Peter 2:12) may be *interpreted* as meaning, "glorify God when he comes to *judge*." However, the NRSV makes the mistake of making that its "translation" rather than leaving it to the commentator.

Many other faults are found in the NRSV. These are only a sampling of its problems.

(Source: Roland Worth, Jr., *The New RSV: A Preliminary Review*, Richmond, Va: 1990.)

V. *New English Bible*

74. CONSCIOUSLY A NEW TRANSLATION RATHER THAN A REVISION

Most major translations claim to be revisions of the King James Version. Those who produced the New English Bible consciously set out, in their own words, to produce "a genuinely new translation." They stressed the word "translation," insisting that they avoided producing a paraphrase or commentary. Its critics, however, have vigorously objected that in actual practice this goal was abandoned (such as in rendering "first day of the week" by the interpretive/commentary phrase "Saturday night" in Acts 20:7). To those less doctrinally oriented, perhaps the biggest practical objection lies in the fact that the NEB tends to fall into "British English" as contrasted with "American English." Much the same problem limited the appeal of the English Revised Version on the American side of the Atlantic.

In the following extract, the translators describe their work and their evaluation of the results.

It is just three hundred and fifty years since King James's men put out what we have come to know as the Authorized Version. Two hundred and seventy years later the New Testament was revised. The Revised Version, which appeared in 1881, marked a new departure especially in that it abandoned the so-called Received Text, which had reigned ever since printed editions of the New Testament began, but which the advance of textual criticism had antiquated. During the eighty years which have passed since that time, textual criticism has not stood still. There is not, however, at the present time any critical text which would command the same degree of general acceptance as the Revisers' text did in its day. The present translators therefore could do no other than consider variant readings on their merits, and, having weighed the evidence for themselves, select for translation in each passage the reading which to the best of their judgement seemed most likely to represent what the author wrote. The translators are well aware that their judgement is at best provisional, but they believe the text they have followed to be an improvement on that underlying the earlier translations.

So much for the text. The next step was the effort to understand the original as accurately as possible, as a preliminary to turning it into English. During the past eighty years the study of the Greek language has no more stood still than has textual criticism. In particular, our knowledge of the kind of Greek used by most of the New Testament writers has been greatly enriched since 1881 by the discovery of many thousands of papyrus documents in popular or non-literary Greek of about the same period as the New Testament. it would be wrong to suggest that they lead to any far-reaching change in our understanding of the Greek of the New Testament period, but they have often made possible a better appreciation of the finer shades of idiom, which sometimes clarifies the meaning of passages in the New Testament. Its language is indeed in many respects more flexible and easy-going than the Revisers were ready to allow, and invites the translator to use a larger freedom.

Our task, however, differed in an important respect from that of the Revisers of 1881. They were instructed not only to introduce as few alterations as possible, but also 'to limit, as far as possible, the expression of such alterations to the language of the Authorized and earlier English Versions.' Today that language is even more definitely archaic, and less generally understood, than it was eighty years ago, for the rate of change in English usage has accelerated. The present translators were subject to no such limitation. The Joint Committee which promoted and controlled the enterprise decided at the outset that what was now needed was not another revision of the Authorized Version but a genuinely new translation, in which an attempt should be made consistently to use the idiom of contemporary English to convey the meaning of the Greek. This meant a different theory and practice of translation, and one which laid a heavier burden on the translators. Fidelity in translation was not to mean keeping the general framework of the original intact while replacing Greek words by English words more or less equivalent. A word, indeed, in one language is seldom the exact equivalent of a word in a different language. Each word is the centre of a whole cluster of meanings and associations, and in different languages these clusters overlap but do not often coincide. The place of a word in the clause or sentence, or even in a larger unit of thought, will determine what aspect of its total meaning is in the foreground. The translator can hardly hope to convey in another language every shade of meaning that attaches to the word in the original, but if he is free to exploit a wide range of English words covering a similar area of meaning and association he may hope to carry over the meaning of the sentence as a whole. Thus we have not felt obliged (as did the Revisers of 1881) to make an effort to render the same Greek word everywhere by the same English word. We have in this respect returned to the wholesome practice of King James's men, who (as they expressly state in their preface) recognized no such obligation. We have conceived our task to be that of understanding the original as precisely as we could (using all available aids), and then saying again in our own native idiom what we believed the author to be saying in his. We have found that in practice this frequently compelled us to make decisions where the older method of translation allowed a comfortable ambiguity. In such places we have been aware that we take a risk, but we have thought it our duty to take the risk rather than remain on the fence. But in no passage of doubtful meaning does the rendering adopted represent merely the preference of any single person.

The Joint Committee appointed a panel of scholars, drawn from various British universities, whom they believed to be representative of competent biblical scholarship in this country at the present time. The procedure was for one member of the panel to be invited to submit a draft translation of a particular book or group of books. This draft was circulated in typescript to members of the panel for their consideration. They then met together and discussed the draft round a table, verse by verse, sentence by sentence. Each member brought his view about the meaning of the original to the judgement of his fellows, and discussion was continued until they reached a common mind. There is probably no member of the panel who has not found himself compelled to give up, perhaps with lingering regret, a cherished view about the meaning of this or that difficult or doubtful passage. But each learned much from the others, and from the discipline of working towards a common mind. In the end we accept collective responsibility for the interpretation set forth in the text of our translation.

It should be said that our intention has been to offer a translation in the strict sense, and not a paraphrase, and we have not wished to encroach on the field of the commentator. But if the best commentary is a good translation, it is also true that every intelligent translation is in a sense a paraphrase. But if paraphrase means taking the liberty of introducing into a passage something which is not there, to elucidate the meaning which is there, it can be said that we have taken this liberty only with extreme caution, and in a very few passages, where without it we could see no way to attain our aim of making the meaning as clear as it could be made. Taken as a whole, our version claims to be a translation, free, it may be, rather than literal, but a faithful translation nevertheless, so far as we could compass it.

In doing our work, we have constantly striven to follow our instructions and render the Greek, as we understood it, into the English of the present day, that is, into the natural vocabulary, constructions, and rhythms of contemporary speech. We have sought to avoid archaism, jargon, and all that is either stilted or slipshod. Since sound scholarship does not always carry with it a delicate sense of style, the Committee appointed a panel of literary advisers, to whom all the work of the translating panel has been submitted. They scrutinized it, once again, verse by verse and sentence by sentence, and took pains to secure the tone and level of language appropriate to the different kinds of writing to be found in the New Testament, whether narrative, familiar discourse, argument, rhetoric, or poetry. But always the overriding aims were accuracy and clarity. The final form of the version was reached by agreement between the two panels.

No one who has not tried it can know how impossible an art translation is. Only those who have meditated long upon the Greek original are aware of the richness and subtlety of meaning that may lie even within the most apparently simple sentence, or know the despair that attends all efforts to bring it out through the medium of a different language. Yet we may hope that we have been able to convey to our readers something at least of what the New Testament has said to us during these years of work, and trust that under the providence of Almighty God this translation may open the truth of the scriptures to many who have been hindered in their approach to it by barriers of language.

(Source: Introduction, *New English Bible: New Testament,* copyright the Delegates of the Oxford University Press and the Syndics of the Cambridge University Press, 1961, 1970. Reprinted by permission.)

VI. *New American Standard Bible*

75. UPDATING AN OLD CLASSIC

The New American Standard Bible intentionally walks in the footsteps of the original turn-of-the-century American Standard Version. It consciously labors to duplicate its literalness in translation, while taking into consideration the latest textual evidence and the need to express it in a readable fashion.

S. H. Sutherland, the president of the Lockman Foundation (which financed and brought out the NASB), describes in the following extract the purposes that lay behind the effort.

The New Testament of the *New American Standard Bible* was produced and copyrighted by the Lockman Foundation in 1963. The whole Bible was released in 1971.

The *New American Standard Bible* was translated with the conviction that the words of Scripture as originally penned were inspired by God. Since they are the eternal words of God, the Holy Scriptures speak with fresh power to each generation, to give wisdom that leads to salvation, that men may serve God to the glory of Christ.

The translators had a twofold purpose in completing this translation: to adhere as closely as possible to the original languages of the Holy Scriptures, and to make the translation in a fluent and readable style according to current English usage. It required an aggregate total of nine years and seven months for the 58 scholars, expert in biblical languages, to complete the major task of researching and translating the many documents that resulted in the final text.

Because this translation follows the principles used in the translation of the American Standard Version of 1901, known as "the rock of biblical honesty," it is named the *New American Standard Bible.* It was completed in adherence to a four-fold aim, and as we glimpse these aims individually we can see why each is important.

The first aim was: "This translation shall be true to the original Hebrew and Greek." Dr. W. A. Criswell, noted Southern Baptist pastor, stated in *Why I Preach the Bible Is Literally True:* "There are those who speak of the inspiration of ideas as though the words were not particularly significant. They speak of the inspiration of ideas instead of the inspiration of words. But we cannot escape the equally vital significance of words.... The self-disclosure and the revelation was made in words. It was not in the general realm of ideas.... We cannot have melody without music or mathematics without numbers. Neither can we have a divine record of God without words, and if that divine record is to be a true revelation of God, it must be without error. It must be infallibly correct."

A formal equivalence test, which discovers how close a Bible translation is to the original words of Holy Scripture, was recently completed. Those Bibles tested included the most popular modern Bibles. This test indicated that the *New American Standard Bible,* as a word-by-word translation, deviates less from the original languages than any other modern Bible tested.

The second aim that guided the translation process was: "It shall be grammatically correct." Many hours were spent in rendering the grammar and terminology in contemporary English. When it was felt that the word-for-word literalness of the translation was unacceptable to the modern reader, a change was made in the direction of a more current English idiom. In these instances, the more literal rendering has been preserved in the margin.

Words are the vehicle of thought, and most languages, especially the English, have a flexibility which economic and cultural progress utilizes. Passing time, with myriads of inventions and innovations, automatically renders obsolete and inexpressive many words that once were in acceptable usage.

The ever-present danger of stripping divine truth of its dignity and original intent was prominently before the minds of the producers at all times. The editorial board therefore was staffed with Greek and Hebrew scholars as well as leading pastors of Bible-believing churches.

The third aim that guided the translators was: "It shall be understandable to the masses." To make God's original revelation understandable to the masses, the translators used marginal readings. In addition to the more literal renderings, the marginal notations have been made to include alternate translations, readings of variant manuscripts, and explanatory equivalents of the text. Only such notations have been used as have been felt justified in assisting the reader's comprehension of the terms used by the original Author. The enthusiastic response of the general public to the *New American Standard Bible* bespeaks the value of this care in making the translation understandable.

The fourth of the four-fold aim was: "This translation shall give the Lord Jesus Christ His proper place, the place which the Word gives Him; no work will ever be personalized." This aim adheres to the goal stated in Colossians 1:18, "so that He Himself (speaking of Christ) might come to have first place in everything."

F. Dewey Lockman, founder of the Lockman Foundation, believed that God made funds available through the claiming of God's promise in Malachi 3:10, "'Bring the whole tithe into the storehouse, so that there may be food in My house, and test Me now in this,' says the LORD of hosts, 'if I will not open for you the windows of heaven, and pour out for you a blessing until there is no more need.'" Mr. Lockman believed that all any of us have to offer to God is our own availability. He believed that God made all of the $850,000 available for the major purpose of translating his Word. He often regretted that United States copyright laws make it mandatory for the producer's name to appear on the translation, because he most definitely believed that only Christ should be glorified by the translation of God's Holy Word.

Because of the fourth aim none of the 58 outstanding Christian scholars who worked on this monumental task have affixed their signatures to their work. If they had, there would be recognized some of the finest Greek and Hebrew New Testament and Old Testament scholars . . .

This four-fold aim was adopted in the beginning of this translation because the Board of the Lockman Foundation was impressed by the Holy Spirit that this was the direction to take. Each of the scholars who worked on this translation was led by the Holy Spirit to accept this responsibility of translation, and they voluntarily adopted the four-fold aim as the guide for their work. These men met in plenary sessions and prayerfully, under the leadership of God's Holy Spirit did the work God had placed before them. No interpretation was ever made by any one single person.

Among those who have been blessed by this translation are the following:

Harold L. Fickett, Jr., pastor, First Baptist Church, Van Nuys, California: "I am convinced that this translation is the most accurate of any on the market today. It is a must in the library of one who is meticulous in the study of the Word of God."

A world-renowned Bible teacher and author, Dr. Wilbur M. Smith: "In my opinion this is certainly the most accurate and the most revealing translation . . . that we now have. I intend to keep it on my desk for immediate access during the years that remain to me."

Duke K.McCall, president, Southern Baptist Theological Seminary, Louisville, Kentucky: "Because of the integrity with which the Hebrew and Greek text was translated, this new edition retains the great value of the original, literal translation. The changes made appear to retain accuracy while facilitating reading and understanding. This is a valuable new tool for a Bible student whose conviction of the inspiration of Scripture produces concern for precisely accurate translation of Hebrew and Greek text."

(Source: S. H. Sutherland, "New American Standard Bible," in *What Bible Can You Trust?* Copyright 1974 Broadman Press. All rights reserved. Used by permission.)

VII. New King James Version

76. PRESERVING THE GREEK TEXT BEHIND THE KING JAMES VERSION

The New King James Version's greatest virtue to many is the fact that it emphatically rejects the "critical" approach to establishing the Greek text. What may ultimately dissatisfy the same theological conservatives is the fact that it rejects both the "critical" text *and* the majority of manuscripts when necessary to preserve the text of the KJV. For example it includes in the main text the "three witnesses" addendum to 1 John

5:7–8, though it concedes in a footnote that, "only four or five *very late* Greek manuscripts contain these words."

Working within these self-assigned perimeters, it is undoubtedly an impressive translation. Perhaps part of this impressiveness is psychological in nature, caused by the translators' wise decision to conform their wording to "the thought flow of the 1611 Bible," thereby minimizing the difficulty of going from the original KJV to the NKJV.

In the following Preface the translators discuss the principles they worked from:

In 1786 the Catholic scholar, Alexander Geddes, said of the King James Bible, "If accuracy and strictest attention to the letter of the text be supposed to constitute an excellent version, this is of all versions the most excellent." George Bernard Shaw became a literary legend in our century because of his severe and often humorous criticisms of our most cherished values. Surprisingly, however, Shaw pays the following tribute to the scholars commissioned by King James: "The translation was extraordinarily well done because to the translators what they were translating was not merely a curious collection of ancient books written by different authors in different stages of culture, but the Word of God divinely revealed through His chosen and expressly inspired scribes. In this conviction they carried out their work with boundless reverence and care and achieved a beautifully artistic result." History agrees with these estimates. Therefore, while seeking to unveil the excellent *form* of the traditional English Bible, special care has also been taken in the present edition to preserve the work of *precision* which is the legacy of the 1611 translators.

Complete Equivalence in Translation

Where new translation has been necessary in the New King James Version, the most complete representation of the original has been rendered by considering the history of usage and etymology of words in their contexts. This principle of complete equivalence seeks to preserve *all* of the information in the text, while presenting it in good literary form. Dynamic equivalence, a recent procedure in Bible translation, commonly results in paraphrasing where a more literal rendering is needed to reflect a specific and vital sense. For example, references to Christ in some versions of John 3:16 as "only Son" or "one and only Son" are doubtless dynamic equivalents of sorts. However, they are not actual equivalents of the precisely literal "only begotten Son," especially in consideration of the historic Nicene statement concerning the person of Christ, "begotten, not made," which is a crucial Christian doctrine.

In keeping with the principle of complete equivalence, it is the policy to translate interjections which are commonly omitted in modern language renderings of the Bible. As an example, the interjection *behold*, in the older King James editions, continues to have a place in English usage, especially in dramatically calling attention to a spectacular scene, or an event of profound importance such as the Immanuel prophecy of Isaiah 7:14. Consequently, *behold* is retained for these occasions in the present edition. However, the Hebrew and Greek originals for this word can be translated variously, depending on the circumstances in the passage. Therefore, in addition to *behold*, words such as *indeed, look, see,* and *surely* are also rendered to convey the appropriate sense suggested by the context in each case.

In faithfulness to our readers, it has seemed consistent with our task to cooperate with competent scholars who are governed by the biblical principle of divine authorship of the Holy Scriptures. Therefore, all participating scholars have signed a document of subscription to the plenary and verbal inspiration of the original autographs of the Bible...

The Style

Students of the Bible applaud the timeless devotional character of our historic Bible. Yet it is also universally understood that our language, like all living languages, has undergone profound change since 1611. Subsequent revisions of the King James Bible have sought to keep abreast of changes in English speech. The present work is a further step toward this objective. Where obsolescence and other reading difficulties exist, present-day vocabulary, punctuation, and grammar have been carefully integrated. Words representing ancient objects, such as *chariot* and *phylactery,* have no modern substitutes and are therefore retained.

A special feature of the New King James Version is its conformity to the thought flow of the 1611 Bible. The reader discovers that the sequence and identity of words, phrases, and clauses of the new edition, while much clearer, are so close to the traditional that there is remarkable ease in listening to the reading of either edition while following with the other.

In the discipline of translating biblical and other ancient languages, a standard method of transliteration, that is, the English spelling of untranslated words, such as names of persons and places, has never been commonly adopted. In keeping with the design of the present work, the King James spelling of untranslated words is retained.

King James doctrinal and theological terms, for example, *propitiation, justification,* and *sanctification,* are generally familiar to English-speaking peoples. Such terms have been retained except where the original language indicates need for a more precise translation.

Readers of the Authorized Version will immediately be struck by the absence of several pronouns: *thee, thou,* and *ye* are replaced by the simple *you,* while *your* and *yours* are substituted for *thy* and *thine* as applicable. *Thee, thou, thy,* and *thine* were once forms of address to express a special relationship to human as well as divine persons. These pronouns are no longer part of our language. However, reverence for God in the present work is preserved by capitalizing pronouns, including *You, Your,* and *Yours,* which refer to Him. Additionally, capitalization of these pronouns benefits the reader by clearly distinguishing divine and human persons referred to in a passage. Without such capitalization the distinction is often obscure, because the antecedent of a pronoun is not always clear in the English translation...

The real character of the Authorized Version does not reside in its archaic pronouns or verbs or other grammatical forms of the seventeenth century, but rather in the care taken by its scholars to impart the letter and spirit of the original text in a majestic and reverent style.

The Format

The format of the New King James Version is designed to enhance the vividness and devotional quality of the Holy Scriptures:

—Subject headings assist the reader to identify topics and transitions in the biblical content.

—Words or phrases in *italics* indicate expressions in the original language which require clarification by additional English words, as also done throughout the history of the King James Bible.

—Verse numbers in bold type indicate the beginning of a paragraph.

—*Oblique type* in the New Testament indicates a quotation from the Old Testament.

—Poetry is structured as contemporary verse to reflect the poetic form and beauty of the passage in the original language.

—The covenant name of God was usually translated from the Hebrew as "LORD" (using capital letters as shown) in the King James Old Testament. This tradition is maintained. In the present edition the name is so capitalized whenever the covenant name is quoted in the New Testament from a passage in the Old Testament.

The Old Testament Text

The Hebrew Bible has come down to us through the scrupulous care of ancient scribes who copied the original text in successive generations. By the sixth century A.D. the scribes were succeeded by a group known as the Masoretes, who continued to preserve the sacred Scriptures for another five hundred years in a form known as the Masoretic Text. Babylonia, Palestine, and Tiberias were the main centers of Masoretic activity; but by the tenth century A.D. the Tiberian Masoretes, led by the family of ben Asher, gained the ascendancy. Through subsequent editions, the ben Asher text became in the twelfth century the only recognized form of the Hebrew Scriptures.

Daniel Bomberg printed the first Rabbinic Bible in 1516–17; that work was followed in 1524–25 by a second edition prepared by Jacob ben Chayyim and also published by Bomberg. The text of ben Chayyim was adopted in most subsequent Hebrew Bibles, including those used by the King James translators. The ben Chayyim text was also used for the first two editions of Rudolph Kittel's *Biblia Hebraica* of 1906 and 1912. In 1937 Paul Kahle published a third edition of *Biblia Hebraica*. This edition was based on the oldest dated manuscript of the ben Asher text, the Leningrad Manuscript B19a (A.D. 1008), which Kahle regarded as superior to that used by ben Chayyim.

For the New King James Version the text used was the 1967/1977 Stuttgart edition of *Biblia Hebraica*, with frequent comparisons being made with the Bomberg edition of 1524–25. The Septuagint (Greek) Version of the Old Testament and the Latin Vulgate were consulted. In addition to referring to a variety of ancient versions of the Hebrew Scriptures, the New King James Version also draws on the resources of relevant manuscripts from the Dead Sea caves. In a few places where the Hebrew is difficult or obscure and where information is now available to resolve the difficulties, the New King James Version follows the Hebrew text; otherwise the King James rendering is retained. Significant variations are recorded in footnotes.

The New Testament Text

There is more manuscript support for the New Testament than for any other body of ancient literature. Over five thousand Greek, eight thousand Latin, and many more manuscripts in other languages attest the integrity of the New Testament. There is only one basic New Testament used by Protestants, Roman Catholics, and Orthodox, by conservatives and liberals. Minor variations in hand copying have appeared through the centuries, before mechanical printing began in A.D. 1450.

Some variations exist in the spelling of Greek words, in word order, and in similar details. These ordinarily do not show up in translation and do not affect the sense of the text in any way.

Other manuscript differences, regarding the omission or inclusion of a word or a clause, and two paragraphs in the gospels, should not overshadow the overwhelming degree of *agreement* which exists among the ancient records. Bible readers may be assured that the most important differences in the English New Testament of today are due, not to manuscript divergence, but to the way in which translators view the task of translation: How literally should the text be rendered? How does the translator view the matter of biblical inspiration? Does the translator adopt a paraphrase when a literal rendering would be quite clear and more to the point? The New King James Version follows the historic precedent of the Authorized Version in maintaining a literal approach to translation, except where the idiom of the original language occasionally cannot be translated directly into our tongue.

The manuscript preferences cited in many contemporary translations of the New Testament are due to recent reliance on a relatively few manuscripts discovered in the late nineteenth and early twentieth centuries. Dependence on these manuscripts, especially two, the Sinaitic and Vatican manuscripts, is due to the greater age of these documents. However, in spite of their age, some scholars have reason to doubt their faithfulness to the autographs, since they often disagree with one another and show other signs of unreliability. The Greek text obtained by using these sources and related papyri is known as the Alexandrian Text.

On the other hand, the great majority of existing manuscripts are in substantial agreement. Even though many are late, and none are earlier than the fifth century, most of their readings are verified by ancient papyri, ancient versions, and quotations in the writings of the early church fathers. This large body of manuscripts is the source of the Greek text underlying the King James Bible. It is the Greek text used by Greek-speaking churches for many centuries, presently known as the *Textus Receptus,* or Received Text, of the New Testament.

Since the latter nineteenth century the theory has been held by some scholars that this traditional text of the New Testament had been officially edited by the fourth-century church. Recent studies have caused significant changes in this view, and a growing number of scholars now regard the Received Text as far more reliable than previously thought. In light of these developments, and with the knowledge that most textual variants have no practical effect on translation, the New King James New Testament has been based on this Received Text, thus perpetuating the tradition begun by William Tyndale in 1525 and continued by the 1611 translators in rendering the Authorized Version. Important textual variants are recorded in footnotes.

A newer group of New Testament scholars are persuaded that the best guide to a precise Greek text is the close consensus of the majority of Greek manuscripts. The Greek text obtained by using this rule is called the Majority Text, which is similar to the Received Text. At important places where the Majority Text or the Alexandrian Text differs from the Received Text, the variants are recorded in footnotes.

VIII. New International Version

77. A WIDE-BASED EVANGELICAL TRANSLATION

Far more so than either the New King James or New American Standard bible, the New International Version represents a strain of evangelicalism willing to abandon traditional wording in an effort to convey the biblical message in contemporary prose. Although it quickly became a major seller, it has been strongly denounced in some quarters because its freer renderings are considered as undermining biblical doctrines concerning man's nature that a more literal wording upholds.

Edwin H. Palmer, the executive secretary for the translation, points out the virtues he sees in the New Testament section:

Long before the present flurry of new English translations of the Bible, *The New International Version* had its beginnings. Back in the middle fifties, theologians who had a high view of Scripture explored the desirability and feasibility of a modern translation. Opinions were garnered from men of wide and diverse theological and denominational backgrounds. The consensus was that, in spite of the fine features of many translations, there was a need for an up-to-date translation that was faithful to the original language. Guidelines were formed and committees established, and in 1967, under the sponsorship of the New York Bible Society International (established in 1809), the actual work of the translation was launched.

A governing committee of fifteen—made up of theologians from different American colleges, universities, and theological seminaries—was established. Dr. Edwin H. Palmer, a former pastor in the Christian Reformed Church and professor of systematic theology at Westminster Theological Seminary, was chosen to be the Executive Secretary.

Over a hundred scholars—in Old Testament, New Testament, systematic theology, and English style—were selected to contribute to the translation. They represented a great number of denominations, such as the Baptist, Brethren, Church of Christ, Episcopal, Lutheran, Mennonite, Methodist, Nazarene, Presbyterian, and Reformed. Such a wide representation of so many different denominations and theological backgrounds has kept the NIV from a provincial, sectarian bias, making it transdenominational in character.

Not only does it cut across denominations at times, but also across the English-speaking nations. Men from the United States, Great Britain, New Zealand, Canada, and Australia have worked on it, giving it an international scope. Although a Commonwealth edition was published—one that would avoid American spellings and idioms—it is remarkable how few changes in wording had to be adopted for it. The NIV does have an international style, one that does not jar the ear of the Englishman, Australian, or American.

The working procedures also gave the NIV a distinctive character. Each book of the Bible was assigned to a team of scholars, some of whom had made that book their specialty either by teaching courses in it or writing a commentary on it. This team produced the first draft of the translation of that book. Next, an Intermediate Editorial Committee of at least five men went over the team translation, with constant reference to the Hebrew, Aramaic, and Greek. Their work then went to a General Editorial Committee, which rechecked it in relation to the original languages and made another thorough revision. Both the Intermediate and General Editorial Committees were composed of no fewer than five men — men who had often worked at a prior level of translation. This cross-fertilization helped to keep a unity of style.

Finally, the product of the General Editorial Committee went to the top committee of fifteen, which had the final responsibility of presenting to the New York Bible Society International an acceptable translation. They, too, went over every translation word by word, checking for accuracy, clarity, idiom, uniformity of style, and dignity.

Before and after the revision by the top committee, English stylists were called in to review meticulously the tentative translations. The translations were also sent out to the many editors and translators, as well as to various other people — young and old, educated and uneducated, ministers and laymen — to be tested for clarity and idiom.

This whole translation process was long and costly. But it helped to produce a mature translation, free from the idiosyncrasies of a single translator or small group of translators, and free from sectarian bias. Regardless of how good an individual translator may be, he has blind spots, foibles, and limited abilities. The risks involved in these problems can be safeguarded by having many pairs of eyes reviewing the same product.

The goals of the translators were fourfold:

1. *Accuracy.* Since all the translators had to subscribe to the belief in the inspiration and infallibility of the Bible, they desired to produce a translation that reflects precisely what God has written through the prophets and apostles. They are adverse to paraphrases and loose translations.

2. *Clarity.* Many people brought up on the King James Version believe they understand it. But the fact is that the archaic words and outmoded sentence structure seriously hamper most laymen — even though they do not realize it — from adequately understanding the rich truths of God's Word. Repeatedly, even the translators, who thought they knew what the Bible said, found that as they tried to put the original into modern English, they did not truly understand it either. And they were forced to translate in a new way so that the meaning of the original could be brought out clearly. However, this did not mean that they were at liberty to water down or alter hard-to-understand biblical truths. Those passages that had innately difficult ideas had to be left as difficult in English as they were in the Hebrew or Greek.

3. *Contemporary idiom.* The one question that was constantly asked during the translation process was: "But how would you say it today?" Again and again scholars, steeped in and mesmerized by the King James, tended to reproduce phrases that seemed natural to them because they had heard and read them so often. For example, the King James says, "Man shall not live by bread alone" (Matt. 4:4). The NIV translated it "on bread alone." Most people reared on the King James will ask: "Why change it? 'By' sounds so natural." Yes, it sounds natural if you have heard that proverb all your life in the King James language. But the question is: "How would you say it today?" Who would say that Japanese live "by fish,"

or Chinese "by rice"? Nobody, for the idiom is "on," not "by." So the question was asked repeatedly: "Is it idiomatic?" And because of the hypnosis the King James holds over most biblical scholars, it was necessary to have many scholars, stylists, and laymen tell the translators what sounded natural or what sounded strained to their ear.

4. *Dignity.* It would be possible for a translation to have these three characteristics and yet to lack dignity or to be coarse in expression. But one goal of the translators was to have a translation suitable, not only for private use, but also for public worship. They wanted one that has dignity without being stuffy, one that is so beautiful, clear, and accurate that a person would want to memorize from it. Calvin Linton, professor of English literature and dean of arts and sciences at George Washington University, expressed it when he said: "High on the list of stylistic characteristics of the NIV is a kind of economical integrity, a quality of simple dignity, of tightly drawn texture, 'wov'n close, both matter, form and stile,' to quote Milton in another connection. Here is no straining after catchy colloquialism, shirt-sleeve casualness, or perky slang."

An unintentional but noteworthy by-product of the working procedures and goals of the NIV is its familiarity together with freshness. As one reads it, he feels at home and not jarred by unusual expressions. There is a freshness to the translation, and yet "the comfort of a tested friendship" (Linton). If 1 Corinthians 13 or John 3 or John 14 are read apart from the King James, one will feel at home with it. Yet, if he will carefully compare these passages with the King James, he will find many improvements.

Source: Edwin H. Palmer, "New International Version," in *What Bible Can You Trust?* Copyright 1974 Boradman Press. All rights reserved. Used by permission.)

SIX

"Immersion" Translations

I. Alexander Campbell

Alexander Campbell's publication of the *Sacred Writings* (as he named the effort) can rightly be called a compiled New Testament. On the title page he pays tribute to the three eighteenth century translators on whose work he primarily relied: George Campbell, James Macknight and Philip Doddridge.

A British edition of a New Testament compiled from these three sources had been printed in 1818. An American edition was proposed but never came to pass. In Campbell's 1826 revision, he corrected some readings found in the 1818 printing on the basis of the three scholars' original, separately published efforts. In addition, where their work did not measure up to the standard Campbell desired, he freely utilized other translations (and his own efforts) to produce what he considered a better rendering.

Most prominent among the changes from the KJV was the replacement of "baptism" with "immerse" and "immersion." This reflected both his own understanding of the meaning of the Greek and the view of at least George Campbell and James Macknight as to the nature of first-century practice. (Neither of these latter two was a member of a church that practiced immersion.)

The word "Christ" is maintained as a proper name, but "Messiah" is substituted in other contexts. Since "hell" had become synonymous in much popular thought with a place of fiery punishment, it no longer functioned as a word that could properly describe the destiny of both the wicked and the righteous; hence he substituted the noncommittal word "hades." Since "church" had definite ecclesiastical overtones in many quarters, he followed an alternative approach used by centuries-earlier English translators and substituted the word "congregation." Since "ghost" now had the connotation of a spooky apparition, he substituted "Holy Spirit" for the KJV's "Holy Ghost."

Perhaps due to the very fact that he was such a devout believer in the inspiration of the scriptures, Campbell saw no reason to perpetuate words and phrases that the best evidence indicated were lacking in the original text. The questionable words were included but distinguished from the text by being printed in italics. (Old Testament quotations were also italicized but distinguished by being placed in quotation marks.) By the third edition (1832) Campbell went so far as to transfer most of the questioned elements to a separate appendix in the rear of the volume. His intellectual honesty can be seen in the fact that the Ethiopian's confession in Acts 8:37 is treated in this manner even though it was a pivotal text in his conflict with the Regular Baptists over the proper prerequisites of baptism.

Considering the period in which it was printed, the fact that Campbell could report 40,000 copies sold (as of 1842) must be taken as a sign of his version's popularity. It is normally assumed that the vast majority of its sales were among those associated with the reform movement that Campbell and Barton W. Stone were spearheading at the time.

78. USING ACCUSATIONS OF HERESY TO DESTROY THE TRANSLATION'S CREDIBILITY

The very fact that Alexander Campbell was responsible for the *Sacred Writings* was enough to discredit it in some quarters, for this Campbell was controversial spelled with a capital "C." If the identification with Alexander Campbell were not sufficient, then the orthodoxy of *George* Campbell (whose work Alexander had utilized) could be attacked, as noted in the following extract.

The New Testament

Some of the priests in Ohio, who pretend to great erudition, have raised an evil report against Campbell's translation of the four gospels, giving out that Dr. Campbell was a Socinian, and the head of a faction of this stamp in the Kirk of Scotland. This is a gratuitous slander. Such a charge was never before exhibited against Dr. George Campbell. Another person named Campbell did, half a century before Dr. Campbell's translation was published, raise some noise in the Kirk of Scotland about Socinianism. If the above slander was not invented by its author in Ohio, he should have known better than to have confounded two persons so essentially dissimilar in views—especially in a matter so important. I am not sure but that the same gentleman will be sorry to find that he was mistaken; for generally they who propagate an evil report wish it to be true.

—Editor.

(Source: Alexander Campbell, "New Testament," in *The Christian Baptist* (7 volumes in 1), 14th edition, Boswell, Chase & Hill, Cincinnati: 1870, pages 280–281.)

79. NO WORD OF GOD WITHOUT THE KING JAMES VERSION?

One of the abiding criticisms of all modern translations is the suggestion that without the KJV we do not truly have the word of God. Alexander
Campbell's version was rebuked with such reasoning, and in the following
extract he exposes the folly.

The Word of God.

So badly taught are many christians that they cannot think that any translation
of the scriptures deserves the title of the Word of God except that of king James.
The translators of the king's version did not themselves think so, as we have shown
most conclusively by publishing their own preface—on which preface we have
some remarks to make, at a more convenient time. But to the intelligent reader
no remarks are necessary to show that they had very different ideas of their version, from those which this generation have formed. Have the French, the
Spanish, the German, and all the nations of Europe, save the English, no Word
of God? If king James' version is the only Word of God on earth, then all nations
who speak any other language than the English, have no Revelation.

Much of the reasoning of both priests and people, on this subject, is as silly as
that of an old lady who, for many years, has been deprived of her reason, from
whom we heard the other day. She once had a sound judgment, and still has a
retentive memory, though she has not been *compos mentis* one day in twenty
years. Her husband was reading in the new version, the account of the cure of the
blind man (Mark viii. 24). He came to these words: "I see men whom I can distinguish from trees only by their walking." In the king's version, "I see men as trees,
walking." After reading these words he paused, and observed to the old lady, to
elicit a reply, "How much better this, than the old version." "That is a good explanation," said she, "but it is not the scriptures, not the Word of God." So our
good logicians reason.

I would thank some of those ignorant declaimers to tell us where the Word of
God was before the reign of king James! Had they no divine book before this good
king, in consequence of the Hampton Conference, summoned his wise men? Yes;
they had version after version, each of which, in its turn, ceased to be the "Word
of God" when a new one was given. This I say after the manner of these
declaimers. Our good forefathers, two hundred and fifty years ago, read and
preached from a different version, which they venerated in their day, as our com-
peers venerate James' Bible.—The English language has changed, and the original
tongues are better understood now than then. The common version is, as many
good and learned men have said, quite obsolete in its language, and in many places
very defective in giving the ideas found in the original scriptures. Taken as a
whole, it has outlived its day at least one century, and like a superannuated man,
has failed to be as lucid and as communicative as in its prime.

There is no version in any language that does not clearly communicate the same
great facts, and make the path of bliss a plain and easy found one; but there is an
immense difference in the force, beauty, clearness, and intelligibility of the
different versions now in use. And that king James' version needs a revision is just
as plain to the learned and biblical student, as that the Scotch and English used
in the sixteenth century, is not the language now spoken in these United States.

And this may be made as plain to the common mind, as it is that the coat which suited the boy of twelve, will not suit the same person when forty years old. As the boy grows from his coat, so do we from the language of our ancestors.

—Editor.

(Source: Alexander Campbell, "The Word of God," in *The Christian Baptist* (7 volumes in 1), 14th edition, Boswell, Chase & Hill, Cincinnati: 1870, page 570.)

II. American Bible Union

In 1834 Adoniram Judson translated the Bible into Burmese and substituted that language's equivalent of "immerse" and "immersion" for "baptize" and "baptism." With their attention thereby forced on the issue, the American Bible Society voted against publishing Judson's effort or any other translation that so rendered the Greek word "baptizo."

This put the Baptists in an embarrassing position. On the one hand they were firmly convinced that immerse and immersion were not only correct translations but, actually, the only correct translations. On the other hand many were fervent defenders of the KJV (which had used "baptize" and "baptism" instead) and had denounced Alexander Campbell's version, which had translated according to the Baptist conviction. Campbell rubbed a little salt into old wounds by publicly urging the Baptists not to allow their animosity toward him to be an excuse to abandon Judson's effort to more correctly translate "baptizo" into English.

80. A BAPTIST BLASTS "IMMERSION" TRANSLATIONS

As indignant Baptists became more and more upset at the rejection of Judson's Burmese version, a tide of sentiment was clearly rising in favor of an "immersion" translation. Among those just as indignant—but *against* such an effort—was a Baptist minister by the name of Octavius Winslow. In the "Christian Review" of March 1837, he vigorously attacked the proposal. Seeing that the idea showed no sign of dying a quick death, he prepared two additional essays, added them to the original critique, and brought out his studies in book form.

In the following extract, Winslow discusses some of his objections.

As far as we have succeeded in informing ourselves of the precise nature of the proposed alterations of the English text, a thorough system of expurgation is contemplated, which shall sweep away all the terms and forms of expression considered obsolete, and offensive to the refined taste of the age, remodel, and retranslate certain passages, with a more particular reference to the terms *baptize*, and *baptism* in the New Testament, to words considered more consonant with the original text. Dissenting as we solemnly and unequivocally do, from such a proposition, in addition to the unanswerable objections advanced in the leading chapter of this book, we respectfully solicit attention to the following: —

1. *The veneration and respect due to antiquity,* might be fairly urged as a reason, why the authorised English version of the Bible, should be permitted to remain as it is, unaltered and unimpaired. We are aware that the plea of antiquity, when urged in favour of any existing form of abuse, whether of a civil or religious character, is an invalid one, and that it has frequently been thus urged in defence of episcopacy and other ecclesiastical institutions, we are not ignorant. Still we honestly believe, that in the present case, it may be fairly and successfully pressed into the service of shielding this "venerable monument of learning, of truth and of piety," from the invasion of a well meaning, but a rash and unhallowed zeal. For more than two hundred years have we, as Baptists, stood by the side of this common version. It has formed the rallying point of the denomination, the vocabulary, from which we derived our name — the authority which we have at all times produced in support of the distinctive principles which that name involves — and to whose decision, unaided by lexicons or lexicographers, we have again and again, in and out our pulpits at home and abroad, submitted the question at issue between our Pedobaptist brethren and ourselves. We have united too with other portions of the Christian church in defending it from every form of attack to which it has been exposed; — we have battled *with* it and battled *for* it, responding to the saying of Chillingworth — the watch-word of the Christian camp, "THE BIBLE, THE BIBLE ALONE IS THE RELIGION OF PROTESTANTS.". . .

There is a sweeping spirit of innovation abroad, at war with every institution bearing on its front the time worn marks of antiquity. Things that are old are set aside or demolished, to prepare the introduction for things that are new. The wisdom of the past ages is denounced as the wisdom of the world's infancy, while that of the present is regarded as only worthy of the name. But where shall we look for wisdom more profound, for eloquence of a sweeter and sublimer order, — for poetry more transcendent — for models in all the fine arts more exquisite, for divinity more sound, or for piety so exalted, as the records of ages gone by will produce? And yet, such is the political, and such the religious Radicalism of the age, no fabric however sacred is secure from its levelling influence, if there be found upon it the dust and the impress of antiquity. — the BIBLE not even excepted!. . .

2. We object to the proposed verbal amendment of the New Testament, on the ground, that the words *baptize* and *baptism* are sufficiently explicit to the mind of an ordinary reader, rendering therefore an alteration entirely unnecessary, a work of mere superrogation. That the Translators of the common English version so understood the word *baptize*, there is but little doubt. For, in numberless passages, where a word of the same root is used, the technical or sacramental sense being out of sight, the Translators have given the primary and obvious meaning. For example, Luke xvi, 24. "Send Lazarus, that he may βαψας *dip* the tip of his finger in water," etc. John xiii, 26. "To whom I shall give a sop when I have βαψας *dipped* it. And when he had εμβαψας *dipped* the sop," etc. Revel. xix, 13. "And he was clothed with a vesture βε βαμμενον *dipped* in blood." That James himself so understood the word *baptize* to signify *immerse,* we gather from a Speech which he delivered to his Parliament in the year 1605, about two years anterior to the commencement of the present version, on the discovery of the Gunpowder plot. Speaking of the destruction of the old world by the flood, he says, "For as God for the punishment of the first great sinners in the originall world * * * did by a generall delluge and overflowing of waters, *baptize the world* to a generall destruction, etc." And in another part, alluding to the overwhelming calamities that would

have ensued but for the discovery of the treason, he says, "I should have been *baptized in blood*, and in my destruction, not only the kingdom wherein I then was, but ye also, by your future interest would have tasted of my ruine."

And for what, as touching the *mode* of the institution, have we been so long contending, — for what, but that *baptize* signifies nothing more or less, than to *immerse*, to *dip*, to *plunge*, to *cover over*. We have, times without number, declared the terms to be one and the same in their meaning, capable, upon just rules of philological criticism of no other interpretation. And when the unlettered enquirer has sought our instruction, anxious to know what was truth respecting this ordinance of the Church, what books have we placed in his hands to guide him in his research? To what authorities have we referred him? With what philological criticisms have we perplexed him? Have we quoted Parkhurst and Campbell and Buxtorf to prove to him that the word *baptism* signifies *immersion*? Nay; such a parade of learning would be lost, as to any beneficial effects, upon two thirds of our enquirers. What course then have we pursued? We have taken the English Testament from his hands, and turning to the passages where the words *baptize* and *baptism* occur, and marking them, have returned the sacred book, and dismissed the disciple with the prayer, that the Eternal Spirit of God would bless His own truth to the enlightening and sanctifying of the mind. And what have been the results of this simple mode of instruction? Results! our answer will be found in the thousands of monthly accessions to the Baptist Church throughout these States of converts recently awakened, and led to follow Christ in the way, by reading, with no other lexicon, but prayer, and with no other interpreter but the Spirit, — the common English version of the Scriptures. What this version has accomplished, it is capable of accomplishing yet again...

3. We object to the proposed expunging of the terms *baptize* and *baptism*, because *we regard it as contravening the providence, and as betraying a diminished confidence in the wisdom and power of God.*

It must be remembered that the question stands distinct from all others of a kindred character. It occupies a position peculiarly its own. It has no connexion whatever with that of *foreign translation.* The proposal is not to translate, for the first time, the word βαπτιξψ and its derivatives, into another and a new language — a language never before hallowed as a vehicle for the conveyance of the sacred Word of God. If *this* were the question, before us for decision, our course would be obvious, and our duty imperative...

But the question before us, though of a kindred character, is not to be regarded in the same light, or decided by the same rules. What is the question? It is proposed to amend certain verbal expressions found in the New Testament, which are supposed to express obscurely the mind of the Holy Spirit on one of the ordinances of the church, and which are considered, therefore, unworthy a place in the sacred canon. But by whom was the translation made? How long have these terms remained there? What has been the effect of their present position? Are they so *very* obscure, and vague, as to leave the enquirer in total darkness respecting the mind of the Spirit, and if so, are the Baptists responsible for that obscurity? These are questions claiming a calm and dispassionate consideration.

It is an historical fact, the truth of which none will question, who have accustomed themselves to trace the onward progress of our distinctive sentiments, that the great majority of those who now swell, and are weekly augmenting the ranks of the Baptist denomination, were led to the abandonment of their pedobaptist sentiments, and to the adoption of their present views, (under the teaching's of the Spirit,) mainly through a simple and prayerful reading of the English version of the New Testament. Ambiguous as the terms which set forth the ordinance are supposed to be; obscure and unintelligible as it is argued, the mind of the Holy Spirit is developed, yet has God, in the goodness and wisdom of His Providence, employed and blest this version, to the uprooting of error, the melting away of long cherished prejudices, and the constraining of thousands to welcome "the truth as it is in Jesus," and to bow their necks to its mild and gentle yoke. What more do we expect from a Baptist version of the New Testament? ...

4. *Such a work must necessarily be an individual, and therefore an irresponsible one.* On this ground we prefer an objection.

From whom ought such a work, supposing it be called for, to issue? From one or more isolated and irresponsible individuals, or from the collected wisdom, learning and piety of the denomination, met at its call, in solemn convention? Surely there can be no hesitation in deciding. And who are the persons from whom the proposal *has* proceeded? We ask for information. Are they men in whose purity of motive, weight of character, ripe scholarship and profound critical acumen the denomination have implicit confidence? Are they such men, as a representative Convention from every Church in the Union, convened for this purpose, would select, and into whose hands such a work would be confided. And when the proposed expurgation has taken place, and the proffered amendments made, who is to guarantee their perfect accuracy? What literary reputation is pledged that the work, when done, has been well done, and done faithfully? We enter our decided protest against this individual and irresponsible assumption of a denominational work, and this committal of an extensive Christian body, to the peculiar opinions and measures of a few of its members. Let these queries be soberly and candidly pondered.

5. We urge as another objection to the proposed measure, *the tendency which it will have to sow the seeds of discord and disunion among brethren now happily agreed in upholding and disseminating the one version, so long the record of their appeal, and the bond of their union...*

That the sentiments of the denomination will be brought to harmonize in the adoption of the proposed amended version we do not believe. The proposed abandonment of the words *baptize* and *baptism,* and the substitution of the kindred terms, *immerse* and *immersion,* will doubtless attract to itself the favourable suffrage of a few. Its plausibility will beguile and its novelty will charm them. But the more reflecting, perceiving that nothing is to be gained by the alterations, while much will be hazarded; caught by no specious reasoning, and won over by no puerile argument, will withhold from the translation their sanction and their patronage, and still retain at the domestic altar, in the study and in the pulpit, the good old English Version, endeared to them by a thousand tender and hallowed associations. Such we think, will be the disorganizing tendency of the question agitated. ...

(One further objection of Winslow's deserves at least passing notice: In the following extract he cites the precedent of Luther's German Bible to prove that even an "immersion" rendering won't change what people actually practice.)

It is generally known that Luther's version of the New Testament, now the standard translation for German Protestants, has the words in dispute, *translated.* It is likewise understood at least among baptists, that the German translation is strong for immersion, and that Luther himself was so. But out of the twenty millions of German protestants in Europe and America none, excepting a few *dunkers,* are found to practise immersion in baptism. If a translation is to be so potent as some would represent, why has not Luther's *version* kept the *Lutherans* right? why, with their translation staring them in the face, have they continued almost with one consent, from the days of Luther to this time, in the practice of sprinkling or pouring? The question admits only one reply. The translation has been of no avail to restrain or correct their practical aberrations. Neither would a translation do us any good.

Source: Octavius Winslow, *Objections to a Baptist Version of the New Testament,* J. P. Callender, New York: 1837, pages 52–64 [first extract] and page 30 [second extract].)

81. HOW TO SIMULTANEOUSLY HAVE AN "IMMERSION" AND A "BAPTISM" TRANSLATION

In 1836 the American and Foreign Bible Society was formed to encourage "immersion" translations in both English and other languages. Although the Baptist element was dominant, a conscious effort was made to seek out a broader base of support. In 1844, for example, the society refused to accept a state charter granted by the New York legislature because it had injected the word "Baptist" into the name of the society Alexander Campbell (opponent of the Baptists in so many matters) financially contributed to the society, encouraged others to do likewise, and spoke with favor of their foreign translation efforts.

While unhesitatingly producing foreign versions with the native equivalent of "immersion," the society refrained from producing an American one. In 1850 the society made the implicit refusal an explicit matter of official policy.

This resulted in a number of its members leaving and forming the American Bible Union with the specific purpose of producing the kind of translation the mother organization had spurned. Campbell spoke at the 1852 convention and was elected one of its vice presidents. In the interest of furthering an immersionist Bible, members of the "Disciples" movement were received with open arms. The appointment of two of these "Reformers" (James Shannon to revise Luke and Alexander Campbell to translate Acts) further outraged those Baptists opposed to the project.

Although an immersion Bible was, indeed, brought out at the end of the Civil War, Baptists remained divided over the wisdom and usefulness of such efforts. The continuing opposition is reflected in the following "Prefatory Note" to the "Improved Edition" of the 1880s:

In 1865 the American Bible Union published a Revised English Version of the New Testament, which has been widely used. The demand for a new edition having been made, and the money necessary having been furnished, the Executive

Board of the American Baptist Publication Society — to which Society the home
Bible work of Baptists was committed by the Bible Convention at Saratoga, N.Y.,
May 22 and 23, 1883 — appointed Alvah Hovey, D.D., John A. Broadus, D.D., and
Henry G. Weston, D.D., a committee to prepare an improved edition of this Re-
vised New Testament of the American Bible Union. To meet the wishes of many
persons, this improved edition is published in two forms, one of which retains the
American Bible Union translations of baptizo (immerse, etc.), the other has the
Anglicised form of the Greek word (baptize, etc.).

(Source: *The New Testament — American Bible Union Version* [Improved Edition], "Edition
with immerse," American Baptist Publication Society, Philadelphia: no date, page 3.)

III. *Schonfield's* Authentic New Testament

82. INTRODUCTION TO SCHONFIELD'S
AUTHENTIC NEW TESTAMENT

Hugh J. Schonfield was the first Jew to translate the New Testament
into English. Because of his studies and religious background, he stressed
the New Testament as a reflection of the Jewish environment in which
Christianity arose and spread during the first century. In order to assist
the reader in overcoming the special word-associations that certain terms
have, he makes an effort to substitute what he considers to be equally accurate equivalents. Baptism becomes immersion, church becomes community, apostle becomes envoy, and bishop becomes supervisor.

Before leaving the text there are certain other matters which call for comment.
In the majority of cases the view taken of glosses is that of leading modern
scholars. Some transpositions of material have been necessary, notably in the
Gospel of John, which is in great confusion. The changes, and the reasons for
them, are briefly explained in the prefaces and footnotes to the books concerned.
Actual emendations of the text have been kept to a minimum, and only those have
been made which in the editor's opinion had the very strongest justification....
   The translator has felt it to be important for his purpose not to employ in his
rendering familiar ecclesiastical terms where they could be avoided, since the use
of them would give the impression that they were peculiarly Christian in origin
and association. This relates to such words as baptism (immersion), church (community), apostle (envoy), bishop (supervisor), and deacon (administrator), but also
sometimes to words like 'salvation,' 'righteousness,' 'faith,' and 'grace,' which occasionally do not accurately represent the sense of the original. Many Greek words
have different meanings, according to the context in which they are placed, or are
interpreting Hebrew words, and it would be quite wrong always to translate them
by the same English expression. Some very telling composite words like *oligopistos*
cannot effectively be rendered by a single word in English, and one has to do one's
best with a phrase like 'feeble in faith.' While, in general, modern speech has been
employed, the older English has been kept for the language of prayer, and here
and there to retain the flavour of an orientalism. Finally, as regards proper names,

these as a rule are given in their most familiar form, whether they relate to Old or New Testament characters, thus Isaiah and Elijah, not Esias and Elias. But there are exceptions, especially where the termination of the name either in Hebrew or Greek has direct reference to God, thus Zechariah, not Zacharias, father of John the Baptist, and Timotheus, not Timothy. Place names also have mostly been retained in the form best known, e.g. Capernaum instead of the more accurate Kefar-Nahum.

(Source: Hugh J. Schonfield, *The Authentic New Testament*, Dennis Dobson, Great Britain: no date, pages xlix–xl.)

SEVEN

Twentieth-Century
Roman Catholic Translations

I. *The New American Bible*

83. AN ECUMENICAL CATHOLIC TRANSLATION

In turning to the NEW AMERICAN BIBLE, we discover an approach dramatically different from that exhibited by Ronald A. Knox's earliest "modern-speech" style version. Knox's loyalty was to the Latin; that of the NAB is to the manuscripts in the original languages that underlie the Latin and other translations. The ecumenical thrust of the translators can be seen in the project's use of non–Catholic translators to supplement the work of those of their own religion.

His Holiness Pope Pius XII issued his now famous encyclical on Scripture Studies, *Divino afflante Spiritu* on September 30, 1943. He wrote: "We ought to explain the original text which was written by the inspired author himself and has more authority and greater weight than any, even the very best, translation whether ancient or modern. This can be done all the more easily and fruitfully if to the knowledge of languages be joined a real skill in literary criticism of the same text."

Early in 1944, in conformity with the spirit of the encyclical, and with the encouragement of Archbishop Cicognani, Apostolic Delegate to the United States, the Bishops' Committee of the Confraternity of Christian Doctrine requested members of the Catholic Biblical Association of America to translate the Sacred Scriptures from the original languages or from the oldest extant form of the text and to present the sense of the biblical text in as correct a form as possible.

The first English Catholic version of the Bible, the Douay-Rheims (1582–1609/10), and its revision by Bishop Challoner (1750) were based on the Latin Vulgate. In view of the relative certainties more recently attained by textual and higher criticism, it has become increasingly desirable that contemporary translations of the sacred books into English be prepared in which due reverence for the text and strict observance of the rules of criticism would be combined.

THE NEW AMERICAN BIBLE has accomplished this in response to the need of the Church in America today. It is the achievement of some fifty biblical scholars, the

162

greater number of whom, though not all, are Catholics. In particular, the editors-in-chief have devoted twenty-five years to this work. The collaboration of scholars who are not Catholic fulfills the directive of the Second Vatican Council, not only that "correct translations be made into different languages especially from the original texts of the sacred books," but that, "with the approval of the Church authority, these translations be produced in cooperation with separated brothers" so that "all Christians may be able to use them."

The text of the books contained in THE NEW AMERICAN BIBLE is a completely new translation throughout. From the original and the oldest available texts of the sacred books, it aims to convey as directly as possible the thought and individual style of the inspired writers. The better understanding of Hebrew and Greek, and the steady development of the science of textual criticism, the fruit of patient study since the time of St. Jerome, have allowed the translators and editors in their use of all available materials to approach more closely than ever before the sense of what the sacred authors actually wrote.

Where the translation supposes the received text — Hebrew, Aramaic, or Greek, as the case may be — ordinarily contained in the best-known editions, as the original or the oldest extant form, no additional remarks are necessary. But for those who are happily able to study the original text of the Scriptures at firsthand, a supplementary series of textual notes pertaining to the Old Testament is added in an appendix to the typical edition published by the St. Anthony Guild Press. These furnish a guide in those cases in which the editorial board judges that the manuscripts in the original languages, or the evidence of the ancient versions, or some similar source, furnish the correct reading of a passage, or at least a reading more true to the original than that customarily printed in the available editions. . .

The basic text for the Psalms is not the Massoretic but one which the editors considered closer to the original inspired form, namely the Hebrew text underlying the new Latin Psalter of the Church, the *Liber Psalmorum* (1944, 1945). Nevertheless they retained full liberty to establish the reading of the original text on sound critical principles. . .

In some instances in the Book of Job, in Proverbs, Sirach, Isaiah, Jeremiah, Ezekiel, Hosea, Amos, Micah, Nahum, Habakkuk, and Zechariah there is good reason to believe that the original order of lines was accidentally disturbed in the transmission of the text. The verse numbers given in such cases are always those of the current Hebrew text, though the arrangement differs. In these instances the textual notes advise the reader of the difficulty. Cases of exceptional dislocation are called to the reader's attention by footnotes. . .

The revision of *Job to Sirach* includes changes in strophe division in Job and Proverbs and in titles of principal parts and sections of Wisdom and Ecclesiastes. . .

In the Psalms, the enumeration found in the Hebrew text is followed instead of the double enumeration, according to both the Hebrew and the Latin Vulgate texts, contained in the previous edition of this book.

In the Prophetic Books *Isaiah to Malachi,* only minor revisions have been made in the structure and wording of the texts, and in the textual notes.

The spelling of proper names in THE NEW AMERICAN BIBLE follows the customary forms found in most English Bibles since the Authorized Version.

The New Testament translation has been approached with essentially the same fidelity to the thought and individual style of the biblical writers as was applied in the Old Testament. In some cases, however, the problem of marked literary peculiarities must be met. What by any Western standard are the limited vocabularies and stylistic infelicities of the evangelists cannot be retained in the exact form in which they appear in the originals without displeasing the modern ear. A compromise is here attempted whereby some measure of the poverty of the evangelists' expression is kept and placed at the service of their message in its richness. Similarly, the syntactical shortcomings of Paul, his frequent lapses into anacolouthon, and the like, are rendered as they occur in his epistles rather than "smoothed out." Only thus, the translators suppose, will contemporary readers have some adequate idea of the kind of writing they have before them. When the prose of the original flows more smoothly, as in Luke, Acts, and Hebrews, it is reflected in the translation.

The Gospel according to John comprises a special case. Absolute fidelity to his technique of reiterated phrasing would result in an assault on the English ear that would be almost unendurable. Yet the softening of the vocal effect by substitution of other words and phrases would destroy the effectiveness of his poetry. Again, resort is had to compromise. This is not an easy matter when the very repetitiousness which the author deliberately employed is at the same time regarded by those who read and speak English to be a serious stylistic defect. Only those familiar with the Greek originals can know what a relentless tattoo Johannine poetry can produce. (A similar observation could be made regarding other New Testament books as well. Matthew and Mark are given to identical phrasing twice and three times in the same sentence. As for the rhetorical overgrowth and mixed figures of speech in the letters of Peter, James, and Jude, the translator must resist a powerful compulsion to tidy them up if only to enable him to render these epistles intelligibly.)

Without seeking refuge in complaints against the inspired authors, however, the translators of THE NEW AMERICAN BIBLE here state that what they have attempted is a translation rather than a paraphrase. To be sure, all translation can be called paraphrase by definition. Any striving for complete fidelity will shortly end in infidelity. Nonetheless, it must be pointed out that the temptation to improve overladen sentences by the consolidation or elimination of multiplied adjectives, or the simplification of clumsy hendiadys, has been resisted here. For the most part, rhetorically ineffective words and phrases are retained in this translation in some form, even when it is clear that a Western contemporary writer would never have employed them.

One other matter should be mentioned. Despite the arbitrary character of the divisions into numbered verses (a scheme which in its present form is only four centuries old), the translators have made a constant effort to keep within an English verse the whole verbal content of the Greek verse. At times the effort has not seemed worth the result since it often does violence to the original author's flow of expression, which preceded it by so many centuries. If this translation had been prepared for purposes of public reading only, the editors would have foregone the effort at an early stage. But since they never departed from the threefold objective of preparing a translation suitable for liturgical use, private reading, and the purposes of students, the last-named consideration prevailed. Anyone familiar with Greek should be able to discover how the translators of the New Testament have rendered any given original verse of Scripture, if their exegetical or theological tasks require them to know this. At the same time, the fact should be set down here that the editors did not commit themselves in the synoptic gospels to rendering repeated words or phrases identically.

(Source: Preface, *New American Bible*, Thomas Nelson, viii–x; copyright 1970 by the Confraternity of Christian Doctrine. Used by permission.)

EIGHT

Contemporary Issues
in Bible Translation

I. The Best Greek Text: Eclectic or Majority Text?

84. IS THE MAJORITY TEXT SUPERIOR?
AN ANALYSIS FROM THE CRITICAL PERSPECTIVE

Nearly all major twentieth century translations have used a Greek text different from that which lay behind the King James Version. We have examined how some of the translators defended the change and some of the differences in English text that have resulted.

In some more conservative circles there is an insistence that the superior Greek text can be found in that which has been generally abandoned: that which lay behind the KJV, sometimes called the Byzantine text-type. Essentially the same thing is also known as the Majority Text, i.e., that text which is reflected by the majority of manuscripts.

In the following extract, D. A. Carson provides a critique of one of the more recent defenses of the Majority Text position.

Of the books that have been written in defense of a Textus Receptus type of text, perhaps none is more convincing than *The Identity of the New Testament Text*. [Wilbur N. Pickering, *The Identity of the New Testament Text* (Nashville: Nelson, 1977).] Written by Wilbur N. Pickering, this little book adopts a line of reasoning quite different from most others that defend its viewpoint. Because of its unique approach to the textual question and because it appeared after most of the preceding pages were written, I have decided to deal with it separately in this appendix.

Pickering has done some hard work. His thesis, in brief, is that eclecticism is not a method to be trusted because there is insufficient evidence that identifiable text-types even existed. The only alternative is to resort to a method of counting manuscripts. It follows inescapably that in those passages where the Byzantine text-type differs from the other text-types, the Byzantine reading will be chosen, for the simple reason that it boasts majority support. Because Pickering does not believe the existence of isolatable text-types has been demonstrated, he prefers to talk about the "majority text" rather than the Byzantine tradition or the Byzantine text-type; but his majority text differs from the Byzantine text in concept only, not in substance.

It is worthwhile outlining the book in a little more detail. The book opens with an approving foreword written by Zane C. Hodges of Dallas Theological Seminary, where Pickering earned a M.Th. Pickering's first chapter is a brief introduction, which raises questions about the propriety of eclecticism as a method and cites a couple of scholars who have voiced their doubts about our ability to achieve certainty concerning the New Testament text. The second chapter marshalls evidence against eclecticism, culled from the writings of those who still use it but who are dissatisfied with it. Chapter 3 offers a thumbnail sketch of the rise of the theory of B. F. Westcott and F. J. A. Hort, and chapter 4 a critical evaluation. Pickering seeks to show that Hort was prejudiced against the Byzantine text-type from the beginning of his work, and that his opinions, far from being the result of careful study, were what prompted the work. Hort, Pickering alleges, succeeded in overthrowing the supremacy of the Byzantine tradition by constructing his genealogical theory. Once accepted, the theory insists that manuscripts relating to one text-type can together offer only one vote for a particular reading. Conversely, two or three manuscripts of different genealogy, of different text-type, provide two or three independent votes. Thus in principle a small number of manuscripts attesting a particular reading could be accepted above a large number of manuscripts that support some other reading. Pickering, however, calls the entire genealogical principle into question. He refers to a number of important studies that could not detect clear genealogical relationships among manuscripts of the Byzantine tradition. More important, many of the ante–Nicene witnesses, including the papyri, are so "mixed" in the type of text they reflect that notable textual critics have raised the question whether "text-type" in the Westcott-Hort sense is a meaningful expression. Pickering has done textual critics a favor by pulling some of this material together.

Chapter 4 also deals with a host of lesser questions that rise out of the Westcott-Hort theory. Pickering cites studies that find evidence of Byzantine readings in the early fathers, and other studies that affirm an early date for the Syriac Peshitta (which reflects Byzantine readings) or that cast doubt on the established principles of textual criticism. He points out that few scholars today treat the Byzantine text-type as if it were a recension; and if not a late recension, as Westcott and Hort proposed, then how did it originate?

That brings us to a crucial question, the one that occupies Pickering's attention in the fifth chapter. Regardless of what textual-critical theory is adopted, that theory must be held in conjunction with a related and believable history of the text. If the Byzantine tradition did not arise as a late recension (as Westcott and Hort suggested), then how are we to account for it? Pickering offers an alternative textual history, one that projects the majority text (the Byzantine text-type) back to the earliest period. Deviations from this must be dismissed as early aberrations, weeded out in the passage of time.

In the sixth chapter Pickering answers various potential objections to his reconstruction. Why, for example, are there no early Byzantine manuscripts? Because, says Pickering, they wore out. Should not manuscripts be weighed, not counted? Pickering thinks counting is to be preferred because he has already dispensed with the genealogical principle — at least to his own satisfaction. Chapter 7 affords Pickering the opportunity of formulating his thesis in terms of

John W. Burgon's old "Notes of Truth," a summary of textual-critical principles Pickering would approve of over against currently adopted textual-critical principles. The last chapter, the eighth, offers a brief conclusion.

The book includes three appendices. The first relates the doctrine of inspiration to the preservation of the text. Pickering says that the affirmation that "God has preserved the original wording of the New Testament text" is "a statement of faith"; but this acknowledgment of the need for faith is coupled with an insistence that such faith is "an intelligent faith, a faith that accords with the available evidence." The second appendix discusses 7Q5, the manuscript fragment from Qumran that the Jesuit scholar José O'Callaghan identified as a piece of Mark 6:52–53. Pickering feels that published criticism of O'Callaghan's work is ill informed and that O'Callaghan is probably right. The third and by far the longest appendix applies the methods of probability statistics to the history of the text. Here Pickering is drawing on his expertise in linguistics (he is a candidate for a Ph.D. in linguistics from the University of Toronto). This is an original approach to the question; but I shall reserve comment for a few moments.

My criticisms of this book are extensive; but before launching into a few of them, I want to commend Pickering for bringing together the cream of significant studies that cast doubt on the reconstruction offered us by Westcott and Hort, and especially for asking many of the right questions. This said, I fear Pickering's alternative is even more problematic than the theory of Westcott and Hort. The tragedy of Pickering's work, I believe, is that his important and pertinent questions will tend to be overlooked and dismissed by scholars of textual criticism, who will find many reasons to reject his reconstruction and therefore his questions, while many conservative Christians will accept his entire reconstruction without detecting the many underlying questions that will still go unanswered.

Specifically I would venture at least the following criticisms:

First, there is a basic flaw in Pickering's overarching argument. Having demonstrated that text-types are not as sharply delineated as some have thought, he argues that the very concept is misguided and concludes therefore that we must view most manuscripts as independent authorities that ought to be counted, not weighed. Yet at the same time he quite clearly preserves the concept of text-type as applied to the Byzantine tradition, even though he prefers to call it the "majority text." For example, he contends that distinctively Byzantine readings are found in the ante–Nicene fathers, but he admits there is not one examplar of the Byzantine tradition per se from the early period. In fact when he asks why there isn't one, he is reduced to the weak answer that they all wore out. However, whatever the merits of this answer, the fact that he can ask the question indicates that the concept of text-types still occupies a large place in his thinking, at least as far as the Byzantine tradition is concerned. But if that is so, then he ought not reject the genealogical principle so categorically: it sounds too much like simultaneously keeping one's cake and eating it.

What recent studies have shown, I think, is that the four classic text-types are too neatly isolated. Perhaps we are forced to conclude that most early manuscripts are mixes. If so, the boundaries between text-types become hazy, like the change from color to color in a rainbow; but it still does not follow that the concept of text-types is entirely dispensable, any more than we could dispense with the colors of the rainbow, or argue that those colors cannot be distinguished from one another. Perhaps p^{66} presents confusing evidence and therefore lives in the hazy zone; but the evidence from p^{75} is remarkably clear. (Later I shall say more on these papyri.) No doubt the four well-known text-types constitute an inadequate basis that still needs much work; but that distinct types of texts exist cannot be dismissed. If the expression *text-type* refers to neatly isolated types of text, then it may be that the pursuit of text-types is an illusory goal; but if *text-type* simply refers to types of text as indexed by several remarkable extremes, it is hard to see how anyone can deny their existence. Once this point is conceded, it follows that simply counting manuscripts will not prove very helpful. Besides, even if it is premature and sometimes misleading to assign this manuscript or that to a particular text-type, nevertheless a few discrete "families" of texts have been found (for example, the so-called Lake family), demonstrating that genealogical relationships do in fact exist. [Since the work of E. C. Colwell, most New Testament textual critics have reserved the word *family* for smaller groupings within a particular text-type.]

On the face of it, because one manuscript was copied from another or from several others, genealogical relationships *must* exist. The only question is whether or not we have identified such relationships, or can identify them. Off the cuff, I suspect we have too often neglected the mobility of the first century. Roman roads and imperial peace meant movement; and just as the overlooking of these factors has contributed to a proliferation of theories concerning "Matthean theology" over against the theology of the "Pauline churches" over against the theology of the "Johannine circle," as if the various groups were almost hermetically sealed off from one another, so also I suspect that early textual history involves more borrowing and cross-fertilization than is often recognized. Yet such fluidity does nothing to mitigate against the *principle* of text-types and genealogical relationships.

Second, Pickering's use of the studies by Edward Miller, though challenging, raises more questions than it answers. Miller, posthumous editor to Burgon, compiled from Burgon's notes and his own studies a complete list of Byzantine readings in the ante–Nicene fathers. He discovered that Byzantine readings invariably outnumber readings of other traditions, but in various ratios. This, it is argued, proves the earliness of the Byzantine text-type.

Textual-critical scholars have responded to this in various ways. First of all, detailed critical editions of the fathers had not been prepared in Miller's day. Many Byzantine readings in the late manuscripts of the fathers may well be due to assimilation to the Byzantine text-type in the post–Nicene period. Of course there is a danger of arguing in a circle here; so let us be conservative and suppose that there were but few assimilations. It then follows that many Byzantine readings are found in the ante–Nicene fathers. However, that fact by itself still proves nothing because textual scholars hold that a primary feature of the Byzantine text-type is its tendency to conflate readings. Obviously, then, the elements of the conflation must antedate the conflation itself. The point is that the vast majority of so-called Byzantine readings in the ante–Nicene fathers are also Western or Alexandrian readings. They become *distinctively* Byzantine only by their conflation in individual manuscripts *after* the fourth century has got underway. The question is whether or not the *Byzantine text-type* existed before the fourth century, not whether or not *Byzantine readings* existed before the fourth century. In the absence of any ante–Nicene manuscript boasting Byzantine text-type, Miller — and Pickering — draw outsize conclusions from the patristic evidence.

Pickering rightly points out that the ante–Nicene fathers also contain some uniquely Byzantine readings: that is, readings that are found in no text-type other than Byzantine. There are not many of them, but there are a few. Pickering seems to think that their presence proves the early existence of the Byzantine text-type.

Of course it does nothing of the kind. Such purely Byzantine words *may* attest to the ante-Nicene existence of the Byzantine text-type; but other explanations are equally possible. For example, the small number of ante-Nicene witnesses (as compared with the larger number of later manuscripts) is well known, and it is frequently pointed out by Pickering himself. Before the discoveries of the best Western, and especially the Alexandrian, witnesses within the last two centuries, one might have supposed that most of the "Byzantine" words found in the ante-Nicene fathers were purely Byzantine. With the discovery of other witnesses, the number of purely Byzantine readings found in the ante-Nicene fathers was reduced to a minute fraction of the total because more and more "Byzantine" readings were also found to be Western or Alexandrian. Perhaps the discovery of a few more manuscripts will reduce that number yet further.

This of course is the converse of the argument of Edward F. Hills (and of Pickering, who cites him). Hort said that the Byzantine text-type is characterized by late readings, yet Hills contends that only about 10 percent of the Byzantine readings are really late; and with new discoveries, this percentage is still falling. True enough; but with each falling percentage point, the number of purely Byzantine readings found in the ante-Nicene fathers is correspondingly reduced.

What this means is that the patristic evidence is at best ambiguous. In the absence of any ante-Nicene exemplar of the Byzantine text-type, the onus of proof, in my view, still rests with the defenders of the Byzantine tradition.

Of course a translation, dated unambiguously early, that clearly boasted the mature Byzantine text-type, would also serve as adequate proof of the early existence of this tradition. That is why the date of the Syriac Peshitta has often been considered important. In point of fact, the textual affinity of the Peshitta to the Byzantine tradition has regularly been overestimated: the close work that has been done on some parts of it (especially Mark and Galatians) reflects Byzantine readings only about 50 percent of the time. In any case, although up until the turn of the century it was almost universally accepted that the Peshitta was a second-century translation, scarcely anyone will defend that position today. As I indicated earlier, F. C. Burkitt convinced almost everyone that it was the fifth-century work of Rabbula of Edessa. Arthur Vööbus disagreed sharply, pointing out a number of instances in which Rabbula's quotations from Scripture are not from the Peshitta but from the Old Syriac. Pickering cites Vööbus enthusiastically; but it is disappointing to observe that he fails to mention Matthew Black's decisive critique of Vööbus. Black sees Rabbula as much less central in producing the Syriac Peshitta. Rabbula emerges as one of the links in the chain of its production, some of which are earlier than Rabbula, and others of which are later (the Peshitta did not thoroughly displace the Old Syriac until the sixth century). Thus even if Vööbus has rightly questioned the Rabbulan origins of the Peshitta version, it appears that Burkitt was entirely correct in seeing this version as a post-Nicene endeavor. And, intriguingly, the spread of textual affinities in the Peshitta — Byzantine, Western, Alexandrian — again testifies to the early fluidity of text-types; but it does not demonstrate that the Byzantine tradition in its mature conflated form existed in the ante-Nicene period. Meanwhile, we may well ask ourselves why, if the mature Byzantine text-type were actually in common use in the ante-Nicene period, the other ancient versions (Old Latin, Old Syriac, Coptic, and so forth) either know nothing of it or make little use of it.

In short, there is still no hard evidence that the Byzantine text-type was known in the ante-Nicene period. But let me hasten to add that even if unambiguous evidence were found in support of its early existence, this would not prove its superiority. It would, to say the least, put it on the same footing as the other text-types; but it would not thereby *necessarily* be promoted to a position of supremacy.

Third, although Pickering rightly points out the importance of reconstructing a believable history of the text, he is persistently insensitive to the broader history in which the history of the text unfolds. He is right in asking that the rise of the Byzantine tradition be accounted for in a fashion that squares with the evidence. He is right when he points out that few accept the Hortian theory of a Lucianic recension at the base of the Byzantine text-type. He is right when he asks how various ante–Nicene Byzantine readings arose. But he is historically naive when he fails to discuss the significance of the professed conversion of Constantine, the immense influence of John Chrysostom in the eastern empire, the rise of monarchical bishops and their pressure for textual uniformity, the division of the Roman Empire and the demise of the Greek language (and the resulting preeminence of Latin) throughout the Mediterranean world, Byzantium excepted. Historically sensitive answers to questions like these may provide the true answer to the problem of why the text-type found in B or p^{75} was neglected for centuries.

When Pickering addresses himself directly to the question of how to account for the Byzantine text-type, however, he never raises such questions. His fundamental appeal, both in the body of his book and in its second appendix, is to probability statistics. The basic argument is simple. If we grant that, on the average, each manuscript is copied the same number of times as the other manuscripts of its generation, then under normal circumstances the older the text-type the greater its chances of surviving in a plurality or in a majority of the extant manuscripts of any later period. But since the oldest text-type is the autograph, it follows that this type must predominate.

This argument depends entirely on what Pickering calls "normal transmission." He repeatedly suggests that the rejection of his statistical argument entails a "radical" break from "normal transmission." But it is precisely at this point that Pickering is, in my view, historically naive. We may be sure that prototypes of the Byzantine text-type were circulating toward the middle of the fourth century; and it was this sort of text that Chrysostom used in his immensely popular preaching in Antioch and Constantinople. It is entirely reasonable, historically speaking, to reconstruct the next one hundred years in terms of the effect of Chrysostom's popularity, the hardening of the Byzantine tradition, the restriction of the Greek language (by and large) to the incipient Byzantine Empire, and the massive displacement of Greek by Latin in the West. The simple convergence of a few such historical phenomena quite adequately accounts for the numerical superiority of the majority text. Granted this is so, then the statistical argument says nothing about the antiquity of the text at any point earlier than the fourth century. And if it says nothing about the text's ultimate antiquity, it equally says nothing about its authenticity.

Pickering introduces another wrinkle into the statistical argument. Suppose, he says, that a manuscript with an error were copied more times than another manuscript of the same generation without an error. It would follow that in the next generation there would be more "bad" copies than "good." But suppose further that another error were introduced into one of the "bad" copies of this new generation. Even if this new, doubly "bad" manuscript were copied more often than its peers, nevertheless in the next generation the new error would be found in a smaller number of manuscripts than those that retained the right reading, because all the thoroughly "good" manuscripts would join with the manuscripts that had only one "bad" reading to make up a majority witness against the second "bad" reading. In the long haul, therefore, as the number of generations increases, bad readings should be found in proportionately fewer manuscripts.

Again, however, I submit that this argument, whatever its reasonableness on paper, is historically naive. As Pickering himself points out, most errors were introduced into the manuscripts within the first two centuries. Errors were not added one per generation, generation by generation, but wholesale, as it were. Pickering's statistical model therefore breaks down. If some of these corrupted manuscripts began to proliferate in an area where Greek was still the lingua franca, and therefore where many copies would be made because the demand would be greatest; and if there was concomitantly rising pressure to secure uniform copies of the New Testament (recall the injunction of Damasus to Jerome), then such basic historical considerations completely nullify Pickering's argument from probability statistics.

An analogy comes to mind, one that serves as a counterexample. One can erect a statistical model in which it is affirmed that there is, in any generation, a certain probability that each pair of parents will have, on average, so many children. This immediately suggests that the total number of offspring from parents of an early generation will outstrip the total number of offspring from parents of a later generation. Adam will have a greater number of descendants than Noah: indeed, he will have the greatest number of all. Similarly one might expect Lamech or Tubal-cain (Gen. 4) to have a greater number of descendants than Noah. According to Genesis, however, such reckoning is false: the "historical accident" of the flood has eliminated that possibility. The mathematical model does not prove convincing once other historical factors are admitted. Similarly, Pickering's mathematical model does not prove convincing. And the use of mathematical symbols does not make his argument one iota stronger, as symbols could equally be used for my counterargument.

A concrete contradiction is in any case built into Pickering's argument about the tendencies of manuscript-copying in the first two centuries. On the one hand, as we have seen, Pickering admits what is generally agreed, that most variants existed before the end of the second century, including most of the worst corruptions. Of course he must concede this if he is to explain the uncials, minuscules, and papyri that he wishes to dismiss as corrupt. His resulting model of the history of the New Testament text brings with it the unpleasant conclusion that the first two centuries of the Christian church can boast of the highest proportion of aberrant texts! Yet on the other hand Pickering elsewhere argues that the earliest believers would, on principle, extend the greatest care to their copying of manuscripts because they would reverence the New Testament writings the way the Jews reverenced their Hebrew Bible.

Pickering has thus constructed a flat contradiction. The plain fact of the matter is that early Christians did not take nearly the pains with their Scriptures that the Jews did with theirs; and this is evidenced not only by the Christians' handling of the New Testament documents but also in their handling of the LXX. We may credit this to what we will—lack of education in some leaders, enthusiastic zeal that outran sober wisdom, the greatness of the demand, or whatever—but facts are facts. And the vast majority of the variants are not demonstrably the result of doctrinal prejudice so much as sheer carelessness.

In these and several other areas Pickering, it seems to me, is historically insensitive.

Fourth, Pickering has not dealt adequately with the papyri. He rightly points out that Byzantine readings are found in p[66], whose textual affinities are, to say the least, highly erratic. Of course, as I indicated in my discussion of the fathers, early Byzantine readings do not necessarily argue for the presence of an early Byzantine text-type, and I need not repeat my argument. But although Pickering discusses erratic papyri like p^{66}, he does not anywhere discuss seriously the implications of the remarkable textual affinities of a papyrus like p^{75}. This papyrus agrees so closely with B, without apparently serving as its parent, that *text-type* is scarcely too strong a term to be used. Moreover, if the recent work by Gordon D. Fee is correct (which Pickering does not discuss), then neither p^{75} nor B is recensional. If p^{75}, a second-century papyrus, is not recensional, then it must be either extremely close to the original or extremely corrupt. The latter possibility appears to be eliminated by the witness of B. If Fee's work stands up, then we must conclude that at least in John's Gospel the Alexandrian text-type is by far the closest to the autograph.

Fifth, Pickering cites the work of A. C. Clark to the effect that in the transmission of classical Greek texts the error to which scribes were most prone was not interpolation but accidental omission. Applied to New Testament textual criticism, this could be taken to suggest that, all other things being equal, the longer reading should be assumed to be correct. Of course this would favor the Byzantine text-type. Most textual critics follow the opposite principle and, all things being equal, prefer the shorter reading (*"brevior lectio potior"*).

In a footnote Pickering admits that Clark's work was criticized by F. G. Kenyon and others (he does not mention that the "others" were William Sanday and Alexander Souter), but he still believes Clark's work "has sufficient validity to be worth taking into account." Unfortunately he does not detail the objections of Kenyon and the others; but the interested reader may turn with profit to the brief treatments in the standard works. More unfortunate yet, Pickering does not mention that Clark himself applied his theory to the famous textual problem of Acts, supporting as a result the longer Western form of the text over against the Byzantine! However, after undergoing rigorous criticism by some of his colleagues, Clark returned some years later to the question of the textual traditions underlying Acts, and to all intents and purposes abandoned his former theory in favor of another, namely, that Luke himself had produced two editions of Acts. On this theory too he faced serious challenge; but the chronicling of this later dispute would transport us beyond the concerns of textual criticism per se. Clark's work on scribal habits, however, does not appear to be so crucial after all.

More work needs to be done in this area of scribal tendencies; but the generalization offered by Pickering and Clark (and B. H. Streeter before them) certainly needs, to say the least, serious qualification. For a start, a distinction would have to be made between accidental and nonaccidental changes. And there are other questions to answer. For example, in the area of intentional changes, would early, reverent Christians be quicker to risk losing sacred words than to risk preserving words that were not sacred but not obviously harmful or untrue? Certainly the later institutional church preferred the latter risk!

Sixth, the criticism I just offered pinpoints a much broader weakness in Pickering's work. Although he is much more fair and restrained than many defenders of the Byzantine tradition, nevertheless in my view he still spends too much time erecting and knocking down straw men, overstating his case, and even unfairly quoting from his opponents. I offer a representative list of examples:

1. Pickering cites authors who insist that the recovery of the original text of the Bible is impossible. "At this point," he says, "I get uncomfortable. If the original wording is lost and gone forever, whatever are we using? The consequences of

such an admission are so far-reaching, to my mind, that a thorough review of the evidence is called for." But this approach projects a distorted image in the mind of the reader, an image that suggests that accepting the Byzantine text entails faithfulness to the Word of God and recovery of the original words of Scripture, and rejecting the Byzantine text cuts a person free from all possibility of knowing God's will. I have already dealt with this under theses 9 and 12. Suffice it to add this additional remark: Pickering himself later admits that following his approach still stops short of ultimate proof that we have the original wording. Only the autographs could provide such confidence. As I indicated earlier, even within the Byzantine tradition no two manuscripts agree perfectly. There is a difference only of degree between the variations found within a textual tradition and the variations scattered across two or more text-types. In that sense it is entirely correct that, as some authors cited by Pickering have argued, we can never achieve perfect certainty on the precise wording of the entire New Testament; and that point stands firm regardless of whether the Byzantine text be followed or not. Of course most of the New Testament is already textually certain; and as I have already argued, the remaining variations may affect the interpretation of various passages, but they do not affect a single doctrine.

2. Pickering's criticisms of eclecticism are sometimes unfair. Even the criticisms offered by Eldon Jay Epp and others are generally actually directed at its worst practitioners; and if I understand Epp correctly, although he rightly pinpoints the many weaknesses of eclecticism (real or potential), he nevertheless offers no better method. His comments are presented as a goad to make us aware of weaknesses and to spur us on to more research in order to achieve greater precision. It is true that eclecticism, to be final, would require omniscient textual critics; but it does not follow that the pursuit of truth should be abandoned in favor of opting for one part of the evidence. In principle the same omniscience would be required to make sound judgments about variants even within the Byzantine textual tradition. Pickering's entire treatment of eclecticism would have more credibility if, with Epp and others, he could see its weaknesses without parodying it.

3. Again and again, Pickering mentions the fact that most manuscripts within the Byzantine tradition have not been neatly related genealogically to others within the same tradition. But he jumps from this fact to the proposition that they are therefore "independent witnesses." That simply does not follow! Precise connections may well have been lost; more links may yet be discovered. In principle, because every manuscript but the original is a copy of at least one other, and perhaps of several others, genealogical relationships must exist. As I have already indicated, the questions to be asked are: If a manuscript were copied from several others, *could* the precise relationships be detected, granted the abundance of attendant witnesses? But all these individual manuscripts cannot be justly said to be independent. Some of them *may* be; but the point must not be assumed.

4. There are too many glib statements, statements not quite true. For example, Pickering tells us it is "common knowledge that all the earliest MSS, the ones upon which our critical texts are based, come from Egypt." In fact we do not know where B and D came from; and certain manuscripts of ancient versions do not boast Egyptian provenance. Again, Pickering speaks of "the known existence of a variety of maliciously altered texts in the second century;" but his ensuing discussion refers to accidental and careless errors such as itacistic spellings.

5. Pickering argues that manuscripts from one geographical area cannot be considered independent witnesses and therefore must be given, collectively, precisely one vote. I am astonished that a person who can see weaknesses in Hort's

genealogical principle cannot see similar weaknesses compounded in his own geographical principle. Pickering is attempting to use this argument to reduce all the witnesses from Egypt to one vote—despite the vast diversity in the textual traditions preserved in Egypt. Incidentally the reason Egypt has brought forth so many ancient manuscripts is that her climate is hot and dry, ideal for preserving such things. But the richness of her textual heritage, far from indicating a provincial isolationism, is strong evidence that she reflected textual traditions from all parts of the empire. Moreover all these finds from Egypt are very early; so when Pickering points out that the relatively uniform Byzantine cursives spring from many countries stretching from Greece to England and from Africa to Gaul, he should in all fairness also point out the following: (1) Not one of them is as early as the non-Byzantine uncials and papyri. (2) Most of them are at least five hundred years later, and some of them one thousand years later. (3) Although they are found in many countries now, in fact we do not know of their ultimate origin; but not a few spread from Constantinople throughout the Mediterranean world during the Renaissance, which followed hard on the heels of the collapse of the Byzantine Empire. And (4) most of those whose origins are truly found in non-Byzantine cities are late copies of manuscripts preserved in the Byzantine Empire; and they were copied at a time when scribes had little choice, ignorant as they were of the later finds of uncials and papyri.

Seventh, I am uncertain what relevance the appendix on 7Q5 has for the thrust of Pickering's book as a whole. In this appendix Pickering argues in favor of O'Callaghan's identification of 7Q5 with Mark 6:52–53, and against O'Callaghan's critics (especially Maurice Baillet). But as I say, I remain uncertain as to the relevance of this appendix to the book as a whole.

In any case, in establishing one's own position it is seldom helpful to focus all attention on the most extreme opposition. Perhaps Baillet's criticisms of O'Callaghan are overdone; yet there are plenty of very sober-minded critics around who remain doubtful that O'Callaghan has proved his point. For example, C. J. Hemer does not insist that O'Callaghan's reconstruction is impossible; but he does show that it is at best speculative and that it could fit other passages just as well. I do not believe that conservative biblical scholarship is helped along its way when every potential conservative find is hailed swiftly or uncritically.

In drawing this appendix to a close, Pickering writes: "It seems to me that 7Q5, 4 and 8 tend to confirm the history of the text presented in this volume. That someone should have a collection of New Testament writings at such an early date confirms their early recognition as Scripture and implies an early notion of a N.T. canon."

I remain unpersuaded that 7Q5 is any sort of basis on which to build propositions concerning the early recognition of New Testament documents as Scripture—propositions that in my view, find much better support elsewhere. However, even if 7Q5 did attest a high view of New Testament documents and an early notion of New Testament canon, it baffles me to see how such attestation in any sense would confirm Pickering's history of the New Testament text. O'Callaghan is not suggesting that 7Q5 contains a Byzantine reading!

That brings me to my final criticism:

Eighth, as do many other defenders of the Byzantine text-type, Pickering ultimately tries to forge a necessary connection between his understanding of textual criticism and a high view of Scripture. Pickering is more careful than most in this regard; but the concluding remarks to his second appendix (on 7Q5) and his entire first appendix ("Inspiration and Preservation"), give away this perspective in the end. But as in other writers, so in Pickering: the connection is based on assertion without evidence, on affirmation without serious theological reflection. I have already dealt with this question under theses 5, 9, and 12, and beg the reader's indulgence if I do not repeat those arguments here. I need only add that *even if* the Byzantine text-type were one day demonstrated to be closer to the autographs than the other textual traditions (an eventuality of which, at this point, I can scarcely conceive), belief in traditional formulations of biblical inspiration would not be affected in the slightest. This granted, the defenders of the Byzantine tradition ought to desist from all statements suggesting or implying that defenders of any other view necessarily risk a heterodox view of Scripture.

(Source: D. A. Carson, *The King James Version Debate: A Plea for Realism*, pages 105–123; copyright 1979 by Baker Book House. Used by permission.)

II. *Sexism*

85. THE RATIONALE FOR GENDER-NEUTRAL TRANSLATIONS

Before the 1970s the claim that available Bible translations are "sexist" would have been looked upon as ludicrous and unbelievable. Yet within recent years those who make this claim have become so influential in mainline denominationalism, that the controversy is certain to remain a focal point of debate far into the twenty-first century.

The religious opponents of this view vary from those who will accept mild alterations in the direction of a gender-neutral text to those who consider the whole affair a terrible example of feminist theology run amok. What disturbs all critics is the danger of mutilating the text by intentional mistranslation: A gender-free rendering in a text that *is* gender-oriented elevates feminist theology above the original meaning and intent of the scripture.

As of the compilation of this volume, there is no complete Bible translation from a gender-neutral approach. (The New Revised Standard Version does not "degenderize" references to the Deity.) What may well turn out to be the foundation-text for such a translation is being produced in a series of lectionaries sponsored by the National Council of Churches. When completed, the three volumes will cover some 95 percent of the New Testament and 60 percent of the Old Testament.

In the following extract, the editors of the "Year B" lectionary describe the principles from which they worked. The reader should note their sensitivity not just to allegedly sexist terminology but also to any phraseology that might be misconstrued as anti–Semitic or racist.

A lectionary is a fixed selection of readings, taken from both the Old and the New Testament, to be read and heard in the churches' services of worship. Most lectionaries are simply tables or lists of readings. They cite the biblical book from which the reading is taken, as well as the chapter and verses: for example, on Christmas Day, Luke 2:1–20. This lectionary contains the full text of each reading.

History of Lectionary Development. The International Commission on English in the Liturgy created an ecumenical group known as the Consultation on Common Texts. One of the tasks of the Consultation was to explore the possibilities of creating a lectionary that would be acceptable to most English-speaking Christians: Anglican, Protestant, and Roman Catholic. To that end, a small working group known as the North American Committee on Calendar and Lectionary was formed. Over a period of five years a revised table of lections, or readings, was developed that took into account the acknowledged critique of the Vatican II lectionary (early 1960s) and its subsequent adaptations by the major Protestant denominations. The report of the North American Committee was approved by the Consultation on Common Texts in 1982, and this "common texts" lectionary has been recommended for trial use in the churches beginning with Advent 1983. It is this Table of Readings and Psalms which this lectionary follows, using the Revised Standard Version as its text. The lectionary attempts to provide comprehensive and balanced coverage of the entire Bible. Over a three-year period about 95 percent of the New Testament is heard, as well as about 60 percent of the Old Testament.

Function of the Lectionary in Congregational Worship. In churches that use the lectionary every Sunday, congregations will hear the same scriptures. Thus the wider church, within denominations and across denominational lines, is united in its hearing and thinking and praying. A lectionary provides a way for Christians to live out the church year, which begins on the first Sunday of Advent and proceeds through Christmas, Epiphany, Ash Wednesday, Lent, Passion (Palm) Sunday, Maundy Thursday, Good Friday, Easter, Ascension, and Pentecost. At least four readings are prescribed for each Sunday and for special days such as Christmas, Easter, All Saints, and Thanksgiving.

It is apparent that any selection of scripture read in a service of worship has been lifted from its biblical context. In the study of the Bible, the context in which a biblical passage occurs is crucial to its interpretation. When passages are read in a service of worship, however, they are read in a new context and in relation to the church year. This radical change in the context of selections is one factor that differentiates a lectionary from the Bible.

A lectionary thus has a special function in the worship of the church. It does not supplant the Bible. The Bible is the church's book—created by and for the church. A lectionary is also the church's book, being a prescribed set of readings selected by the church from its scripture for its own special use in worship. The unique feature of AN INCLUSIVE-LANGUAGE LECTIONARY is that it recasts some of the wording of the Revised Standard Version in order to provide reader and hearer with a sense of belonging to a Christian faith community in which truly all are one in Christ.

Why Inclusive Language? The lectionary readings are based on the Revised Standard Version and the original Greek and Hebrew texts, with the intent of reflecting the full humanity of women and men in the light of the gospel. A growing number of people feel they have been denied full humanity by a pattern of exclusion in English usage. Consider, for example, the traditional English use of the word "man." A man is a male being, as opposed to a female being. But in common usage "man" has also meant "human being," as opposed to "animal." On the other hand, "woman" means female, but never *human being.* No word that refers to a female person identifies her with humanity. So the common English idiom has been subject to the understanding that "man" has been defined by his humanity, but "woman" by her sex, by her relationship to man. "Woman" becomes a subgroup under "human." "Man" is the human race; "woman" is man's sexual partner in traditional English usage.

These are some examples of how language *reflects* the way in which we think but also *informs* the way in which we think. The mandate to the Inclusive-Language Lectionary Committee is to seek "language which expresses inclusiveness with regard to human beings and which attempts to expand the range of images beyond the masculine to assist the church in understanding the full nature of God." In the Appendix the reader will find specific examples of how these kinds of exclusive imagery have been dealt with in this lectionary.

HOW THE REVISED STANDARD VERSION HAS BEEN RECAST

The RSV is highly respected by biblical scholars and is widely used in this country. However, in this lectionary the wording of the RSV has been recast to minimize the male bias and other exclusive imagery reflected in its language about human beings and the male bias reflected in language about Christ and God. Except for these changes the text of the RSV has been retained.

Male bias, however, is not unique to English translations of the Bible; it is characteristic of its original languages. Both the Old Testament and the New Testament were written in languages and in cultures that were basically patriarchal; and as the English language is also patriarchal, the patriarchal character of both Testaments has slipped easily into the great English versions of the Bible.

Language About Human Beings. In a few instances the RSV Bible committee has already avoided male bias in reference to human beings. For example, in Rom. 7:1 the RSV has used "person" ("the law is binding on a *person*") as a translation of the Greek word *anthropos* (meaning "man" or "person"). But most of the time *anthropos* is translated "man" or, in the plural, "men." For example, Matt. 5:16 in the RSV reads, "Let your light so shine before *men*" where the meaning of "men" is obviously "people," but not male people exclusively. This verse can be rendered, "Let your light so shine before *others*"—i.e., men and women, which represents the clear intention of the words.

Male bias also appears when masculine pronoun subjects are supplied with third person singular verbs when the context does not require them. Compare, for example, the RSV of John 6:35-37: "Jesus said to them, 'I am the bread of life; *he* who comes to me shall not hunger, and *he* who believes in me shall never thirst . . .; and *him* who comes to me I will not cast out." What is the intention of this passage? It surely is not that only *men* come to Jesus and believe in Jesus. Why, then, does the RSV read "he" and "him"? It is because of the assumption that "he" also means "she," though we know that it does not.

In this lectionary all readings have been recast so that no masculine word pretends to include a woman. For example, the word "brethren" has been rendered in a variety of ways, including "sisters and brothers." Formal equivalents have been adopted for other male-specific words and phrases. For example, "kingdom" is rendered "realm" or occasionally "reign"; "king" in reference to God or a messianic figure is rendered "ruler" or "monarch."

Where appropriate, references to women have been added, for example, "Abraham [*and Sarah*]." Contemporary English usage also suggests that we refer to a "person with a disabling condition" rather than to a "cripple" or a "crippled person." So the biblical reference to "the blind and the lame" is rendered "those who are blind and those who are lame" (see Jer. 31:8). Where "darkness" is set in contrast with "light" and has a moral connotation, a substitute word for darkness is supplied—for example, "The light shines in the *deepest night*" (John 1:5).

Language About Jesus Christ. Jesus was a male human being. But when the Gospel of John says, "The Word became flesh" (John 1:14), it does not say or imply that the Word became *male* flesh, but simply *flesh.* Of course, to "become flesh," the one from God had to become male or female, but the language used in this lectionary tries to overcome the implication that in the incarnation Jesus' *maleness* is decisive—or even relevant—for the salvation of women and men who believe. From the very beginning of the church the salvation of women has been assumed to be equal to the salvation of men.

In this lectionary the fact of Jesus' maleness is taken for granted. Jesus is referred to as a man, and the pronouns "he," "his," and "him" are used when the reference is to the historical person. However, the name "Jesus," as well as other proper names, is occasionally substituted for pronouns both for the sake of clarity and to avoid pronoun repetition. The use of the proper name also deemphasizes Jesus' maleness, so that in hearing the gospel, the church may be reminded of the inclusiveness of all humanity in the incarnation. Pronoun references to the preexistent and postcrucifixion Jesus are replaced by the proper names—Jesus, Christ, or Jesus Christ. Formal equivalents adopted for "the Son of man," "Son," and "Son of God" are, respectively, "the Human One," "Child," and "Child of God." (For a discussion of these terms, see the Appendix.)

Language About God. The God worshiped by the biblical authors and worshiped in the church today cannot be regarded as having gender, race, or color. Such attributes are used metaphorically or analogically. God the Father is only one metaphor for God; other personal metaphors include God as mother, midwife, and breadmaker. Less familiar, but equally appropriate, are such impersonal images for God as Love, Rock, and Light. This lectionary tries to speak of God so that when the church hears its scripture read, it is not overwhelmed by the male metaphors but is also allowed to hear female metaphors for God.

In the RSV Old Testament, the major names for God are "God" (*elohim*), "LORD" (*Yahweh*), and "Lord" (*adonai*), and several variations of these nouns, for example, "the LORD God" and "the GOD of hosts." In this lectionary, "LORD" (*Yahweh*) is rendered "GOD" or "SOVEREIGN ONE" and "Lord" (*adonai*) is rendered "God."

In the New Testament passages in this lectionary the formal equivalent adopted for "God the Father" or "the Father" is "God the Father [*and Mother*]" or "God the [*Mother and*] Father." The words that have been added to the text and that may be omitted in reading are italicized and in brackets. If the reader chooses to omit the bracketed words, the sentence will read exactly as rendered in the RSV. Where God is called "Father" several times in a single passage, as is frequently the case in the Gospel of John, the word "Father" is rendered "God." (For an explanation of metaphor, and of specific ways in which this lectionary has recast scriptural language about God and images for God, see the Appendix.)

TOWARD THE FUTURE

AN INCLUSIVE-LANGUAGE LECTIONARY is a first attempt to rethink the language of scripture as inclusive of both men and women, and as such it is provisional and experimental. Although scripture is written in patriarchal language, it is clear that God is not a patriarch. Our mandate for affirming the inclusiveness of the scriptures is found in the scriptures themselves. The apostle Paul wrote: "There is neither male nor female, for you are all one in Christ Jesus" (Gal. 3:28)...

Metaphor

A metaphor is a figure of speech used to extend meaning through comparison of dissimilars. For example, "Life is a dream" is a metaphor. The character of dreams is ascribed to life, and the meaning of "life" is thus extended. "Dream" is used as a screen through which to view "life." Two dissimilars are juxtaposed.

The statement "God is Father" is also a metaphor. Two dissimilars, "Father" and "God," are juxtaposed, and so the meaning of "God" is extended. Although "God the Father" has been a powerful metaphor for communicating the nature of God, like any metaphor it can become worn. It may even be interpreted literally, that is, as describing exactly. The dissimilars become similar. The metaphor becomes a proposition.

Now, if one were to say "God is Mother," the power of the metaphor would be apparent. To offer the image "God the Mother and Father" as a lens through which to view God elicits the response of a true metaphor, just as the statement "God is Father" once did. In this lectionary, "God the Father and Mother" is used as a formal equivalent of "the Father" or "God the Father." "God the Father" is clearly a metaphor, just as "God the Mother" is. God *is* not a father any more than God *is* a mother or than life *is* a dream. By reading and hearing "God the Father and Mother" we provide a metaphor for God that balances the more familiar *male* male imagery for God with *female* imagery.

There are many female images for God in the scriptures. For example, God as mother is found in the Old Testament: "Now I will cry out like a woman in travail" (Isa. 42:14) and "As one whom his mother comforts, so I will comfort you" (Isa. 66:13); and God is compared to a nurse carrying a suckling child (Num. 11:12). In the New Testament, the parable of the woman seeking the lost coin (Luke 15:8–10) functions as a female image for God. Metaphors are figurative and open-ended. Their meanings vary from hearer to hearer, but they are not dispensable, for there is no other way by which to say directly what the metaphor communicates. A metaphor provides a new way of seeing.

[God] the Father [and Mother]
(RSV the Father; God the Father, God our Father)

One of the outstanding characteristics of the Christian faith is its emphasis on the personal nature of God. While God is also described in impersonal terms (Rock, Light, Love), personal imagery prevails.

"Father" is one such personal term. The Gospels record that when Jesus prayed he called God "Father" (see Mark 14:36), and frequently, especially in the Gospel of John, Jesus refers to God as Father. To refer to God as Father has little precedent in the Old Testament. For Jesus, *Abba* ("Father") was a sacred word, pointing to the mysterious intimacy Jesus had with God ("No one knows the Son except the Father, and no one knows the Father except the Son," Matt. 11:27), and pointing to the intimate relationship his disciples also had with God ("Call no man your father on earth, for you have one Father, who is in heaven," Matt. 23:9). Jesus' own use of the word "Father" in addressing God supported the church's claim that Jesus was the "Son."

That Jesus called God "Father" is the basis for our thinking about Jesus Christ as one of the three Persons of the Trinity. As the words of the Nicene Creed state, Jesus Christ is "begotten, not made, being of one substance with the Father," a relationship that cannot be claimed by any created being. The relationship that the Father/Son imagery of the New Testament seeks to describe is that of Jesus being of the same substance as God. But if God the Son proceeded from God the Father alone, this procession is both a male and a female action, a begetting *and* a birth. God is the motherly father of the child who comes forth. It was the ortho-dox dogmatic tradition which most dramatically defended Trinitarian language about God, and it is this tradition which speaks most boldly of God in images of both genders. According to the Third Council of Toledo, "it must be held that the Son was created, neither out of nothingness nor yet out of any substance but that He was begotten or born out of the Father's womb (*de utero Patris*), that is, out of His very essence."

The phrase used in this lectionary, "God the Father and Mother," is an attempt to express in a fresh way the same intimacy, caring, and freedom as is found in Jesus' identification of God as *Abba*. It is also an attempt to hold on to the impor-tant Christian belief that Jesus is the Child of God. Just as we do not create our children, but give them birth out of our very selves we believe that God did not create Jesus, but that God gave birth to Jesus.

It is also the case that Christians rejected as pagan the view that God is father of the world. For Christians, God is Father in relation to the Son. Christians are brought into this relationship because they are adopted as "sons," or heirs (Rom. 8:15, 23; Gal. 4:5; Eph. 1:5).

God, the Almighty Father, considered as the author of all things, is a Zeus-like figure, sitting on Mt. Olympus, a remote and solitary power. Such an authoritarian God causes earthly authorities to take their cues from "Him." God as Almighty Father legitimates the authority of the fathers of the church, the father of the country or of the family. This is not the way Jesus spoke of God as Father. *Abba* is an accessible, caring, revered figure.

The image of God as Father has been used to support the excessive authority of earthly fathers in a patriarchal social structure. The metaphor "God the Father and Mother" points to the close relationship between language about God and language about the human community. The mutuality and coequality of the per-sons of the Trinity is a model for human community and especially appropriate, therefore, for readings prepared for worship. Those who worship in the Christian church are struggling to bring about a community where there is no longer male or female, but where all are one in Christ Jesus and joint heirs according to the promise (Gal. 3:28). . . .

Sovereign, God the SOVEREIGN ONE, etc.
(RSV Lord, LORD, etc.)

According to Hebrew tradition, the personal name for God, *Yahweh*, was in-troduced by Moses at the time of the exodus. Sometime after 538 B.C. the name was no longer pronounced for fear that it would be profaned, even though it con-tinued to be written in the text of the scriptures. From that time on, the chief word read in place of the divine name was *adonai*—an honorific title translated "my lord." In those places in the RSV where the underlying Hebrew text contains the divine name, and not simply the word *adonai*, the typography is changed to LORD. Where the divine name (*Yahweh*) is found in the original text (RSV "the LORD"), this lectionary renders it as "GOD" or "the SOVEREIGN ONE." The latter equivalent is used especially where the name is emphasized or where literary concerns seem to make that wording preferable. Occasionally the divine name is found in combination with the word for God (*Yahweh elohim*) or with the word for Lord (*adonai Yahweh*). These are rendered in the RSV as "the LORD God" and "the Lord GOD," respectively. In this lectionary, the former is rendered as "God the SOVEREIGN ONE" and the latter as "the Sovereign GOD." In this lectionary, the Hebrew word *elohim* is rendered "God," as in the RSV.

When the Old Testament was translated into Greek, *elohim* was usually translated by *theos*, meaning "God." Both the name *Yahweh* and the title *adonai* were usually rendered by the word *kyrios*, meaning "Lord." It was the Greek translation of the Hebrew Old Testament which the New Testament authors read. In the New Testament, therefore, the primary terms used to designate God are *theos* ("God") and *kyrios* ("Lord"); and the word *kyrios* was also taken over by the church as a primary way of designating Jesus: "Jesus is Lord."

Kyrios has a wide range of other meanings. It is used for the *owner* of possessions, for the *head* of a family, or for the *master* of a house or of slaves. In the vocative it often means "Sir." *Kyrios* is usually translated into English by "Lord" (in reference to God or Jesus) or "lord" (in reference to a man), a word that in common usage means a man with power and authority, such as a titled nobleman.

Because it is a gender-specific word, "Lord," when used of either God or Christ, connotes a male being. However, since the church believes that God transcends gender and that the risen Christ is one with God, in this lectionary *kyrios*, occasionally rendered "God" or "Christ," generally has been translated as "Sovereign," a word which, like "Lord," also means one who is supreme in power and authority. No theological difference is intended by the change, but "Sovereign" is free of purely male connotations. Women as well as men are sovereigns. Elizabeth II is currently sovereign of England.

"Sovereign" thus has another advantage for the translator over "Lord." It is a word in contemporary usage in the political arena, and is not confined to religious usage as is virtually the case with the word "Lord" in the United States. Not only are there living sovereigns in monarchical societies but nations as well are said to exercise sovereignty. The designation of Jesus Christ as *kyrios* by the early church carried precisely such a political meaning: Jesus, not Caesar, was *kyrios*. Christians believed that Jesus Christ is supreme over all earthly authorities. Hence, the status of the authority of the *Sovereign Jesus Christ* in relation to any national sovereignty is expressed in a contemporary idiom which brings to the fore the revolutionary significance of the statement *Kyrios Iēsous* (Jesus is Lord [Sovereign]) for the history of the church...

Child, Child of God
(RSV Son, Son of God)

"Son" is used as a designation of Jesus as the Messiah (Matt. 1:1; 9:27). At Jesus' baptism there was a voice from heaven: "This is my beloved Son" (Matt. 3:17). Jesus also refers to himself as "Son," though seldom except in the Gospel of John, where the self-designation is common.

A son is male, and of course the historical person Jesus was a man. As the Gospels depict Jesus, his maleness is not said to have any significance for salvation. It is the fact that Jesus was *human* that is crucial, both for Jesus' designation as the Christ and for Jesus's work of salvation.

If the fact that Jesus was a male has no Christological significance, then neither has the fact that Jesus was a *son* and not a *daughter*. Therefore, in this lectionary the formal equivalent "Child" or "Child of God" is used for "Son" when the latter has Christological significance, and the masculine pronouns that refer to "Child" ("Son") are rendered as "Child." Thus, all hearers of the lectionary readings will be enabled to identify themselves with Jesus' *humanity*.

In traditional language, Jesus as "the Son" makes believers "sons" and therefore heirs. In this lectionary, Jesus as the Child of God makes believers — men and women — children of God and therefore heirs. When Jesus is called "Son of God" it is not Jesus' male character that is of primary importance but Jesus' intimate relationship with God (see Matt. 11:25–27). Other connotations of "sonship" are divine authority (see Matt. 28:18–20), eschatological revelation, and freedom (see Rom. 8:21).

The Human One
(RSV the Son of man)

The term "the Son of man" is found frequently in the Gospels and almost nowhere else in the New Testament. Only Jesus uses the term (with a single exception), and the Gospel writers always intended the term to refer to Jesus. How do the Gospel authors interpret its meaning?

Much light would be shed on the meaning of the term if there were clear antecedents to its use in the Gospels, but any such antecedents are now impossible to demonstrate. It cannot be shown that Jewish use of the term "Son (son) of man" has influenced its use in the Gospels; in fact, the term does not appear to have functioned as a title prior to its application to Jesus by the church. Its meaning varies in different contexts, but one basic connotation is hard to miss: it speaks about a male human being, a "son" of a "man." In this lectionary, the term "the Human One" is used as a formal equivalent for "the Son of man." That formal equivalent is not derived from or dependent on any particular judgment as to the background of "the Son of man" in Judaism, and is not intended to prejudice in any way the ongoing discussion of that question. We believe, however, that the title "the Human One" is open to the same nuances of interpretation allowed by the title "the Son of man."

Realm of God
(RSV Kingdom, Kingdom of God)

The Greek word used frequently in the New Testament and usually translated by the male-specific word "kingdom" has generally been rendered in this lectionary as "realm." The Greek word refers either to the activity or God (i.e., God's "kingship" or "reign" or "rule") or to the state of affairs brought about by God (i.e., God's "kingdom" or "realm"). In this lectionary, the word "realm" has been used rather than the word "reign." "Realm" is closer in meaning to "kingdom," which is the customary English rendering, and is preferred to the word "reign" because of the possible confusion of that word with the homonyms "rain" or "rein." The Hebrew word usually translated "kingdom" in the RSV is occasionally rendered "kingdom" in this lectionary but is also rendered as "sovereignty" or "realm."

Ruler, Monarch
(RSV King)

The word "king" is used in the Bible both in reference to earthly royal figures and as a metaphor for God. In this lectionary "King" as a metaphor for God is rendered as "Ruler," "Sovereign," or occasionally as "Monarch." The word "king" is retained in reference to specific earthly kings, such as David, and in stories and parables about kings.

Sisters and Brothers, Friends, Neighbors, Followers
(RSV Brethren)

The contemporary use of such phrases as "sisters and brothers in Christ" to address members of the church is helpful in clarifying how the words "brother" and "brethren" are used in the Bible. In Hebrew usage, the same word could refer to a sibling, a more distant relative, a neighbor, or a member of one's community or race. Paul appears to reflect such a broad use of the word "brethren" in Rom. 9:3, where "my brethren" (translated in this lectionary as "my own people") is the same as "my kinsmen by race." In Greek, "brother" was often used to refer to a friend, or to a person with whom one shares a common purpose, but not necessarily a blood relative.

In the New Testament, the plural form of the word "brother" appears to have been intended to include both women and men. For example, in Luke 21:16 "brothers" is certainly intended to mean "sisters and brothers"; and when Paul addressed Christians as "brethren" (see Rom. 8:12; 1 Cor. 2:1) he was surely including women as well as men. In such cases of direct address, "brethren" has been rendered in this lectionary either as "sisters and brothers" ("brothers and sisters") or as "friends." In postresurrection sayings attributed to Jesus, "brethren" is translated as "followers" (Matt. 28:10) or "friends" (John 20:17), to make clear that the reference is to the nascent church and not to Jesus' siblings.

Addition of Women's Names to the Text

In several instances, women's names have been added to the text in this lectionary. These names are offered where generation or origin of the people is a major concern. The additional names therefore make explicit what was formerly implicit, namely, women's obvious role in childbearing. An example is, "As God spoke to our ancestors, to Abraham, [*Sarah,*] and their posterity for ever" (Luke 1:55). Other passages in Series B are Ps. 105:6; Isa. 63:16; Acts 3:13; Rom. 4:16; Heb. 2:16. The addition to the text is placed in brackets and is italicized to make clear that it is an addition. If the additional words involve a change in the verb form, the RSV rendering is in the footnote.

The Jews

The term "the Jews" occurs very frequently in the Gospel of John. Sometimes it refers in a straightforward, historical way to the ethnic people of whom Jesus was one and among whom Jesus lived out his life. Sometimes, however, it is used almost as a code word for religious leaders who misunderstand the true identity of Christ. When "the Jews" is used in the former sense in the lections from the Gospel of John, it remains unchanged in this lectionary. When it is used in the latter sense, it is rendered "the religious authorities" so as to minimize what could be perceived as anti–Semitism in the Gospel of John.

Other Exclusive Imagery: Darkness

The New Testament imagery of light versus darkness (John 1:5; Rom. 13:12) is used to contrast good with evil. The equation of darkness with evil, or that which is done in secret and out of the light, has unfortunately led some persons and groups to condemn and reject anything that is black or any dark-hued person as evil or somehow condemned by God. This color symbolism has its equally inaccurate and unfortunate correlative in the equation of light with white — with what is true, good, and loved of God. For example, the William Bright hymn "And Now, O Father" has the line, "From tainting mischief keep them white and clear...," and in the Bible "Wash me, and I shall be whiter than snow" (Ps. 51:7). While the biblical context may be free from racist intent, the too-easy misconception that dark people are also condemned and to be avoided has led to the use in this lectionary of terminology other than "darkness" as a metaphor for sin and evil.

Use of "They," "Them," "Themselves" and "Their" as Singular Pronouns

In some cases, indefinite singular pronouns are rendered in this lectionary by "they," "them," "themselves," or "their." This usage is recognized as appropriate by the National Council of Teachers of English in its *Guidelines for Nonsexist Use of Language in NCTE Publications*. The *Oxford English Dictionary* says that "they" is "often used in reference to a singular noun made universal by *every, any,* or *no,* etc., or is applied to one of either sex (= 'he or she'). Those grammarians who oppose this usage follow common practice established by an 1850 Act of Parliament declaring that "he" is generic and legally includes "she." That declaration in turn was based on a rule invented in 1746 by John Kirby: the male gender is "more comprehensive" than the female. This lectionary follows the precedent of St. John Fisher (1535), who wrote that God "never forsaketh any creature unlesse they before have forsaken themselves," and William Shakespeare, who urged "everyone to rest themselves." See Thomas Emswiler and Sharon Neufer, *Women and Worship,* revised and expanded edition (Harper & Row, 1984).

(Source: *An Inclusive-Language Lectionary: Readings for Year B.* Prepared by the Inclusive-Language Lectionary Committee of the Division of Education and Ministry of the National Council of the Churches of Christ in the U.S.A. Published for the Cooperative Publication Association by the John Knox Press [Atlanta], Pilgrim Press [New York], and the Westminster Press [Philadelphia]: 1984, pages 5–9 and 241–248. Used by permission.)

III. Anti-Semitism

86. THE RATIONALE FOR "DE-ANTISEMITIZING" THE NEW TESTAMENT

The assertion that traditional renderings of the biblical text are either anti–Semitic in fact or through misunderstanding has already been touched upon in the previous extract dealing with gender-free translations. Since the 1970s it has increasingly been suggested that it is time to tackle the question and revise the New Testament renderings accordingly. Those opposed to the movement are not (with very few exceptions) anti–Semitic; rather, they feel that it is one thing to be extra cautious where the text allows for it but that it is theological axe-grinding to alter the text when it is quite clear and specific.

The following extract presents the very brief rationale included at the beginning of the *Judaean Version of the New Testament.*

The Judaean and Authorized Version may be described as "The New Testament Without Antisemitism." Amendments herein of the 1611 translation can all be established from the sources. They have been adopted with one aim: to eliminate, as far as truth will allow, those unfortunate renderings which tend to sow enmity between Christians and Jews. The authentic New Testament teaching involves love (not murderous hate). Thus, this Judaean version claims to be a truly Christian translation. In all other respects, the text remains as in 1611.

(Source: *New Testament: Judaean & Authorized Version,* Judaean Publishing House, Jerusalem: 1970, back of title page.)

87. REPRESENTATIVE READINGS OF THE JUDAEAN VERSION

To provide the reader with an idea of what such a revision entails (at least to some of its advocates), the following representative samples are reprinted from the *Judaean Version.* The differences between it and the King James Version are noted in brackets as recorded in the footnotes to the Judaean Version itself.

Matthew 2:1-4

Now when Jesus was born in Bethlehem of Judea in the days of Herod the king, behold, there came wise men from the east to Jerusalem, saying, Where is he that is born King of the Judaeans? [KJV: Jews] For we have seen his star in the east, and are come to worship him. When Herod the king had heard these things, he was troubled, and all Jerusalem with him. And when he had gathered all the ministers [KJV: chief priests] and scribes of the people together, he demanded of them where Christ should be born.

Matthew 3:1, 7

In those days came John the Baptist, preaching in the wilderness of Judaea.... But when he saw many of the Separates [KJV: Pharisees] and Sadducees come to his baptism, he said unto them, O generation of vipers, who hath warned you to flee from the wrath to come?

Matthew 10:5

These twelve Jesus sent forth, and commanded them, saying, Go not into the way of the nations [AV: Gentiles], and into any city of the Samaritans enter ye not.

Matthew 16:21

For that time forth began Jesus to shew unto his disciples, how that he must go unto Jerusalem, and suffer many things of the lawyers [KJV: elders] and ministers [KJV: chief priests] and scribes, and be killed, and be raised again the third day.

Matthew 26:55

In that same hour said Jesus to the rabble [KJV: multitude], Are ye come out as against a thief with swords and staves for to take me? I sat daily with you teaching in the temple, and ye laid no hold on me.

Acts 2:36

Therefore let all the house of Israel know assuredly, that God hath made that same Jesus the crucified [KJV: whom ye have crucified] both Lord and Christ.

Romans 2:10-15

Tribulation and anguish, upon every soul of man that doeth evil, of the Hebrew [KJV: Jew] first, and also to the Gentile; For there is no respect of persons with God. For as many as have sinned without Bible [KJV: law] shall also perish without Bible [KJV: law]: and as many as have sinned in the Bible [KJV: law] shall be judged by the Bible [KJV: law]; (For not the hearers of the Bible [KJV: law] are just before God, but the doers of the Bible [KJV: law] shall be justified. For when the Gentiles, which have not the Bible [KJV: law] do by nature the things contained in the Bible [KJV: law], these, having not the Bible [KJV: law], are a law unto themselves: Which shew the work of the Bible [KJV: law] written in their hearts, their conscience also bearing witness, and their thoughts the meanwhile accusing or else excusing one another.)

(Source: *New Testament: Judaean & Authorized Version,* Judaean Publishing House, Jerusalem: 1970.)

IV. Postscript

88. SOME STRANGE BIBLE MISPRINTS AND UNEXPECTED TRANSLATIONS

In the first American printing of the English Revised Version, Professor Isaac H. Hall includes the following assortment of distinctive editions of the Bible.

Singular Renderings

The Bug Bible. This is Matthew's Bible, 1551, and is so called because of the rendering of Psalm xci., 5. Instead of, "Thou shalt not be afraid for the terror by night," as in our version, it has, "So that thou shalt not nede to be afrayed for any Bugges by night." Dore suggests that the translator may have meant *bogies,* which, perhaps, is a little nearer than bugs to the idea of terror, though there might be a difference of opinion on that subject. Coverdale and Taverner's Bibles likewise have the word *bugs.*

The Breeches Bible. The Genevan Bible, 1560, renders Gen. iii., 7, "They sewed fig-leaves together and made themselves *breeches.*" Wycliffe, 1382, had the same; so there was a "Breeches Bible" before the Genevan. *The Golden Legend,* 1483, also made the same rendering.

The Treacle Bible. This is the Bishops' Bible, 1568. It has, in Jer. viii., 22, "Is there no *tryacle* in Gilead?"

The Rosin Bible. The Douay Version, 1610, has, in Jer. viii., 22, "Is there no *rosin* in Gilead?"

An Improved Version. In 1754 there was published in London, GENESIS, *the first Chapter by way of Essay towards an Interpretation of the whole Pentateuch.* Cotton quotes from the "Gentleman's Magazine" for August, 1754, the following as a specimen: 1. "AElohim, beginning, created *lucide* and *illucide* matter. 2. And the *illucide*, void of co-adjunct cohesion, was unmodified, and distinguishableness was nowhere upon the face of the *chaos*: And the *Ruach* of AELOHIM emanated over the periphery of the fluctuation. 3. Until AELOHIM said that *Aether* should coallesce to the production of light. 4. And AELOHIM saw the light was good, when it was become a separation from obscurity. 5. And AELOHIM deemed *this* daylight, and the obscurity was yet as night, which was light, and obscuration the consummation of the first day."

Typographical Errors.

Cotton Mather tells of a Bible printed before 1702, in which David is made to say, in Psalm cxix., 161, "*Printers* have persecuted me without a cause."

The beautiful Cambridge Bible, of 1629, has, in spite of the care bestowed on it, at least one error, which ran through many subsequent editions. In 1 Tim. iv., 16, Paul says, "Take heed unto thyself and to the doctrine." This book has, instead, "*thy* doctrine."

The edition of 1638, though more correct even than the former, has in it one famous error, which was serious in its day because of the disputes between the Independents and the Episcopalians. In Acts vi., 3, it has "whom *ye* may appoint," instead of "whom *we* may appoint," which latter is correct.

In 1653 an edition of the Authorized Version was printed in London, in which 1 Cor. vi., 9, was made to read, "Know ye not that the unrighteous shall inherit the kingdom of God?"

Another example of the omission of the negative is found in an Oxford Bible of 1711, in which we read in Isaiah lvii., 12, "I will declare thy righteousness and thy works, for they shall profit thee."

In an Oxford Bible of 1792, in Luke xxii., 34, the Saviour is represented as telling *Philip* that he should deny him thrice before cock-crowing.

Another Oxford Bible of 1804 makes Paul say, in Gal. v., 17, "For the flesh lusteth *after* the Spirit."

Still another Oxford Bible of 1807 has in Heb. ix., 14, "Purge your conscience from *good* works," instead of *dead* works.

A Genevan Bible, published in 1562, has two singular errors. In the chapter heading of Luke xxi. are the words, "Christ *condemneth* the poor widow," instead of *commendeth.* In Matt. v., 9, instead of "Blessed are the *peacemakers*," it has, "Blessed are the *place-makers*."

The *Vinegar Bible* is an edition of the Authorized Version published in Oxford in 1717, by J. Baskett. In the running title of Luke xx., instead of *The Parable of the Vineyard,* it has *The Parable of the Vinegar.* This Bible, issued in two folio volumes, is remarkable for its beautiful typographical appearance, but so numerous are the mistakes in it that a punster of the day declared that it was "a *Baskett*-full of printer's errors."

Another famous Bible is called the *to remain Bible.* It is a Cambridge Bible of

1805. In examining the proofsheet containing Gal. iv., 29, in which are the words "persecuted him that was born after the Spirit, even so it is now," the proof-reader is said to have had a doubt about leaving the comma after the word Spirit. He sent a query to the editor, who wrote on the margin of the proof the words "to remain," meaning that the comma was to be retained. The compositor, in correcting the proof, found these words written in the margin, and, mistaking them for a correction, deliberately took out the comma, and substituted the intrusive words, so that it reads "persecuted him that was born after the Spirit to remain even so it is now."

But the worst of all errors is found in the celebrated *Wicked Bible*. This is an edition of the Authorized Version printed in London, by Barker & Lucas, in 1631. In Exod. xx., 14, the negative particle is left out of the seventh commandment, making it read, "Thou shalt commit adultery."

(Source: Isaac H. Hall, *The Revised New Testament and History of Revision*, Hubbard Brothers, Philadelphia: 1881, pages 116–119.)

Name Index

Abbott, Ezra 100–104, 106–107, 113
Alcaeus 32
Alexander 40
Ambrose 35, 54, 56, 59, 61, 63
Andreas 7, 8, 12
Aphtonius 26
Apollinaris of Lacodicea 35
Aquila 19–20, 21, 24, 28, 31, 32
Aratus 20
Aristeas 1, 4, 5–9, 10
Aristobulus 2–4
Asinius Pollio 38
Asterious of Scythopolis 35
Athanasius 57
Augustine 33–34, 35–37, 39, 54, 56, 58, 59, 60, 63

Bancroft, Bishop 87–88
Basil 54, 57, 63
Baskett, J. 187
Beatty, A. Chester 118
Bede 54
Beza 103, 112
Bois, John 91–92
Bomberg, Daniel 147
Bowie, Walter R. 125
Bright, William 184
Broaddus, John A. 160,
Burgon, John W. 167, 168
Burkitt, F. C. 169
Burrows, Millar 129

Calvin, John 49, 127
Campbell, Alexander 113, 152–155, 159
Campbell, George 152
Celsus 31
Challoner, Bishop 162
Chayyim, Jacob ben 147
Chromatius (Bishop of Aquileia) 40
Chrysostom 20–21, 54, 57, 63, 170
Cicerco 20
Cicognani, Archbishop 162
Clark, A. C. 172
Coverdale (Bible) 71–75, 186
Cranmer, Archbishop 76–77, 84–86
Criswell, W. A. 143
Crosby, Howard 104–107
Currentuis 21
Cyprian 63
Cyril 54

Day, George E. 108
Demetrius, Bishop 23
Demetrius (Phalerus) 1, 2, 3, 4, 8, 9, 10, 11, 13, 14
Didymus of Alexandris 35
Dionsius Bar-Salibi 26
Doddridge, Philip 152
Dorotheus 12, 13

Eleazar 7, 8, 9, 11, 12, 13, 14
Elias of Salamia 26, 27
Emser, Jerome 47–49